Pius XII and the Holocaust

Current State of Research

The workshop on which this publication is based was organized
in cooperation with
the **Salesian Theological Institute of Saints Peter and Paul in Jerusalem**.

Pius XII and the Holocaust

Current State of Research

Edited by
David Bankier, Dan Michman and Iael Nidam-Orvieto

Yad Vashem * Jerusalem
The International Institute for Holocaust Research

David Bankier, Dan Michman and Iael Nidam-Orvieto

Pius XII and the Holocaust

Current State of Research

Language Editor: Leah Goldstein
Production Editor: Gayle Green

P.O.B. 3477, Jerusalem 91034, Israel
publications.marketing@yadvashem.org.il

ISBN 978-965-308-421-6

Typesetting: 2w-design.com
Printed in Israel by Offset Nathan Shlomo Press.

Contents

Introduction

DAN MICHMAN AND IAEL NIDAM-ORVIETO

Dilemmas, silence, active rescue, passivity. These are a few of the words often mentioned when dealing with the controversial figure of Pius XII. Eugenio Maria Giuseppe Giovanni Pacelli was born in Rome in 1876, to a well-known family of the "black nobility."[1] Ordained to priesthood in 1899, by 1901 he had already been selected for a diplomatic career within the Vatican foreign office. In 1917, Pacelli was appointed Apostolic Nuncio in Bavaria, and in 1920, the first Apostolic Nuncio to Germany. In 1930, he was elected by Achille Ratti—Pope Pius XI—to be the Vatican Secretary of State.

Following Ratti's death in 1939, Pacelli was elected Pope, and took the name Pius XII. His papacy is considered, both in historiography and in the public discourse, to be one of the most contentious, primarily due to his alleged and non-alleged responses to the extermination of the Jews during the Holocaust. This controversy unfolded during the 1960s, particularly after the release of the play *The Deputy* by Rolf Hochhuth and the publication of Saul Friedländer's book *Pius XII and the Third Reich,*[2] and continues to split public opinion as well as the academic community.

1 The term refers to those aristocratic families who kept their loyalty to the Pope following the unification of Italy.

2 Saul Friedländer, *Pius XII and the Third Reich: A Documentation* (New York: Alfred A. Knopf, 1966).

Positions within the Controversy

Pacelli's critics emphasize that his main failure was his silence—that is, the lack of a public and direct condemnation of the persecution of the Jews and, later, their extermination by Nazi Germany. Others add to this the absence of condemnation of the mass killing of the Poles by the Germans, the crimes committed by the fascist nationalist Ustashe in Croatia under the leadership of the Catholic Ante Pavelić, the policies of the Slovak regime headed by the priest Jozef Tiso, and so on. Pius's famous radio speech of Christmas 1942 is considered by many to reflect this silence, as the pontiff neglected to mention the Jews or Nazi Germany, and only generally referred to the deaths of hundreds of thousands of people "who, without any fault on their part, sometimes only because of their nationality or descent [the original Italian word *stirpe* is often translated as "race" or "ethnicity"], have been consigned to death or to a slow decline."[3]

The different critics raise a vast range of motivations for this silence, from political to ideological reasons, such as a desire to keep the Vatican out of the conflict because Catholics were to be found on both sides of the raging battle; the determination to combat Communism; and a fear of German repercussions, in the case of condemnation. Some scholars further state that Pius XII was pro-Nazi or even antisemitic.

In his important book, John Morley analyzes Pacelli's responses from the position of the Vatican's own self-perception.

> The Holy See was very conscious and proud of its diplomatic status, and maintained that it benefited not only the Catholic Church and its members but also all other men because of its commitment to the ideals of justice and brotherhood [...] The Holy See has loudly and repeatedly proclaimed its uniqueness as a religious and moral power.[4]

3 This sentence is often quoted. See, for example, Paul O'Shea, *A Cross Too Heavy: Eugenio Pacelli; Politics and the Jews of Europe, 1917-1943* (Kenthurst: Rosenberg Publishing, 2008), p. 291. For the original Italian text see *Acta Apostolicae Sedis: Commentarium Officiale*, 35 (1943), p. 59.

4 John F. Morley, *Vatican Diplomacy and the Jews during the Holocaust, 1939-1943* (New York: Ktav Publishing House, 1980), pp. 4-5. Note that Morley based his book on the ADSS volumes published at the time of his research, and therefore did not deal with the years 1944-1945.

He concludes that the main reason for the wartime Vatican policy was a parochial interest aimed at the self-preservation of the Church.

> It must be concluded that Vatican diplomacy failed the Jews during the Holocaust by not doing all that was possible for it to do on their behalf. It also failed itself, because in neglecting the needs of the Jews and pursuing a goal of reserve rather than humanitarian concern, it betrayed the ideals that it had set for itself. The nuncios, the Secretary of State and, most of all, the Pope, share the responsibility for this dual failure.[5]

The Italian scholar Giovanni Miccoli added significantly to the dense historiographical debate by describing the dilemmas that motivated Pacelli politically. He reached the conclusion that the activity (*operato*) of Pius XII was, among other things, anachronistic, and he failed to find an appropriate reaction to the unprecedented horrors of the war.[6]

In any case, the critics emphasize that by keeping his official view vague, Pius XII left the moral decision of what to do to certain individuals and the lower Church echelons, thus limiting the extent of assistance given to the Jews.

On the other side of the debate, Pacelli's defenders do not consider his behavior as "silence." They emphasize that already in his first encyclical of October 1939, Pius XII referred to the natural laws and the unity of the human race, thereby objecting to the very essence of the Nazi racial policy. Later on, during the entire war period, the Pope proclaimed the need to help the innocent victims of war. These scholars claim that to a Catholic ear his speeches were clearly referring to the Jews and their suffering, albeit not specifically mentioned. Moreover, they believe that the large-scale rescue activities carried out by Catholic clergy throughout Europe[7] are clear proof of the inspiration given by the Pope

See *Actes et Documents du Saint Siège relatifs à la Seconde Guerre Mondiale* (Vatican City: Libreria Editrice Vaticana, 1965-1980).

5 Ibid, p. 209.

6 Giovanni Miccoli, *I dilemmi e i silenzi di Pio XII: Vaticano, Seconda Guerra mondiale e Shoah* (Milano: Rizzoli, 2000).

7 A large number of Religious (a term that refers to members of an institute of consecrated life—either a religious order or religious congregation), as well as men and women of the

on different occasions. Some of his defenders maintain that the lack of a direct confrontation with the Nazi regime was a strategic choice meant to avoid a worse catastrophe, such as repercussions against Catholics as well as Jews, or an invasion of the Vatican. The renowned case of the Netherlands, where the episcopacy openly condemned the arrests and deportations of the Jews shortly after they began, is often mentioned as indicative of this choice. Sister Pascalina Lehnert, Pacelli's close aide, wrote in her memoirs that Pius XII prepared a denunciation of the mass killing of the Jews in the summer of 1942. However, after hearing that the Germans retaliated by arresting and immediately deporting converted Jews[8] (among them was the nun Edith Stein), Pacelli feared that his own denunciation might cause an even worse retaliation, and therefore decided to maintain neutrality and avoid criticism of war atrocities committed by any belligerent party.[9] Pierre Blet, in his book, emphasizes the dilemmas faced by Pacelli in his search for the best strategy to be taken: "The Pope envisioned the eventuality of a public declaration and it was not easy for him to decide in favor of silent action. In several letters to the German bishops he confided his hesitations and doubts." For example, Blet quotes from such a letter written on March 3, 1944, where Pius wrote, "Frequently, it is painful and difficult to decide what the situation demands: reservation and prudent silence, or on the contrary, frankness and vigorous action."[10] Finally, his defenders maintain that this strategy, based mainly on political neutrality, enabled secret rescue activities throughout Europe.

As much of the relevant material is still unavailable to the scholarly community, one must remember that the interpretations of and explanations for and against Pacelli's actions—or lack of them—on behalf of

clergy, have been recognized as Righteous Among the Nations over the years. Dan Michman refers to this phenomenon in his introduction to *The Encyclopedia of the Righteous Among the Nations: Belgium* (Jerusalem: Yad Vashem, 2005), pp. XIX-XXVII.

8 Jacob Presser, *Ashes in the Wind: The Destruction of Dutch Jewry* (London: Souvenir Press, 1968), p. 148.

9 Pascalina Lehnert, *Ich durfte ihm dienen: Erinnerungen an Papst Pius XII* (Würzburg: Naumann, 1982); Margherita Marchione, *Pope Pius XII: Architect for Peace* (New York: Paulist Press, 2000), pp. 22-24.

10 Pierre Blet, *Pie XII et la Seconde Guerre mondiale: D'apres les archives du Vatican* (Paris: Perrin, 1997), p. 321.

the Jews during the war and their repercussions for the behavior of the Church in general and Catholic individuals in particular are often based on assumptions and fragmentary documentation. Many researchers use mainly postwar oral documentation, engendering criticism by those scholars who demand a more critical methodology in examining these testimonies, similar to the approach used in examining Jewish survivors' testimonies. Most historians agree that only the systematic opening of all material in the Vatican Secret Archives will facilitate a clearer picture. But even that will not be enough. Much more research will have to be carried out on the behavior of Religious Orders, seminaries, and Church leaders on the basis of their archives.

New Documentation

In recent years there has been an increase of interest in the topic of Pius XII and the Holocaust, and previously unknown documentation is becoming available. For example, the material from the papacy of Pius XI was recently opened to the public, enabling new research that sheds light, among other things, on Vatican policy during the 1930s, as well as on Pacelli's activity as Secretary of the Vatican State. The recent opening of other archives throughout the world, such as the American Federal Government's archives, has resulted in the publication of new books that offer enlightening information. Moreover, several studies attempting to summarize the general topic of the Vatican and Pacelli's activities during the war and to analyze recent research, have been published in the last few years.[11]

The picture presented in new research reveals the complexity and breadth of the topic due to several historical reasons. First, we are dealing with a personality whose authority reached many countries and institutions worldwide. Second, the period we are addressing is characterized

11 See, for example, Hubert Wolf, *Papst und Teufel, Die Archive des Vatikan und das Dritte Reich* (Munich: Verlag C. H. Beck, 2008); ibid, *Pope and Devil: The Vatican's Archives and the Third Reich* (Cambridge, Mass.: Belknap Press of Harvard University Press, 2010); Paul O'Shea, *A Cross Too Heavy*; Andrea Tornielli, *Pio XII: Eugenio Pacelli, un uomo sul trono di Pietro* (Milan: Mondadori, 2007). For a review of Hubert Wolf's book, see Doris Bergen, "Speak of the Devil: Hubert Wolf on Pope Pius XI and the Vatican Archives," *Harvard Theological Review* 105/1 (January, 2012).

by a world calamity. We must also remember that due to the nature of the regimes much of the activity was not documented but concluded orally, which presents a significant methodological challenge.

The Yad Vashem Workshop

On March 8-9, 2009, the International Institute for Holocaust Research at Yad Vashem and the Salesian Theological Institute of Saints Peter and Paul in Jerusalem, represented by Father Roberto Spataro, convened an international workshop on this much-debated topic.

The idea was first proposed inside Yad Vashem by the late Prof. David Bankier, Head of the International Institute for Holocaust Research, whose scholarly work dealt extensively with the variety of reactions by non-Jews, especially of non-Nazis, to the Holocaust. The upsurge in the general interest in Pius XII's behavior and policies vis-à-vis this issue triggered the idea of convening a workshop of scholars, in which both the literature and original documents could be discussed. When the Apostolic Nuncio in Israel, Msgr. Antonio Franco, approached Yad Vashem with a similar idea, it was accepted by the Institute and integrated into the already existing series of international workshops dealing with topics that are currently at the forefront of research.[12]

As Yad Vashem is at the forefront of Holocaust research, the Institute conducts seminars on various topics, discussed by groups of researchers in their respective fields of expertise. The workshop was restricted, as is common in the academic world when one aims to achieve an atmosphere free of external influences and pressures deriving from the broad

12 To our regret, in a recently published book, the author Matteo Napolitano, himself one of the participants in the workshop, depicts a distorted picture of the background to the workshop and Yad Vashem's role and intentions. Additionally, the author wrongly presents the convening of the workshop as part of some "secret" negotiation between the Vatican and Yad Vashem in regard to the description of Pope Pius XII in Yad Vashem's new museum, which opened in 2005. It bears noting that, contrary to the author's opinion, the contents of Yad Vashem's museum are never the result of "negotiation" but rather reflect updated relevant historical research. Issues regarding the Pius XII caption in the museum as well as the question whether Pius XII was ever a candidate to be a Righteous Among the Nations were not discussed during the workshop (as was suggested by Mr. Napolitano) and is clearly evidenced in the presentations and discussions throughout this volume. See: Matteo Luigi Napolitano, *The Vatican Files, La diplomazia della Chiesa, Documenti e segreti* (Milan: Edizioni San Paolo, 2012), pp. 171-188.

interest in a topic. Similarly, the number of participants was limited in order to create the most conducive atmosphere for a lively and open discussion, where each participant could express his or her scholarly opinion and interpretation of the archival material presented.

The main aim of the Pius XII workshop was to review the current state of research on the topic in light of recent publications and, even more so, the archival material that has recently been discovered or opened to the public.

Father Spataro, on behalf of the Nuncio, invited several scholars (Andrea Tornielli, Matteo Napolitano and Grazia Loparco from Italy, Jean-Dominique Durand from France, and Thomas Brechenmacher from Austria) to the workshop; Yad Vashem invited experts who have conducted some of the most serious studies on the topic based on primary documentation (Paul O'Shea from Australia, Michael Phayer and Susan Zuccotti from the U.S.A., and Sergio Minerbi and Dina Porat from Israel), yet they did not represent any Yad Vashem stance or "the Jewish side,"[13] but rather their scholarly findings and convictions; Yad Vashem itself was represented by David Bankier, Dan Michman (at the time, Yad Vashem's Chief Historian), and Iael Nidam-Orvieto (at the time, a researcher in the Research Institute). The fact that each of the participants was invited either by Yad Vashem or the Salesian Institute created a certain initial division that reflected the difference of opinions. Yet, in fact, the array of opinions was much more subtle, multi-layered, and varying on different issues.

The main questions posed by the organizers of the workshop were:

- Can materials that recently became available shed new light on the existing controversy surrounding the activity of Pius XII?
- Can historiography reach a better and more comprehensive understanding of the crucial questions related to this topic?

The workshop sessions were organized according to specific historiographical questions that are still under debate, following a pattern of academic discussion and not the medieval type of "quaestiones."[14]

13 As wrongly assumed by Napolitano, *The Vatican Files*, pp. 181-185.

14 As wrongly assumed by Napolitano, *The Vatican Files,* p. 186.

In each session, a presenter and a respondent were asked to relate to one question previously presented to them, using both known as well as new documentation. An open discussion with all participants followed.

The workshop was a unique gathering, bringing together researchers who align themselves with all ranges of opinions on Pius XII, from fierce critics to ardent defenders. It dealt with a very sensitive topic that raised significant interest from the media and other bodies. It was therefore decided to have the proceedings published as a contribution to the scholarly and public debate.

This Volume

This publication consists of the transcript of the presentations of each speaker in the workshop. Nevertheless, in order to safeguard the academic value of the publication, the participants were asked to edit lightly the raw recording of his/her contribution and to add minimal footnotes and bibliographies, as well as some necessary explanations for the reader. As the initial idea was to reflect on original documentation, each presenter was asked to add a few documents (listed in the Appendix) relevant to his or her conclusions. The only two exceptions to the latter were Loparco and Napolitano, who presented documents that belong to archives that are still inaccessible to the public; it was therefore not possible to quote here all of the documents they examined. Each session included an open discussion among the participants. These discussions were not reviewed by the participants and footnotes were not added.[15]

It should be emphasized that the opinions, findings, and conclusions presented at the workshop and in this volume do not necessarily reflect any official opinion of either of the two organizing institutions (Yad Vashem and the Salesian Theological Institute). The texts published here must be considered representative only of the personal opinion of each participant.

15 Quite often during the discussion speakers referred to documents that they are familiar with and which they quoted from memory. Therefore, these quotations represent the essence and not always the precise formulation of what can be found in the original document.

The range of topics presented begins with the pre-papacy period of Pacelli's life and continues until the aftermath of World War II. The leading question posed to all participants was whether the new documentation changes the historical understanding of Pius XII. Different speakers related to this topic by presenting some new insights and documents: Durand, Brechenmacher, and Tornielli demonstrated how the new documentation enables a better understanding of Pacelli's background and opinions vis-à-vis Nazism and antisemitism. They emphasized the aversion of Pacelli to National Socialism, which he considered one of the worst heresies of modern times. Pacelli's background was rooted in traditional anti-Judaism, and the place of anti-Jewish tradition was raised by several experts, who highlighted the existence of an old anti-Jewish tradition that undoubtedly influenced the opinion of clerics, whether publicly or privately. Nevertheless, this was not necessarily an obstacle to the aversion felt by many toward Nazi antisemitism and Germany's murderous policy.

Phayer noted that European culture was engrossed in antisemitism and anti-Judaism, and suggested that the fear of splitting Catholic public opinion was one of the reasons why Pacelli avoided a clear, public, and unequivocal condemnation of Nazi Germany's murder of the Jews. In O'Shea's opinion, the responsibility for not having spoken out clearly should be shared by the entire Catholic Church.

The newly available documentation on Pius XI's papacy enabled a clear presentation of the historical and political circumstances that brought forth the concordat with Nazi Germany in 1933. This implies a new evaluation of general foreign policy of the Vatican under Pius XI and the role of Pacelli in this context. It also led to a better understanding of the internal tensions within the Vatican, which resulted in different political choices. The dynamics of the relationships between the Pope, the Secretary of State, and the nuncios were approached with additional documentation, which enabled a more complex view of the circumstances that influenced the activity of different nuncios around Europe. The figure of Cesare Orsenigo, the Papal Nuncio in Nazi Germany, was newly presented using materials from the archives of Pius XI, which suggested a more variegated picture of a nuncio who was indeed trapped in a harsh situation and yet on many occasions endeavored to protest the persecution of human rights in Nazi Germany.

Phayer suggested re-evaluating the famous speech Pius XII gave in December 1942. One cannot speak of "silence," he claimed, as the Pope's speech was understood by many contemporaries, from both sides, as a clear denunciation of the genocides perpetrated by the Germans. And yet, Phayer still believes that the Pope's diplomatic choices must be considered in their entirety, as they were clearly not intended for the benefit of the Jews but rather for internal Church interests. Phayer emphasized that Pacelli did not choose a path of systematic contact with bishops in order to encourage a more favorable attitude toward the Jews.

Another innovative study deals with the rescue of Jews in Italy. Thanks to new material gathered in different archives, Loparco presented a picture that indicates a more direct involvement of Pius XII in the rescue of Jews in Rome and throughout Italy. Loparco emphasized that hospitality to the Jews, while remarkable in Rome and Italy, cannot be dissociated from the help offered to political figures and their families, deserters, young men in danger of being seized, evacuees, orphans, Italians, Englishmen, German soldiers, and partisans—all in the name of Christian charity.

Finally, the participants addressed the postwar period, touching upon two sensitive topics: the so-called "ratlines" (the organized evacuation of Nazi criminals from Europe), and the question of Jewish children in religious houses and institutions. Phayer described the involvement of all ranks of the Vatican hierarchy in the ratlines, bringing new documentation from U.S. Federal archives to substantiate his claims. Napolitano discussed the topic of Jewish children, differentiating between baptized and unbaptized children, and between children whose parents came back to get them and those who were left orphaned, in which case Jewish institutions tried to organize their return to the Jewish community. When the surviving parents requested the children, it seems that the policy of the Vatican and the Pope himself was to return them to the family, even in the cases of baptized children. However, in instances of baptized orphans, the return of the children proved to be a more complex issue.

One of the much-debated questions was whether the Pope was able to view the murder of the Jews as an extraordinary case of genocide that demanded unprecedented measures and responses. For example, did Pacelli reach an understanding that the situation of the Jews called for a suspension of rules set by the Church, in order to deal with the unprecedented challenges of the moment? Historiography has already shown many cases in which individual clerics and members of the episcopacy understood that the situation was unprecedented, raising the question of whether the political center was able to grasp what the periphery had already comprehended due to their day-to-day contact with the victims. Connected to this issue is whether the aid given to Jews should be viewed as a separate phenomenon or as part of a general pattern of Christian charity, embedded in tradition. According to Tornielli, there was definitely no awareness of the existence of a specifically Jewish problem, and therefore the Catholic Church behaved inadequately with respect to the tragedy of the Shoah. Napolitano, on the other hand, suggested that since the Holocaust had crossed the boundaries of any imagination, regular diplomacy could never have been sufficient. Instead, "an alternative diplomacy," which he named "catacomb diplomacy," was required, which could concentrate on more direct contact with the grassroots through the network of clerics throughout Europe, whose main purpose was to rescue victims.

David Bankier, head of the International Institute for Holocaust Research, added a central question to the debate: Can one find in the behavior and activity of Pius XII the moment of what he called "enough is enough"? That is, a moment in which a new understanding of an unprecedented calamity causes individuals to choose an alternate strategy of action, no matter the consequences. Bankier pointed to the fact that such turning points have been found among Germans, even in the Nazi leadership, the Jews locked in ghettos, and bystanders. This particular question should also be researched regarding Pacelli and his deeds should be evaluated accordingly; Prof. Bankier pointed to the fact that existing research has not yet shown that Pacelli ever reached that moment.

The participants often posed questions that were highly divisive, which brought to the forefront basic disagreements. One of these questions was whether one could consider Pius XII responsible for, or even the initiator of, the actions taken by his clerics. The question was posed twice: in the context of the rescue of Jews during the Holocaust, and in its aftermath, regarding the operation of the so-called ratlines. In both cases, the participants pondered Pius XII's possible involvement as an initiator of the activity, if he encouraged it, or whether he simply accepted the actions of his clerics and religious followers. The discussion demanded a basic understanding of the dynamics of the Vatican's modus operandi. More than one participant noticed that if one "accuses" Pius XII of being involved in the ratlines operation, as head of the Vatican autocracy, one must also see him as encouraging the rescue of Jews during the Holocaust. But equally, if he was directly involved in the rescue of Jews, as head of the Vatican autocracy, how can one say he was not involved in the ratline activity?

Another question emerged in relation to converted Jews. The existing published documentation shows that much of the aid activity throughout occupied Europe was carried out on behalf of converted Jews. Should this fact influence one's understanding of the activity of Pacelli and the Vatican? Here too, opinions differed greatly. Some participants claimed that help given to converts must be considered as help given to Jews due to the fact that according to Nazi racist principles, converts were considered and persecuted as Jews. Other participants argued that Nazi policy should not be taken into consideration when trying to evaluate the activity and motivation of the Vatican. The help given to converts must be considered instead as the fulfillment of the parochial interest of the Church, i.e., to preserve mainly the rights of Christians. "Full" Jews, who chose not to abandon their faith, were less likely to receive help, thus diminishing the impartiality of the aid offered by the Vatican.

Another major question was if the rationale behind the Pope's policy was due to fear of communism, a lack of concern for the Jews who were considered "lesser victims," or strategic neutrality? The term "catacomb diplomacy," which was raised by Napolitano, aimed to describe the lack of open condemnation as instrumental to the rescue of more Jews. On the other hand, Minerbi suggested that Pius XII possibly chose not to confront the Germans and even tolerated the deportation of the Jews from Rome in October 1943 in order to appease the Germans and avoid an invasion of the Vatican.

It was the prevalent opinion that only by the opening of all relevant material—in the Vatican archives and of Catholic organizations—could a better understanding of all raised topics be reached. As O'Shea pointed out, "until the archives of the Secretariat of State are opened for the period 1939-1945, it is impossible to compile a complete picture of what the Pope and his coworkers did or did not do for the Jews of Europe. The published documents are a valuable source, but only give the end result, not the details or the processes that led to the result."[16] Recent innovative research, based on newly released archival material, proves beyond doubt the need to accelerate the opening of classified material in the Vatican Archives.

Despite the persistence of basic disagreements between the participants, this publication presents the fruits of an effort to share and clarify opinions, and to reach scholarly agreements on modes of inquiry, as well as regarding where the major problems lie. It was the beginning of an effort that will lead to a better and fuller understanding of this still controversial topic in historiography and in the public discourse.

* * *

During the preparations of this volume, Prof. David Bankier lost his five-year battle with cancer. During the workshop, he made an enormous effort and joined us briefly, contributing, as always, some crucial questions and thoughts. He passed away in February 2010 and did not have the chance to add his final input to this introduction. In the last year of his life, we spent many hours talking about the workshop and this publication.

Prof. Bankier believed it was a significant example of academic cooperation and a possible step toward future joint research. As always, he believed in posing difficult questions along with honest discussion, something which is often absent in the Pius XII debate that is conducted in the media. He was convinced that the existing gaps should not disturb or deny mutual respect or the exchange of opinions. Moreover, it

16 See Session Four, page 96.

was his belief that the new documentation brought some new important insights, which changed some previous understanding of the topic. He therefore longed wholeheartedly for the opening of the full archive on Pius XII's papacy.

This volume is dedicated to Prof. Bankier's blessed memory and in particular to his legacy of honest academic research and moral values, which made him such an admired and beloved scholar and teacher.

Introductory Speeches

AVNER SHALEV

Good morning and welcome to everybody here, especially our guests who have come from all over the world: Australia, Europe, the United States, and Israel. I am pleased to welcome our participants and our guests—scholars who have gathered here at Yad Vashem, in Jerusalem, this morning; scholars who will take part in the discussions that will follow the presentations during the coming two days.

This academic workshop was conceived by Yad Vashem's International Institute for Holocaust Research. We were joined by the Salesian Theological Institute of Saints Peter and Paul in Jerusalem.

I'm gratified that this gathering has convened here today, and I believe that this is not the last time we will meet—we shall continue our academic meetings for as long as the participating parties, including scholars from around the world, feel that there is something new to discuss in this field.

We know well that Holocaust research is an ongoing process, and although a great deal of research has been published and well documented through the years, I believe that research about the Holocaust is certainly far from reaching its conclusion. In my opinion, this is a welcome phenomenon. Holocaust research is an ongoing worldwide activity, and increasing numbers of scholars, shapers of public opinion, and the public at large are finding interest in the research, in Shoah-related publications, and in the Shoah itself. This is not only because much remains to be revealed and studied, but also because the fundamental issues with regard to the story and the history of the Shoah are still open and will remain open, I believe, for eternity, as they relate to the very basic values of human existence. With such moral issues at stake, the subject matter is all the more compelling. Each generation seeks to fathom it in its own way, dealing newly with these issues and trying to articulate some kind of response.

This is the essence of what we are going to discuss over the coming two days: fundamental, historical, and moral questions.

When we come to the very important chapter within the history of the Shoah, regarding the Vatican, and specifically Pope Pius XII, we know that we face a very complex and very sensitive subject. Over time, research regarding this chapter has grown significantly. I would estimate that during the last six or seven years at least a dozen books related to this topic have been published, as well as hundreds of articles. Some of them are quite serious and well documented, others less so. They reflect a variety of approaches, an array of related sources and disciplines and, in some cases, a range of conclusions that researchers and scholars have reached.

Much controversy indeed revolves around this issue, which is reflected here today by the presence of representatives of the media who are with us this morning for the opening of the workshop.

We know that one of the obstacles that still lies in the way of in-depth research is the lack of comprehensive documentation. As we know, thorough, serious research must be well documented. Regardless of the topic, the researcher has to have read and reviewed a substantial number of documents. Unfortunately, for a variety of reasons, the archives of the Vatican, with regard to the period in question, have yet to be opened. But I am pleased to note that following many requests, the Vatican is now moving forward in this regard, which is encouraging. A variety of sources confirm that the current Pope has called for the acceleration of the procedures and steps required to bring the hundreds of thousands of relevant files and documents to the point where they could be declassified. We have been told that the longest we will have to wait is approximately five years, but that the intention of the Holy See is to speed up this process and perhaps open the archives three or four years from today. As I said, this indicates a positive and encouraging approach on the part of the Church. I consider it a step forward, one that promises to open a new stage of serious and in-depth research into this subject.

From time to time new documents are revealed, new approaches and analyses are undertaken by researchers and, of course, we here at Yad Vashem are receptive to listening and sharing. Genuine research should not be affected by political or ideological assumptions or by underlying tendencies. Yad Vashem—well known and respected by academics and scholars all over the world—is a completely independent institution, established by a special law of Israel's parliament, the Knesset, in 1953.

We are proud of our high academic standards and norms of research and we are open to listening to, discussing, and publishing any piece of research that has appeared, provided that it is well documented and meets the standards of serious study. Over the years, we have published materials that have diverged from existing research. Dissent, even controversy, are therefore not foreign to Yad Vashem's proceedings or publications. This is an essential principle that we are dedicated to upholding. I cannot stress enough that Yad Vashem dutifully collects any piece of documentation relating to the Holocaust. We unremittingly attempt to retrieve, copy, and safely store any piece of relevant documentation; we have done so since our founding, and we shall continue to do so through the generations, in order for a comprehensive history of the Holocaust to be forever available here in Jerusalem, the center of Jewish and world research.

Of course, via Yad Vashem's other activities—our school, museum, and exhibitions—we seek to present the story, or rather the stories, of the Shoah in the most objective way possible. And so, when we established the new Holocaust History Museum at Yad Vashem, we attempted, as we have done in other endeavors with which Yad Vashem is connected, to immerse ourselves in the best of the research being conducted throughout the world, to evaluate it, and present it as objectively as possible.

I want to stress that we are involved here in a serious effort to reveal the truth. What we believe and the values we want to uphold are founded on truth. Without the truth nothing can be achieved.

I still recall the words, the very important words, of the previous Pope, John Paul II, who visited Yad Vashem. While visiting our Hall of Remembrance, he noted that remembering the Shoah and dealing with its history and remembrance are essential values for the Christian world, and especially for Catholics. As I understand it, he also offered his reflection about how it happened, because the basic question that is addressed again and again—and it is of course a tremendous challenge to humanity—is: How could it have happened—humanly and morally?

Of course, as the leader of the Catholic world, John Paul II had to address that question. He tried to deal with it. The Holocaust transpired during a period in which many people had abandoned their religious values. As Pope John Paul II perceived it, this was the only way that such total evil could have occurred, why so many could have remained indifferent and so many neighbors were able to look the other way.

These remain open questions—ones to which we shall refer together and share. I think that the only way to deal with these questions in a humane, scholarly, historical, and moral manner, is through discourse, holding precisely these kinds of encounters, encouraging this kind of sharing, enabling this kind of joint study, and listening very closely to one another.

The only way that all of us can achieve greater openness, more sensitivity, and a kind of watchfulness among sensitive, moral human beings is by doing whatever we can, not only to remember what happened during the period of the Shoah, but also to utilize this remembrance as a basic element, a vehicle if you will, to practically educate and raise the generations to come to live morally, to maintain and adhere to values, and to stand up whenever anyone threatens those values. This, then, is the main goal of our gathering.

I shall conclude with thanks and appreciation—first and foremost to my colleague and friend, Prof. David Bankier, Head of the International Institute for Holocaust Research, who initiated this workshop.

I wish to thank my associate at Yad Vashem, Dr. Iael Nidam-Orvieto, and our colleague, Father Spataro, who together prepared this workshop under the auspices of our international institute.

I would also like to thank the Apostolic Nuncio, Monsignor Franco. I wish to express my appreciation to Your Excellency for the counsel and knowledge that you make available to us as the representative of the Holy See in the Holy Land. I know that you have come here seeking a fruitful, successful workshop this morning and over the coming two days.

Thank you very much for the honor of working with you all.

MONSIGNOR ANTONIO FRANCO

As Director Shalev was saying, this meeting evolved from a relationship built on trust, a trust unmotivated by hidden agendas or contingent interests, but rather an honest search for truth. Our only interest is to ascertain the facts. For this, I thank you all for showing the understanding and goodwill in coming together today. I also wish to say, especially to the media, that this meeting is not a confrontation, but a dialogue. This dialogue is based on the trust that inspires each of us, that we simply wish to shed more light on what were extremely complex events. We understand, of course, that this meeting will not answer all the questions. Nevertheless, we hope it will be the starting point of a new phase in our relationship, and it will help build a stronger alliance in the search for the truth.

We live a short span of time in history and this is our modest contribution towards building a world, a future in which the horrors of the past never happen again. Our contribution is working together, using our common heritage to answer the question—How was it possible? Together we can sow the seeds of a new relationship that will make the events we deplore impossible to repeat.

Over the past months there have been some very sad moments in the relationship between the Vatican and the Jewish world. I refer to the case of Bishop Richard Williamson, who belongs to the society of St. Pius X, and his denial of the Holocaust and the lifting of his excommunication. However, these events and their interpretations have also led to certain clarifications that Yad Vashem will welcome.

In essence, I say today that one cannot be Catholic if one denies the Shoah. Of course, the Shoah is not a dogma of faith, but an historical truth, and a Catholic cannot deny historical truth. This has been stated in such clear terms that there can no longer be any discussion on the issue.

This brings me to a consideration that, let me clarify, is not intended as a provocation. Historians are working hard to find a written document of the order given by Hitler to eliminate the Jewish people; a document yet to be found. I believe the same criteria could be applied to the Church. We must widen our search—not just for a document regarding the activity of the Church during the Holocaust, but also for testimonies, for facts. No one can deny the Shoah, we have said, because of the facts, and no one can deny the activities of the Church during that time, because of the facts. This is vital. We must arrive at a better understanding of the Church, of how the Church works, of how there is a communion from the Pope to the faithful, and through the Bishops to everybody, so that we can talk about and analyze the Church in its unity during the events of the Second World War.

This is the task you historians and researchers face. I am not an historian, but I vowed that when I retired, I would dedicate myself to the study of the Shoah and uncover more documents that could illuminate the topic.

It is my sincere hope, therefore, that this meeting will be a success—even if that means simply that we end it with a pledge to meet again. Yad Vashem and the Holy See must continue in our joint efforts to reach a common understanding of the issues. Let me be clear: You have a partner in the Catholic Church that shares the same values of safeguarding and learning from the memory, as affirmed by John Paul II within these walls, and which Pope Benedict XVI will likewise affirm in his upcoming visit.

So, I wish you all success in building a beneficial relationship, a personal relationship that will form the basis of mutual research in the months and years to come. Thank you again for being here, and may God bless your person and the work that you start here today.

Jerusalem, March 2009

Presentations

Session One: Pacelli's Personality and the Jews

Is there a gap between the private and public Pacelli before and during his pontificate? To what extent did the Pope's character affect his feelings and his bearing toward Jews during the war?

Presenter: Andrea Tornielli

My task is to talk about Eugenio Pacelli prior to his pontificate, and to see whether there is a gap—a difference—between the public and private Pacelli.

I would like to remind you that Eugenio Pacelli had a different education from that which ecclesiastics usually received at the time. In fact, Pacelli attended public school, which, in Rome at the end of the nineteenth century, had a strong anti-clerical undertone. Pacelli had anti-clerical professors, and it was at school, at the Visconti secondary school, that he met and befriended a Jewish student, Guido Mendes, who came from a family of great medical tradition, claiming even to have served in the British Royal Court. In an article published in *The Jerusalem Post* a day or two after the death of the Pope, on October 10, 1958,[1] Guido Mendes describes his friendship with Eugenio Pacelli, how he went to his home, and how Pacelli himself had been to Mendes's home, had asked him for a book by Rabbi Elijah Benamozegh, *Teologia Dogmatica ed Apologetica,*[2] and had read it. In the same article, Mendes also reported that later on, when the shameful racial laws were publicly issued in Italy in 1938, the Secretary of State helped the Mendes family leave the country. I can also produce a letter by Guido Mendes's son,

1 Mark Segal, "Ramat Gan physician recalls schooldays with Pius XII," *The Jerusalem Post*, October 10, 1958.

2 Elijah Benamozegh, *Teologia Dogmatica ed Apologetica* (Leghorn: 1877).

a diplomat in Italy, which describes the relationship between his father and the Holy See.[3]

I mention this episode in order to demonstrate that Pacelli had known Jews and had had a Jewish friend even during his childhood. As his upbringing was different from that of other ecclesiastics, we do not find in him any expression of the traditionally anti-Jewish legacy that used to belong to the Catholic Church.

Before he became Apostolic Nuncio, Eugenio Pacelli arranged for the Zionist leader Nahum Sokolow[4] to have an audience with Benedict XV. There are documents, preserved in the Zionist Archive and later published (I read them for the first time in an Italian translation of a book by Pinchas Lapide, published in Italy in 1967),[5] which demonstrate that Pacelli facilitated this interview and paid attention to the requests of the Zionist Movement. Immediately after becoming Nuncio (illustrated by documents of the Nunciature in Bavaria, but also cited in the Zionist Archive), Pacelli personally intervened on behalf of the Jewish population of Jerusalem by sending a letter to the Bavarian Minister of Foreign Affairs on November 16, 1917.[6] In the letter, Pacelli demanded that the German government safeguard the Jews endangered by the Turkish leader Ahmed Jamal Pasha, who had threatened to persecute and expel them. In this case too, it was the Germans who actually protected the Jewish population in Jerusalem, as is documented in the reports and microfilms preserved in the Zionist Archive and published many years ago.

In addition to documents originating from the Vatican's secret archives, we also know of other archives, in particular that of Cardinal Eugène Tisserant, Dean of the Sacred College and Prefect of the Oriental Congregation, whom we often find cited in various documents. Documents from Tisserant's archives reveal that in 1938, Secretary of State Pacelli intervened on behalf of the Polish Jewish

3 See letter of Meir Mendes to Paule Hennequin, niece of Cardinal Tisserant, Rome, February 28, 1972, Ass. Amis Card. Tisserant, no. 44/2. See also letter of Cardinal Tisserant to Professor Guido Mendes, January 14, 1939, Ass. Amis Card. Tisserant, No. 844/28.

4 Sokolow was first Secretary-General and then President of the World Zionist Congress. He died in 1936.

5 The reference is to Pinchas Lapide, *Three Popes and the Jews* (New York: Hawthorn Books Inc., 1967).

6 See letter from Pacelli to the Bavarian Minister of Foreign Affairs, November 16, 1917, Archivio Segreto Vaticano (ASV), Nunziatura apostolica Baviera, no. 2240.

population, which was threatened by a law that would have forbidden ritual slaughtering. Cardinal Tisserant notified Pacelli, then Secretary of State, asking him about this law, and Pacelli immediately requested clarification from the Apostolic Nuncio in Poland. In a letter he then sent to Tisserant (a signed document from Tisserant's personal archives, kept by his niece in France), he clearly stated that a law that would forbid ritual slaughter in accordance with the requirements of Jewish law "would constitute a real persecution against the Jews." A response from the Apostolic Nuncio explained that the law had only been approved by one of the two Polish Chambers, and therefore would not be enforced.

Why do I think this is important? Because in this case, we are not talking about saving human lives, we are not talking about a vicious persecution like the one that unfortunately occurred subsequently—we're talking about a law that would have affected a religious tradition. The fact that Pacelli intervened in writing, clearly demonstrates his friendship with Guido Mendes since secondary school, and his absolutely non-anti-Jewish attitude.

We have also found a letter in the Vatican's secret archives dated April 4, 1933 (almost contemporaneous to the letter Edith Stein sent to Pope Pius XI) from Cardinal Pacelli, Secretary of State, to Monsignor Cesare Orsenigo, Apostolic Nuncio in Berlin. In the letter, Pacelli explained that one of the missions of the Holy See was to exhibit peace and charity towards all people, no matter which social class or religion they belonged to, and asked the Nuncio to intervene in favor of the German Jewish community. This was written after some eminent representatives of that community had addressed the Holy See seeking help.[7] The letter is, therefore, another document illustrating Pacelli's direct intervention on behalf of the Jewish community.

The archives of the Knights of Columbus contain the private documents of Count Enrico Galeazzi, Governor of the Vatican City, a layman and a close collaborator of Pacelli during his offices as Cardinal and Pope. Galeazzi was probably the most authoritative direct go-between

7 Secretary of State Pacelli to the Apostolic Nuncio in Berlin, Monsignor Orsenigo, April 4, 1933, ASV, N. 915/33, Archivio della Congregazione degli Affari Ecclesiastici Straordinari (AES), Germany, pos. 643 p.o., file 158, f. 4.

in the relationship between the Pope and the United States of America. There are multiple correspondences between Galeazzi and James McDonald, High Commissioner for Refugees (Jewish and non-Jewish) from Germany. In one of these letters, McDonald wrote with satisfaction about a meeting and a conversation he had had with Pacelli.[8] They would meet several times thereafter. Clearly, these meetings were aimed at helping persecuted people who had escaped from Germany, both Jewish and non-Jewish.

Further demonstration of the similarity between the private and public Pacelli is a Vatican document—a letter dated May 1, 1924 from Eugenio Pacelli, Apostolic Nuncio in Munich, Bavaria (the city where the Nazi Party was coming into existence), to his superior, Cardinal Pietro Gasparri, Secretary of State, in which Pacelli defined nationalism as "probably the most dangerous heresy of our time."[9]

In addition, in a dispatch dated May 4, 1924, Pacelli wrote of "the heresy of nationalism, which puts the national element or race above all, above truth and justice," and then quoted a sentence by the Nazis, the nationalists of that period: "The German nation above all."[10]

Therefore, in his official dealings, Pacelli manifested from the very beginning his aversion to Nazism, and demonstrated to have clearly understood the danger embedded in that ideology. However, in order to emphasize the lack of difference between the public and the private Pacelli, we must also look at the Pacelli private archives—documents released to historians and researchers only two years ago. These consist of hundreds of letters Pacelli sent when he was Apostolic Nuncio to his brother Francesco in Rome. Among these letters is one dated April 28, 1924,[11] in which Pacelli talks about the extremely disturbing situation in Germany, due to the advance of the fanatically anti-Catholic nationalist parties. Again, the importance of this letter—a private letter—lies in the fact that it demonstrates how, though his reports to Gasparri were

8 McDonald to Galeazzi, April 22, 1940, private archive of Galeazzi, box 25, file 10.

9 Pacelli to Gasparri, May 1, 1924, AES, Bavaria 3, Nunziatura di Monaco, 396/7, in P. Chenaux and F. Cavarocchi, *Pio XII: Diplomatico e pastore* (Cinisello Balsamo: Edizioni San Paolo, 2004) p. 127.

10 Pacelli to Gasparri, May 4, 1924, AES, Bavaria 3, Nunziatura di Monaco, 365/7, Pos. XIV.

11 Letter of Eugenio Pacelli to his brother Francesco, April 28, 1924, private archive of the Pacelli family.

reserved, the public and official Pacelli was not at all different from the private Pacelli.

I would also like to cite the public speeches of the Pope following his election—in particular, one given in 1940, when he stated: "Not less of a comfort is it for us that we were able to console, with both the moral and spiritual assistance of our representatives and with the support of our donations, a high number of refugees, exiles and emigrants, even among the 'non-Aryans.'"[12] Then he talked about the Poles.

There are documents of the Holy See in which, when people of the Semitic race or non-Aryan people are mentioned, the word "baptized" is added, but not in this case. He talked only of "those of the Semitic race." By publicly relaying the message that he was pleased about having helped persecuted persons, *even those of the Semitic race*, the Pope was giving a signal to the entire Church that it was a good thing to be able to help these people.

I conclude with a final document regarding the darkest period for the Jewish community of Rome. His Excellency Monsignor Franco mentioned that current historians are seeking written proof of an order given by Hitler for the horrific Final Solution. Certainly, as of today, no written order by Pius XII indicating that the Jewish people had to be *helped* has surfaced either; however, like the Apostolic Nuncio said, there are traces. *La Civiltà Cattolica* was and still is a journal tightly connected to the Holy See. The editor of *La Civiltà Cattolica* used to have a fortnightly private audience with the Pope, even during the war. During these meetings, he discussed the magazine with the Pope, but he also learned about the Pope's *mens* (mind), his opinions, and his judgment regarding the various events that were taking place. As soon as he came out of these meetings, the editor would record a short written note, a private diary, that he would later use to convey the information to the writers of *La Civiltà Cattolica*, namely a few Jesuit priests who wrote essays for the magazine. The editor of *La*

12 Originally, the Pope said, "even among the non-Aryans." *Acta Apostolicae Sedis*, 1941, Annus XXXIII, series II, vol. VIII, p. 10. In a second version of the published speech the sentence was changed to "even among those of Semitic Race." *Discorsi e radiomessaggi di Sua Santitá PIO XII*, vol. II (Vatican City: Tipografia Poliglotta Vaticana, 1955), (Speech delivered at the Sacred College of Cardinals and at the Roman prelature, December 24, 1940), p. 347.

Civiltà Cattolica was therefore the intermediary between the Pope and its writers. In this private diary, the original copy of which is conserved in the archives of *La Civiltà Cattolica*, Father Giacomo Martegani, Editor-in-Chief of *La Civiltà Cattolica* at the time, summarized in some twenty lines his meeting with Pius XII on November 1, 1943, less than two weeks after the roundup in the ghetto of Rome. Among other things, the Pope told him what he had been doing to safeguard Rome. Then Martegani wrote the following sentence: "The Holy Father also took an interest on behalf of the Jews." He did not say what he did, but he said that the Pope had evidently informed him that he had taken steps in their favor. This is the diary of the editor of *La Civiltà Cattolica*, and those who are familiar with the mode of operation of the magazine at the time, as well as the tight relations between the editor, the Pope, and the writers, consider this important document a testament to the fact that everything happening in Rome during that time was certainly desired by Pius XII.

Respondent: Michael Phayer

First of all, I wish to thank the Nuncio. As a Catholic myself, I very much appreciate you saying that you cannot be a Catholic if you deny the Shoah.

We were asked to direct our remarks in this first session to the personal, political, and theological aspects of Pope Pius XII. Andrea Tornielli has given us some insights into Pius's background that we all value. My knowledge of his personal feelings and his emotional constitution come principally from Monsignor Domenico Tardini, who, as you probably all know, worked closely with Pius XII for longer than anybody else.[13]

The image Tardini gave of Pius XII was a man able to empathize deeply with other people. He mentioned that, standing at almost 5'11", the Pope weighed only about 125 pounds by the end of the war, meaning that he personally suffered what other people were suffering. On the other hand, Tardini said that Pius was not a fighter, and so his response

13 Domenico Cardinale Tardini, *Pio XII* (Vatican City: Tipografia Poliglotta Vaticana, 1960).

to events was to empathize with the people who were suffering, but not to fight for them.

I see no reason to disagree with Andrea Tornielli about the difference between the private and the public Pacelli, but we have to remember that there is a difference between how a person responds privately and how he responds as pontiff of the Catholic Church. In a letter Pacelli wrote to Bishop Konrad von Preysing of Berlin in April of 1943, he showed his ongoing sympathy for the Jewish people. Pius wrote that as Jewish life was coming to an end, his fatherly love and concern went out to them in the greatest measure during their period of hopeless desolation.[14] Therefore, at the time of the Holocaust, he deeply empathized with the Jewish people.

Were his personal feelings allowed to overrule his judgment? That is clearly a different question that we must consider. The short answer is no, they did not, but we need to explore the question.

Now, let me move on to the political side of Pacelli. In answer to the question, "Is there a difference between the Pacelli of before, during, and after World War II?" I would say no. He is on record as being anti-communist in the mid-1930s if not before, he is on record as being anti-communist during the war, and he is very much on record as being anti-communist after the war. This orientation consistently dictated the policies of Pius XII. But we have to nuance that "no." Certainly, a change did come about, specifically in 1943. In the Pope's Christmas address in 1942,[15] he spoke about genocide. While there is a difference in opinion about how effective he was, he did speak about genocide. He was speaking about what was happening in Poland. But by 1943, his fears and concerns about what was hap-

14 Pius XII to von Preysing, April 30, 1943, *Actes et Documents du Saint Siège relatifs à la Seconde Guerre Mondiale* (ADSS) (Vatican City: Libreria Editrice Vaticana, 1965-1980), vol. II, pp. 318-327.

15 On December 24, 1942 Pius XII delivered his annual Christmas speech on Radio Vatican. At the very end of the speech he said, "*Questo voto l'umanità lo deve alle centinaia di migliaia di persone, le quali, senza veruna colpa propria, talora solo per ragione di nazionalità o di stirpe, sono destinate alla morte o ad un progressivo deperimento*" (Humanity owes this vow to those hundreds of thousands of persons who, without any fault on their part, sometimes only because of their nationality or descent [the original Italian word *stirpe* is usually translated as "race" or "ethnicity." M.P.], have been consigned to death or to a slow decline). This sentence became the center of the controversy as it did not directly and clearly mention the systematic extermination of the Jews by the Nazis.

pening in Poland were diminishing. So much so, that by the end of 1943, the Polish Church wrote to the Pope that they understood why he didn't ever say anything about their persecution. The reason for this is very interesting. The brilliant historian Christopher Browning pointed out that in the middle of 1943, the order was given by Hitler and Himmler to execute all the Jews in the ghettos who were working for the German army.[16] Who took their place? Polish Catholics. But, all of this wasn't known until recently. So of course, Pope Pius XII did not know either.

What happened in 1943 was that Pius's concern about Poland of the previous year became a concern for what might happen to the Catholic Church in general. There were two reasons for this. Firstly, his fear of communism, which was so evident in the mid-1930s when he and Pius XI overruled two studies (this comes from information made public by the recent opening of the secret archives)—a study by Dutch Jesuits and a study by the Congregation of the Holy Office in the mid-1930s—that found that the greatest danger to the Catholic Church was racism. They decided that the greatest danger to the Catholic Church was actually communism. I always suspected that Pius XI began to waiver on this decision. But I don't think Pius XII ever did.

1943 was the year of Stalingrad, making it very likely that Russia was going to play a major part in Eastern European, if not European, affairs after World War II. In 1942, Pius did not believe that the Allies could win the war. By 1943, however, he knew that was not true, because he listened to the BBC radio broadcast at 11:30 every night. He was very informed. Now his concern was how the war was going to end, and that fear overrode the fear that he formally had for what was happening in Poland.

Secondly—and this point has not been thought about enough, principally because European scholars are not sufficiently familiar with American archives—a second great fear of Pope Pius XII in 1943 was the destruction of the Catholic Church, the physical Catholic Church, i.e., the bombing of Rome. Simultaneous with Stalingrad, Erwin Rommel was dispatched from Northern Africa. The writing was on the

16 Christopher Browning, *Nazi Policy, Jewish Workers, German Killers* (New York: Cambridge University Press, 2000).

wall. Rome—in fact, all Italian cities—were now going to be bombed, by the Allies. If you could read the letters, coming again and again from the Vatican to President Roosevelt, begging him to tell the British not to bomb Rome, you would understand his great concern with regard to the physical church. So in 1943, Pius XII was very concerned on a *practical* level about his church, and not about what was happening to the Jews in the gas chambers.

Let me conclude this part of my remarks with this comment. The concern about the destruction of the church by aerial bombardment is really the same concern the Pope had about communism—the destruction of the Catholic Church. So while his concern about communism was there before, during, and after the war, in 1943 this concern was overridden by the very real danger of the Catholic Church being destroyed by the aerial bombardment of Rome and the Vatican.

I turn now to the theological side of Pacelli. I owe my insights into the Pope's theological views to my colleague Paul O'Shea, the first person to write about, what some consider to be, the most important encyclical that Pope Pius wrote—*The Mystical Body of Christ*. In that encyclical, Pope Pius expressed the usual supersessionist view of Jews, i.e., that because the Jews had crucified their Messiah, they were now going to be the victims of death. Now I ask you, could anybody have written those words on June 29, 1943, without meaning them explicitly? Modern historians see ideas in *The Mystical Body of Christ* that came to fruition at the Second Vatican Council, but from a historian's point of view, it's clear he was talking about what was happening to the Jews at that time. However, more importantly, the encyclical goes on to discuss the meaning of the Catholic Church, and he wrote that *The Mystical Body of Christ* is now the visible Church—the buildings of Rome, the Vatican, and the Pope. And if those buildings were destroyed, it would destroy the faith of Catholics everywhere in the world.

My conclusion, therefore, is that the sympathy—the empathy—that Pope Pius XII had for the Jewish people in private was not allowed to interfere with his actions as the Roman pontiff.

Discussion

Paul O'Shea: My first question is to Professor Tornielli. One of the issues I have about Pacelli as Secretary of State concerns, as you mentioned, *La Civiltà Cattolica.* My understanding of how *La Civiltà Cattolica* operated was that the editor of the journal had a meeting with the Secretary of State, or in some cases the Pope, to determine the editorial content of the journal. Up until the late 1930s, in fact just before *Kristallnacht* in November 1938, *La Civiltà Cattolica* was publishing profoundly Judaeophobic articles on a regular basis—viciously Judaeophobic. My question is: How do we understand Pacelli's role as Secretary of State if he both empathized with Jews and allowed the publishing of very anti-Jewish material in this Jesuit magazine, which was read as far away as Sydney, the "shtetl" of Sydney, on the other side of the world, by seminarians and all sorts of other people? Can you shed some light on that, please?

Sergio Minerbi: I have a short statement: I cannot understand why one would try to rewrite history. Nahum Sokolow (of the Zionist Movement) arrived in Rome in 1917 following Mark Sykes, one of the two signatories of the famous Sykes-Picot Agreement on the Middle East.[17]

When he arrived in Rome, Sykes decided that the next visit of Sokolow, two or three weeks later, had to absolutely include the Vatican. Moreover, he left clear, accurate, written instructions, visible today, to Sokolow, telling him that his colleague, the British representative at the Holy See, would do everything possible in order to obtain an audience for him with His Holiness. Sykes was Catholic and had excellent connections with the Vatican. It was for the British Embassy in Rome to obtain for Sokolow first a meeting with Pacelli—the Minister of Foreign Affairs at the Secretariat of State at the time—then a meeting with the Secretary of State Gasparri, and finally, a meeting with the Pope. With your permission I refer you to my book on this subject.[18] I

17 The Sykes-Picot Agreement was a secret agreement signed in 1916 between Sir Mark Sykes and François Georges Picot. The agreement was meant to define the sphere of influence and control in the Middle East following the downfall of the Ottoman Empire.

18 Sergio Minerbi, *The Vatican and Zionism: Conflict in the Holy Land 1895-1925* (New York, Oxford University Press, 1990).

also have with me relevant documents from the Zionist archive. So the explanation by Mr. Lapide seems to me completely unfounded.

As far as the rest is concerned, I do not wish to question every single detail, although it would be possible to do so. But let's take one example: the assistance given to the refugees. According to the Vatican documents, the refugees were primarily those who had been baptized. There is the issue of the 3,000 visas to Brazil obtained for baptized Jews, which were cancelled by the Brazilian government after the first 700 arrived in Brazil. Why were they cancelled? Maglione, then Secretary of State, wrote that it was due to their *misconduct*. What could the misconduct of a Jewish refugee, let's say from Germany, who arrives in Brazil, have been? What happened? Did he engage in some tricky business? What exactly did he do? I asked Mr. Graham, one of the four editors of the Vatican documents, if by any chance this "misconduct" could have been the return of those baptized to the Jewish faith. And he said: Yes, of course. This is why the Brazilian government put an end to the arrival of the rest of the Jews. So it's a very complex and confused situation, and no conclusions should be drawn on such an inadequate basis.

Dina Porat: I want to ask Professor Tornielli a question regarding archives. You mentioned the private archives to which access was given only very recently, over the last two years or thereabouts. Are these archives, the private archives, different from the secret archives of the Vatican, i.e., the private archives are now open to all researchers while the secret ones—the political, general ones—are not? That's one question. You also mentioned another, private diary you had access to. Is this diary accessible? And still, with regard to material and documents, I'm not sure that Pinchas Lapide is such a good source. This is an ongoing problem; while perhaps one cannot deny its full value, as far as research has gone, Lapide's book is problematic. It has been contested and cannot be relied upon. It was published in 1967, but since then so much research has been done—Professor Phayer is a good example of that.

Another comment I would like to make regards the really very pertinent question of the difference between the private and the public Pacelli. What is private? Private is not only what one thinks, because nobody else could know about that. Private is more what a person tells the people who are close to him, and not what one expresses in public.

I had access to the private archive of Haim Barlas, head of the delegation of the Yishuv (the Jewish community in the Land of Israel) to Istanbul, where he befriended Angelo Roncalli.[19] The archive describes Roncalli's relationship with the Pope, who spoke very delicately about his attitude to the Holocaust, and Roncalli very delicately expressed much concern and even disappointment. So one more way to research the private Pacelli is what he said to others—not only what he wrote in letters—and what his relationships were like with those who were close to him.

Matteo Napolitano: I have a short observation, a marginal observation, without anticipating what will be said in the afternoon session. I doubt that the Holy See's assistance was limited only to Catholic Jews. I do not doubt this based only on the documents, I also doubt it from a logical point of view. Even if it was true, we are talking about people who were escaping the Holocaust on the basis of hasty conversion processes. Obviously, all these people were escaping the Shoah. Hitler did not distinguish Catholic Jews from non-Catholic Jews. Conversion does not change one's blood. This point needs to be made.

Moreover, there is no doubt, and it has been proven by documents, that there were organizations interested in Catholic Jews. The Pope's approach, duc in part to his cducation (as pointed out by Andrea Tornielli), was an approach that basically made no difference. We're talking about rescuing people from the Shoah. Catholic Jews also faced the Shoah; they were not saved by conversion.

What did the Pope write to von Preysing during the war? "I need not reassure you that our love and paternal concern are focused on the 'non-Aryans' and the Catholic 'half-Aryans', who are now sons of the Church like anybody else, in the downfall of their material existence and their moral anguish."[20] Why did the Pope need to distinguish between Catholic "half-Aryans" and "non-Aryans" if he himself had discriminated between the two types of Jews?

19 Apostolic Delegate to Turkey and Greece during WWII. In 1958 he was elected Pope, taking the name John XXIII.

20 Pius XII to von Preysing, April 30, 1943, ADSS, vol. II, pp. 318-327.

Thomas Brechenmacher: I would like to add some remarks concerning the 1938 document written by Cardinal Tisserant, which Andrea Tornielli cited earlier. Tisserant wrote of Pacelli's efforts regarding the religious liberty of Jews in Poland in 1938. There is a very interesting complementary document I found several years ago in the Zionist Central Archive, which has so far gone relatively unnoticed. It is the record of two Yishuv representatives who visited Rome in May 1938: Dr. Dante Lattes,[21] and the person who wrote the record, Moshe Waldmann. The document details a meeting with the Chief Rabbi of Rome, Rabbi David Prato, in which the Vatican's reaction to the situation in Europe, to National Socialism and especially to the persecution of the Jews, was discussed—above all regarding Germany, but also with an eye on the other Fascist regimes in Europe. During the discussion, Prato tells Waldmann the same thing that Tisserant had noted, namely that Pacelli had made an effort to promote the religious liberty of Polish Jews. Of interest is the context in which this was embedded: "Following my conversation with Lattes, I called upon Dr. Prato and he told me, among other things, the following: The hostility of the Vatican against the new paganism of National Socialism is fundamental. Due to this fact, a peculiar psychological state had developed, i.e., a greater open-mindedness regarding Jewish demands."[22] Thus, in their talk with the Chief Rabbi of Rome, both Jewish politicians ascertain that because of the persecution of Jews, a new position had been established at the Holy See regarding Jewish concerns in Europe. This document hints to a development that I would like to refer to in general. Of course, Pacelli stands in the tradition of Catholic theology, which, as we all know, was characterized by strong anti-Judaic verdicts, for example, that the Jews murdered God or that they have not recognized the Messiah. The theological Pacelli of the 1930s, is not the same as the theological Pacelli of the late war years. As the persecution of the Jews intensified, Pacelli began to focus more on the questions: Are we not obliged, as Holy See, to care much more about the Jewish issues, regardless of our theological background?

21 Dante Lattes was still residing in Italy at the time. He emigrated to Mandatory Palestine in 1939.

22 Central Zionist Archives, S25, 3759.

Are we not called to their help, for they are not the outcasts of God but the chosen people of the first covenant?

These theological matters must be viewed in relation to the political and personal development of Pacelli, and the sources show this. In 1933, Pacelli suddenly recognized that they not only had an obligation to their Catholic Church, which they surely had to protect, but also to all people. He restated this position in his telegram to Orsenigo, saying it was the duty of the Catholic Church to stand up for all people, regardless of their social background.

I would like to conclude with a final remark on the telegram from Pacelli to Orsenigo, cited by Andrea Tornielli earlier today. The audience minutes, accessible since 2006, reveal that on the first day of the boycott against Jewish shops in Germany, on April 1, 1933, Pius XI addressed the topic in a meeting with Pacelli. Pope Pius XI instructed Pacelli as follows: "We witness horrible things happening in Germany, and now we have to react to them."[23] So even before the letter of Edith Stein arrived at the Vatican, the topic had been discussed at the Holy See and in the Secretariat of State. The consequence of this audience was the telegram to Orsenigo of April 7 or 8, 1933, in which Pacelli wrote along the lines of: We have to act upon it. For it is the good tradition of the Holy See to stand up for all people, regardless of the group they may belong to.

Dan Michman: I would like to continue the questions and remarks raised by Professor Phayer and Professor Brechenmacher. From an historian's point of view, it's not just the private and public aspects that must be taken into account. There are actually three levels, which were mentioned earlier: the private or other feelings, the political, and the theological-moral. And these change over time. In the beginning, in 1933, the most urgent problem was the situation of the Church in Germany, i.e., its status, its rights, and the persecution of priests. But things develop over time, and therefore we must be very careful about stages and turning points. One of the topics that should be addressed is how the importance of each level changed at certain turning points.

23 As noted in the Introduction, quotations represent the essence and not always the precise formulation of what can be found in the original document.

The relationship between the theological and political aspects had certain turning points, one of them being *Kristallnacht*, and definitely December 1942, when it was well known that a systematic murder was taking place. At that point, the theological-moral aspect of the Pope's role became much more important than all the others. The others didn't disappear, but we historians must tackle how this aspect was expressed. While this will be talked about over the next two days, perhaps, as we are discussing his personality now, it can be brought up.

Andrea Tornielli: The first thing I would like to ask Professor Phayer is the exact citation of that phrase in the encyclical *Mystici Corporis* he mentioned earlier. I did not know that this sentence appeared in that text. I knew about a similar sentence, not in *Mystici Corporis*, but in the famous anti-racism encyclical draft that was, in the end, never published. But in the first encyclical of Pius XII, *Summi Pontificatus* (on the Supreme Pontificate) in 1939, the Pope spoke about the unity of origin and the uniformity of nature of all human beings, no matter which people they belong to. The anti-racism encyclical draft was entitled *Humani Generis Unitas* (Unity of the Human Race), and appears in the first encyclical of Pius XII. The first encyclical of a Pope is important, since it is his keynote speech. Therefore, I would like to know the exact location of the sentence that you quoted from *Mystici Corporis*.

Concerning Professor O'Shea's question—there is no doubt that a change occurred. *La Civiltà Cattolica* published articles imbued with anti-Judaic sentiment in the 1920s. However, this changed when the racial laws appeared and the persecution of Jews began. The previous anti-Judaic attitude should be condemned; there is no doubt that Christian and Catholic anti-Judaism did indeed exist. However, when the persecution and discrimination of Jews began, *La Civiltà Cattolica* published articles condemning the racial laws, including those issued in Italy.

To Ambassador Minerbi I would like to say that I have no wish to rewrite history. I was probably mistaken to have cited such a controversial and disputed book as that of Pinchas Lapide, but I believe that even here, in Yad Vashem's bookstore, they sell John Cornwell's book, which is no less controversial in my opinion.[24] What I am saying is that different opinions are valid. But I was speaking about Pacelli's attitude vis-à-vis the Zionist movement. What emerges from Sokolow's report—and not from what Lapide said—is that Sokolow found Pacelli to be very cordial, more so than Gasparri. I was only talking about this cordiality.

On the other hand, I spoke about a letter written by Eugenio Pacelli in 1917 intervening on behalf of the Jewish community in Jerusalem, whose members, of course, were not baptized.

With regard to Professor Porat's question—I have consulted the recently recovered private family archive, not yet cataloged but which the family makes available to researchers upon request.

The document relevant to Father Martegani from *La Civiltà Cattolica* is found in the archives of *La Civiltà Cattolica*, a totally different archive from the family archive.

I was impressed by Professor Porat's statement that in order to form an opinion on these issues, one cannot rely on written documents alone, one must also take into account oral testimonies. This is a very important point. You also quoted a "silence" in a conversation the Apostolic Delegate Roncalli had with Eugenio Pacelli-Pius XII, when the Pope asked Roncalli to elaborate on his attitude towards the Germans. You, however, referred to a silence concerning the Holocaust. As a matter of fact, that conversation took place in 1941, prior to the Final Solution. On that occasion the Pope intended to say that he had not yet taken a clear position on Germany. Later on, in a 1942 radio broadcast, he *would* speak about this subject (also cited by Professor Phayer), about the genocide of hundreds of thousands of people due only to their nationality or race (*stirpe* in Italian). Here, I would like to remind you that although it is true that the Pope never said the word "Jew," the word *stirpe* had a precise meaning for Catholics in particular, since the Latin liturgy often speaks of *stirps Judaeorum*, the Jewish race. So in 1942, the Pope talked about hundreds of thousands of Jews being transported to extermination facilities. This is December 1942, just a few months after the initiation of the horrible Final Solution.

24 The reference is to John Cornwall, *Hitler's Pope: The Secret History of Pius XII* (London: Penguin Books, 1999).

Therefore, while Roncalli's testimony is important, it should be remembered that it is from 1941, preceding the Final Solution.

Remarks from the audience.[25]

Andrea Tornielli: No, it was dated 1943-1944 in an Italian newspaper, but the dialogue in the diary is from 1941. This is verified in the documents from the Apostolic delegate's audiences with the Pope. Had it been 1943-1944, it would certainly have been serious. But it's not. It was an error by the Italian newspaper to postdate something that had happened earlier. In this case, however, the dates are crucial.

Iael Nidam-Orvieto: We need to verify whether it was the same meeting, or a different one.

Andrea Tornielli: I think it was the same one, because it speaks about his attitude towards the Germans, no? That's what Professor Porat said.

Susan Zuccotti: I wish to point out that in his Christmas message of 1942, the Pope did not speak of the extermination of the Jewish people or of people due to their race; he referred to people "sometimes dying" because of their nationality or race. This was in December 1942, with the Pope knowing what was happening and still using the term "sometimes dying." There is a difference.[26]

Michael Phayer: That's true, but he also went into a little more detail than that, and talked about people being dragged from their homes to another place and left desolate, etc. He didn't say specifically that it was Jews because he couldn't, since he hadn't said anything about the Polish Catholics who had been killed in great numbers. So he was tied in that respect.

25 The remarks from the audience were impossible to transcribe.

26 The actual reference is to the message of June 3, 1943. The Pope spoke of his compassion for "those who have turned an anxiously imploring eye to us, tormented as they are, for reasons of their race or ethnicity (*stirpe*), by major misfortunes, and by more acute and grave suffering, and destined sometimes, even without guilt on their part, to exterminatory measures." *Discorsi e radiomessaggi*, vol. V, pp. 75-76.

Susan Zuccotti: My only point is that the "sometimes" is an unfortunate qualification.

Michael Phayer: If I could just respond quickly to Andrea Tornielli—I found the quotation in *Mystici Corporis Christi*, 1943 as follows: "On the Cross then the Old Law died, soon to be buried and to be a bearer of death."[27] He goes on in that encyclical to say that Christian love must embrace all people, regardless of their race. So that doesn't exclude what you said earlier.

And if I could just respond briefly to Professor Michman's remark—we have to ask ourselves why the Pope spoke out on Christmas 1942. If you recall, earlier I remarked that the opinion of the congregation of the Holy Office was overruled by Pius XI and Pacelli. That congregation is the one responsible for defining Catholic dogma, which believed that the Pope spoke infallibly. The dogma upheld the moral infallibility of the Pope, defined at the first Vatican Council.[28] In 1942, four Catholic countries in South America and two Catholic countries in Europe wrote to the Pope, challenging his moral authority because he had not spoken out about what was happening in Poland. So, when you talk about his moral responsibility, he was probably thinking about retaining the moral responsibility he had as the infallible Pope, not the moral responsibility regarding what was happening to the Jewish people. That was less important than upholding the Catholic Church.

Andrea Tornielli: I would like to thank Professor Phayer for the quotation, since the way I had heard it, it seemed as if the Pope was speaking of the death of the Jewish people while, in fact, he was talking about the law of the Old Testament and the theological viewpoint that there was a new alliance with Christ—with death, therefore, as the old alliance. Thus, there was clearly a misunderstanding with respect to your earlier quotation.

27 *Mystici Corporis Christi*, June 29, 1943; http://www.vatican.ca.

28 The first Vatican Council was opened in December 1869 and continued until October 1870.

Session Two: Pacelli before His Pontificate

What can we learn about Pacelli's attitude toward Nazi Germany, racial policies, and Jews during his period as Nuncio in Germany? What was the role of Cardinal Pacelli as Secretary of State in inspiring the anti-Nazi attitude of Pope Pius XI?

Presenter: Jean-Dominique Durand

I will talk mainly about the period of Pacelli's activity as Secretary of State because, among other reasons, I have lately become interested in the preceding pontificate, that of Pius XI. This is a very important period because the "good" Pope, Pius XI, is often contrasted with the "bad" Pope, Pius XII, or Secretary of State Pacelli.

I'll begin with some methodological thoughts. I believe it would be a major error to view the relationship between a secretary of state and a pope as political in nature, such as that between a head of state and his prime minister, which is often a relationship resulting from public opinion and votes.

In the Vatican, the political aspect is nonexistent. The pope is totally free to choose his secretary of state based on trust, and thus the secretary of state is hardly ever replaced during a pontificate.

Therefore, these two men have too often been misrepresented. Of course, Pius XI and Pacelli were naturally very different in character, but a dissimilarity of character does not necessarily mean opposition.

The recent opening of the Vatican archives of the pontificate of Pius XI allows us to understand better how this relationship worked. Of particular value are the minutes from the audiences—notes Cardinal Pacelli took during his meetings with the Pope. These, together with many other documents, help us better understand the decision-making processes.

The operation of the Holy See is extremely complex. In his very critical preface in the famous book dedicated to the unpublished encyclical on racism, the great French historian Émile Poulat says that in order to understand the Vatican, we have to, and I quote: "Take the example of the ethnologists; patiently become familiarized with the rules and habits of this particular society." Poulat also speaks out against the culture of suspicion: "Suspicion is the method of the poor." This topic dominates so many of his works. "Suspicions and insinuations are not worthy of proof," he writes further.[1] He also underscores how long the preparation of an encyclical can be, but I'll return to that topic later.

Concerning the period I am addressing, however, one must consider other problems: the role of the German bishops, the Episcopal Conference, the individual public figures, their relationship with the Nuncio in Berlin and the Secretary of State, and the not-always-clear role of Pacelli's successor in Berlin, Monsignor Cesare Orsenigo. With these in mind, and returning to the documents, we must focus upon four cases.

The first instance is Nuncio Pacelli facing the development of Nazism in Germany during the 1920s. Pacelli had a long stay in Germany, first in Munich and then in Berlin, 12 years altogether, from 1917 to 1929. His familiarity with the country, its culture (he spoke perfect German), and its political and religious life played a fundamental role. When he was called to Rome to serve as secretary of state, he was considered "the utmost expert on Germany within the Roman Curia,"[2] as he himself wrote. While this did not make him an expert on Nazism, he was qualified to express his aversion towards this movement.

In November 1923, Pacelli advised Rome on Hitler's attempted putsch.[3] On November 12, he announced Hitler's arrest and the return

1 Émile Poulat, "Préface," in Georges Passelecq & Bernard Suchecky, *L'Encyclique cachée de Pie XI: Une occasion manquée de l'Église face à l'antisémitisme* (Paris: La Découverte, 1995), p. 24.

2 Hubert Wolf, *Il papa e il diavolo: Il Vaticano e il Terzo Reich* (Rome: Donizelli, 2008), p. 139.

3 The Munich Putsch, also known as the Hitler-Ludendorff-Putsch, was a failed attempt by the Nazis to bring the Weimar Republic to collapse. It took place on November 8-9, 1923. As a result of the putsch, Hitler and other Nazi leaders were arrested and charged with high treason. Hitler was sentenced to five years in prison.

to tranquility.[4] On November 14, he noted the anti-Catholic character of the extreme right press, emphasizing its violent verbal attacks on the Archbishop of Munich for his homily in the cathedral, in which he deplored the persecution against the Jews.[5]

Later on, in May 1924, he spoke about National Socialism (as mentioned by Andrea Tornielli), as possibly "the most dangerous heresy of the time."[6] Heresy is a very powerful word in Catholicism.

Hence, at a time when few contemporaries understood the uncommon nature of this political movement, he had obviously already understood the true meaning of National Socialism, which was based on hatred and violence and which lacked any historical precedent.

The second case is the Secretary of State facing the Nazi rise to power. Pacelli—above all a diplomat who believed in discrete negotiations, verbal engagements, and the signing of treaties, particularly in the truly binding nature of concordats—thought that Hitler could be treated like any other head of state.[7] Doubtless, he must have shared some of the illusions of other European democracies that thought they could pacify Hitler through dialogue and negotiation. Facing a regime that did not conceal its use of violence, he contemplated a concordat aimed at defending whatever could be defended, namely the Catholic organizations.

As Nuncio, he had previously prepared concordats.[8] His notion of a concordat was, first of all, the means to ensure the bilateral freedom and independence of the Church.[9] Such conviction was shared by the papal diplomacy. The breach of the concordat with France at the beginning of the century was considered a drama. The Holy See wanted to have agreements with as many countries as possible, even the Soviet Union. Indeed, when he was Nuncio in Berlin, Pacelli was tasked with

4 Pacelli to Gasparri, November 12, 1923, Archivio Segreto Vaticano (ASV), Munich Nunciature, vol. 396, file 7. Also see Hubert Wolf, *Il papa,* pp. 143-144.

5 Pacelli to Gasparri, November 14, 1923, ASV, Munich Nunciature, vol. 396, file 7. Also see Philippe Chenaux, *Pie XII. Diplomate et pasteur* (Paris: Cerf, 2003), pp. 140-141.

6 Pacelli to Gasparri, May 1, 1924, ibid.

7 On Pacelli's mentality and his formation as a diplomat, see the biography of Philippe Chenaux, *Pie XII.*

8 With Bavaria in 1924. He had taken part in the preparation of the concordat with Serbia in 1914 and then tried to obtain, without success, a concordat with Prussia.

9 Philippe Chenaux, *Pie XII,* p. 126.

trying to find the means to sign an agreement with the Soviet Union. Regardless, a concordat does not imply approval of any ideology or political regime.

Negotiations with the Reich had been going on since 1931, long before the Nazis took control. But from 1933, these negotiations took place in a climate of such violence and tension that in a now well-known communication to the secretary of the foreign office, the British diplomat Sir Ivone Kirkpatrick described a private conversation he had had with Pacelli: "Cardinal Pacelli criticized the German government's internal policy, the persecution of the Jews, their actions against their political opponents, and the regime of terror to which the whole nation was submitted [...] These reflections on the dreadful attitude of Germany led the Cardinal to explain, in order to justify himself, how he came to sign a concordat with such characters. He said that he had had a pistol pointed at his head and was left with no alternative."[10] The concordat, as we know, was signed in July 1933, and in fact it proved to be very weak in defending the Catholic associations. Pacelli did not delude himself about its efficacy, but believed that the concordat could have formed the legal basis for possible protests.[11]

Hence, the archives show us that there were no ideological compromises; rather, it was diplomatic strategy. The Holy See was informed about the persecution of the Jews time and again. During his dialogue with the Pope on April 1, 1933, the first day of the boycott against Jewish shops in Germany, Monsignor Pacelli made a note to write to the Nuncio of Berlin about Jewish prominent figures who had presented to the Holy Father the dangers of the antisemitic actions in Germany. "See whether you can say or do something," the Pope had said. The Secretary of State then apparently added in parenthesis: "Thus, may the day come in which it can be said that something had been done. And this should be considered as part of the good traditions of the Holy

10 Kirkpatrick to Vansittart, August 19, 1933, *Documents of British Foreign Policy*, 2nd series (London: Her Majesty's Stationery Office, 1956), V, p. 524; Sir Ivone Kirkpatrick, *The Inner Circle: Memoirs of Ivone Kirkpatrick* (London: Macmillan, 1959).

11 See the interpretation given by the semi-official periodical, *La Civiltà Cattolica*: Enrico Rosa, "Il Concordato della Santa Sede con la Germania," November 18, 1933; Giovanni Sale, *Hitler, la Santa Sede e gli ebrei* (Milan: Jaca Book, 2004), p. 87.

See."[12] This is a very important remark. Three days later—this document was also indicated by Andrea Tornielli—Pacelli sent more precise instructions to Nuncio Orsenigo: "Prominent Jews have addressed the Holy Father to invoke his intervention against the danger of antisemitic extremism in Germany. The Holy Father delegates your Excellency to see if and how it would be possible to act in this regard."[13]

Yet, on the other hand, there are many other questions, such as the letter of Edith Stein, already cited earlier.[14]

Now, the third issue: I would like to dwell on the encyclical *Mit brennender Sorge* of March 14, 1937. This well-known encyclical was drafted in a particularly tense environment, with the Vatican engaging in in-depth contemplation on racism and nationalism, in particular in relation to the Holy Office.[15] Rosenberg's book was placed in the Index in 1934.[16] But here, the personal action of Pacelli stands out. He convoked to Rome the three German Cardinals—Bertram of Breslau, Faulhaber of Munich, and Schulte of Cologne—as well as two Bishops—von Preysing of Berlin and von Galen of Münster—for meetings held on January 16-17, 1937, and also for a meeting with the Pope (who in fact was very ill at that time). They decided to prepare an encyclical, on very short notice. The various versions, all of which are marked by Pacelli's handwriting, demonstrate an extensive work, at the end of which the Pope expressed his opinion and added his own corrections.[17]

The first part, written entirely by Pacelli, deplored the German lack of respect towards the concordat. The second, written mostly by the

12 Note of Pacelli, April 1, 1933, ASV, Archivio della Congregazione degli Affari Ecclesiastici Straordinari (AES), pos. 430a, file 348.

13 Pacelli to Orsenigo, April 4, 1933, ASV, AES, Germany, pos. 643, file 158. Document published by Thomas Brechenmacher.

14 Published in German in Hubert Wolf, *Il papa,* pp. 200-201; and in Italian in Emma Fattorini, *Pius XI, Hitler e Mussolini: La solitudine di un papa* (Turin: Einaudi, 2007), pp. 231-232. Wolf dedicates ample space to these requests of intervention that demonstrate with what fervent expectations the Papacy was regarded as a moral authority.

15 The Holy Office is the oldest of the nine Roman Congregations of the Roman Curia. It was established in connection with the Inquisition of 1542 to deal with heresy and oversee matters of doctrine. In 1965 it changed its name to the Sacred Congregation for the Doctrine of the Faith.

16 The reference is to Alfred Rosenberg's *Der Mythus des 20. Jahrhunderts: Eine Wertung der seelisch-geistigen Gestaltenkämpfe unserer Zeit* (Munich: Hoheneichen-Verlag, 1930).

17 Philippe Chenaux, *Pie XII,* p. 215.

Cardinal of Munich, insisted on the incompatibility of Nazism with the Christian faith, due to the divinization of race, blood, and state.

Pacelli personally and closely followed the delicate phrasing and then propagation of the encyclical, written in German, which was read in German churches on Palm Sunday, March 22, 1937.[18] This document is supplemented by the long diplomatic note Pacelli wrote in response to the message of protest from the German Ambassador to the Holy See.[19] An Italian scholar, Giovanni Sale, wrote: "This document is certainly one of the strongest and most courageous documents issued by the Holy See deploring National Socialism."[20]

On the fourth and last point I would like to say a few words, even though it's already been discussed, about the unpublished encyclical on racism and the election of Cardinal Pacelli for papacy.

As we well know, tension increased further in 1938 with the Anschluss,[21] Italy's alignment with German policy, etc. The Holy See reacted to the subsequent racial laws. We could mention the circular of the Congregation of Seminars and Universities, which was considered an anti-racist syllabus,[22] and was published on May 3, 1938, in order to warn, and I quote, "against the extremely pernicious defamations and doctrines of racism."[23] Highly spirited speeches were also made by various Italian bishops, such as Cardinal Schuster in Milan.

As to the Pope's request, three Jesuits were commissioned to prepare a draft encyclical on the unity of the human race, bearing the title "Humani Generis Unitas." Much has been said, unfortunately in controversial terms, about the non-publication of this document. Without going into the dispute itself, it seems to me that three facts should nevertheless be mentioned.

18 For the drafts see ASV, AES, Germany, pos. 719, file 316.

19 Pacelli to the German Ambassador to the Holy See, April 30, 1937, ASV, AES, Germany, pos. 717, file 317.

20 Giovanni Sale, *Hitler,* p. 139.

21 The annexation of Austria to Nazi Germany in March 1938.

22 In the historical memory the term *Syllabus* refers to a text published by Pius IX in 1864, which listed 80 condemned proposals. The text was, in fact, a condemnation of all "new" ideas, from liberalism to socialism, which, according to the pontiff, posed a danger to the Church's teachings.

23 As noted in the Introduction, quotations represent the essence and not always the precise formulation of what can be found in the original document.

First, we must remember that when the Pope died, everything in the Vatican came to a halt. All the functions came to an end, including those of the Secretary of State, except for the Camerlengo of the Sacred College of Cardinals, who was charged with overseeing the everyday secular problems until a new Pope was elected. It was also Pacelli's duty, as Camerlengo, to destroy all the documents the deceased Pope had not yet published. The same applied to the famous last speech of Pius XI, supposed to have been delivered the day after his death, discussing Italian Fascism, which Pope John XXIII later made public and was published afterwards in various books. As a matter of fact, this speech was not so opposed to Mussolini's regime.

In any case, this is how things work. Evidently, the new pontiff is absolutely free to recover the documents of his predecessor, if he wishes to do so. However, this was not the case with regard to the encyclical on racism, since this encyclical was merely a draft, or rather, several drafts. They had not yet reached a final version, ready for possible publication. It was a draft, still in the thinking process.

The drafting procedure of an encyclical is lengthy and complex and this secret encyclical (though not called "secret") was obviously not finished. And if I may add, it is fortunate that it was not published as is, because even if racism—and particularly antisemitism—was clearly condemned, like the Holy Office had already done in 1928, some segments still relied on a traditional theology on Judaism. It was still full of anti-Jewish prejudice, which might have justified the undertaking of certain segregation measures by some countries.[24] Therefore, it would have been dangerous at the time, and it would also have possibly blocked the evolution that led to the Second Vatican Council, etc.

I don't honestly know whether it was for this reason that Pius XII chose not to publish this document after having read it, but as an historian who pays attention to documents, I can comment that in his first encyclical, *Summi Pontificatus*, of October 20, 1939 (and as we know, and as someone here said, the first encyclical always outlines the program for the pontificate), Pius XII recovered an entire and very important segment on the unity of the human race—namely, the incongruity of

24 Jean Dujardin, *L'Église catholique et le peuple juif: Un autre regard* (Paris: Calmann-Lévy, 2003), p. 190.

racism in a Catholic person. And so I believe that the segment I have in front of me, and paragraphs 34-36 in particular, is very important in demonstrating the spirit in which the Pope began his papacy.

Respondent: Paul O'Shea

May I begin first by thanking the Nuncio and Chairman Shalev for their welcome, and in particular the Nuncio for saying that no one who denies the Shoah can be a Catholic. That should be written large and clear.

I'd like to begin with a quote from Pius XI about Cardinal Pacelli. In July 1937, Pacelli went as the Pope's delegate to the dedication of the Basilica of St. Thérèse in Lisieux, Normandy. In his message to the crowd, the Pope said: "Our dear son, the Cardinal *legate a latere* represents our person in your midst, speaks to you in my name, and interprets our thoughts in his pious and eloquent words."[25] When looking at Eugenio Pacelli in his role as Nuncio and then Secretary of State, we see, as Professor Durand pointed out, a continuity of the relationship between the two men—the Pope and the Secretary of State, the Pope and his nuncio. The two men agreed on a worldview, the two men agreed theologically, there's no surprise in that. It would have been surprising if there had been a disagreement.

The list of topics he had to address, first as Nuncio in Bavaria from 1917 to 1920 and then as Nuncio to the German Reich from 1920 to 1929, reveals Pacelli as a man who acted as his master's voice. He was sent as nuncio to speak and listen on behalf of the Pope. He was never meant to be an original thinker, he was never meant to be a shaper of policy; he was meant to be someone who executed policy. Certainly in the early years of the Weimar Republic, much of Pacelli's work was spent listening to the German bishops, responding to what Pope Pius XI saw as the dangers affecting Germany. Of course, Pius XI's knowledge of Germany was profoundly influenced by what his nuncio sent him and paramount in those concerns was the ever-present fear, the phobia, of Bolshevism and the civil unrest caused by the extremes of both left and right.

25 Pius XI to the Faithful in Lisieux, July 17, 1937, in Paul O'Shea, *A Cross Too Heavy*, p. 180.

What comes through very clearly in Pacelli's nunciature—and has already been alluded to—is that the relationship with the bishops was very interesting. Pacelli, I suppose the easiest way to describe him, was an autocrat. He was the representative of the last absolute monarch on Earth, tasked with executing policy. The German bishops were not particularly united. The older German bishops had lived through the *Kulturkampf*[26] of Otto von Bismarck and they were determined to show themselves as good Germans, as good citizens of the new Reich, a republic they weren't particularly keen on. People like von Galen in Münster came from aristocratic Westphalian families that had no particular sympathy towards democracy and liberalism but had to live with them. The relationship between Pacelli and the German bishops was also profoundly affected by his relationship with Cardinal Michael von Faulhaber of Munich, with whom he had developed a very profound friendship in 1917. Faulhaber and Pacelli maintained that friendship until the end of Faulhaber's life, and in the documents both from the Vatican and in the archives of Faulhaber, we see a very close working relationship. They had many things in common. Once Pacelli returned to Rome, he relied intensely on the information provided to him by a number of key German bishops with whom he had strong personal relations, particularly Faulhaber, whom I think he listened to. If Faulhaber had written, "We have a problem here," then Pacelli would have been likely to agree.

I also believe that Pacelli trusted people like Faulhaber and von Galen. He also came to trust von Preysing, an interesting individual because he was one of the few bishops who actually—"criticized" is too strong a word—but during the war years said to the Pope, this is what is happening. We see this in the letters published in the *Actes et Documents du Saint Siège* (ADSS) and in what we heard today.

I now come to a couple of particular points. One of the major issues of Pacelli's nunciature was, of course, the rise of National Socialism. He was one of the few diplomats in Germany who not only understood National Socialism, but also had a general idea of the direction in which

26 The term *Kulturkampf* (cultural struggle) refers to the policy started by the German Chancellor Otto von Bismarck in 1871, meant to reduce the political and social power of the Catholic Church. Von Bismarck instituted state control over the Church's activity and every resistance was met with severe sanctions, including imprisonment, and even exile.

it was heading. In the letter, already cited, that he wrote to Cardinal Pietro Gasparri after the Munich Putsch on November 9, 1923, he basically said National Socialism and Hitler was bad for Germany, it was bad for the Catholic Church, and it was bad for Jews. Regarding this, there is no ambiguity.[27]

I question whether he believed negotiation with Hitler was at all possible. I don't think he ever trusted Hitler; he knew his enemy all too well. He understood that if Hitler came to power by whatever means—and Pacelli was realistic enough to understand that Hitler would use whatever means possible to come to power—that once in power, the only thing that would get him out of power would be a revolution, another putsch, or perhaps something worse. This leads me to comment on the Reich Concordat.

The conversation he had with Ivone Kirkpatrick in 1933 ended almost on a note of...what's that wonderful German word? *Schadenfreude*. Kirkpatrick says to Pacelli, "Why did you sign it?" And Pacelli says, "They held a gun to my head, what was I going to do?" And then he says, with a smile, "But I don't think even the Germans would break all the articles of the concordat at the same time."[28] He knew his enemy and he knew his enemy well.

So what could he do and what could be done? He was now in Rome; he relied on the German bishops to do what they were consecrated to do—to be the successors of the Apostles, to be the teachers of the faith, to provide through witness and moral living the Christian response to the situation in which they found themselves. And I honestly think it caused him and Pius XI a considerable amount of pain that the German bishops were so disunited throughout most of the 1930s.

Adolf Hitler never had to attack the Catholic Church head on; he never had the need to do that. The Church in Germany was divided. The bishops couldn't agree on policy—if one looks at those acts of the German bishops that have been published, you find that in their meetings, at the Fulda Bishops' Conference[29] and in correspondence

27 A loose interpretation of Pacelli's report to Cardinal Gasparri, ASV, AES, Bavaria ANM, pos. 396, file 7, f. 6, November 14, 1923.

28 Kirkpatrick to Vansittart, August 19, 1933, *Documents of British Foreign Policy*, 2nd series (London: Her Majesty's Stationery Office, 1956), V, p. 524.

29 German bishops' conference at the Shrine of St. Boniface.

between different bishops, they couldn't even agree on a response to the 1933 boycott. Although Faulhaber had written to him saying they had to do something, Cardinal Adolf Bertram in Breslau basically said it was not their problem, so they weren't going to do anything about it.[30]

The other area of Pacelli's pre-papal life, once he had left the nunciature in Germany and become Secretary of State in 1930, can be found through what Pius XI did. He made him travel. We have to remember that Pius XI had also said that Pacelli would make a good Pope. Popes don't say things lightly. This was as close to anointing a successor as was canonically possible within Catholicism, and evidently in 1939 the cardinals took the Pope at his word.

But if you look at where Pacelli went in the 1930s, and at what he said, where he went, a pattern emerges: Argentina in 1934, for the Eucharistic Congress; the Pope, Pius XI, was keen to ensure that South America was not forgotten. There was a bastion of Catholicism in the New World, with a gradual shift towards the right in Latin American politics. Pacelli went to Argentina to bring the Pope's message to the Eucharistic Congress, which saw the Nazis' attitude towards Catholicism as the Church being put on trial, just as Jesus was tried by Pilate. He spoke of the decisions that they, the Catholic people, would have to make; that there were new and false crosses being raised. It didn't take much to figure out what the false crosses might mean. He spoke of Neo-Paganism. Woven into that, very subtly, was a hint to the racial element coming out of Germany.[31]

In 1935 he went to Lourdes in the south of France, the premier shrine to Mary in the Catholic world, for the Jubilee Year of Redemption, the supposed 1900th anniversary of the resurrection, and during three days of solemn liturgy and prayer Cardinal Pacelli spoke in the same way. This time he was speaking not to Latin American Christians, but to European Christians and, to use the English expression, every man and his dog was there. All the imperial and royal houses of Europe, both reigning and defunct, turned up, including the ex-Empress Zita of

30 Acts of the German Bishops (ADB) 1.17, 42, note 3, response from Bertram, March 31, 1933; ASV, AES, Germany, pos. 643, file 158, f. 6, Orsenigo to Pacelli, April 10, 1933 and file 158, f. 11rv, Faulhaber to Pacelli, April 10, 1933.

31 Cardinal Pacelli preaching at the closing mass of the Eucharistic Congress in Buenos Aires, October 14, 1934, in *Catholic Mind* 32, pp. 474-475.

Austria, hundreds of cardinals, bishops, priests, deacons, and ordinary Catholics, and he spoke very, very clearly. The Catholic world, the whole world, needed to repent of its sins and return to the purity of the Christian faith in order to avoid what might follow. It didn't take much to figure out "what might follow" meant, since this speech was given shortly before the declaration of the Nuremberg Laws in September 1935,[32] on which the Vatican made no public comment.

The Reich Concordat: This is one of those points in diplomatic history, and I think my colleague Matteo Napolitano might illuminate further. When the concordat was made, the Church or the Vatican State entered into a formal agreement with another sovereign state, in this case the Third Reich. With the establishment of that relationship—done at Hitler's request, not the Pope's—the Vatican State and its emissaries, including the Nuncio in Berlin, had no right to interfere in the domestic politics of the Reich. The Nuremberg Laws were domestic policies. As distasteful, as repellent, as they were, the Pope as head of the Vatican State had no legal diplomatic right to comment on what was essentially an internal German domestic matter. So the comments that were made were veiled. They were full of circumlocutions.

In 1936 he went to the United States. The Pope was worried about the United States, after Leo XIII's condemnation of what he called "Americanism." I'm not sure what exactly that meant, but I think it meant that they tended to think for themselves. The American Church was growing, it was wealthy, and it had a handful of outspoken cardinals, including the Archbishop of Chicago, Cardinal George Mundelein, who would rise to fame 12 months later with his description of Hitler as "a second rate paper-hanger" that caused an enormous diplomatic uproar. He (Pacelli) travelled to the United States purportedly on vacation. Of course, no one believed that. He flew all over the States. The fact that he flew was, in itself, considered amazing, but it points to a sense of urgency. He went to meet people. He went to meet the electors of the next Pope, namely all the American cardinals. He met bishops of influence in positions of authority. He heard about Charles Coughlin, the

32 Antisemitic laws that were announced at the annual Nazi Party rally in Nuremberg in September 1935. The laws classified people racially according to their parents and grandparents. The laws deprived Jews of many of their civil rights.

antisemitic radio priest in Detroit. He also met with President Roosevelt just after the November 1936 elections. There is a very interesting account of the conversation he had with President Roosevelt in Hyde Park. One of the ironies is that Eleanor Roosevelt, a woman for whom I have enormous esteem, was quite anti-Catholic, and while she had overcome her antisemitism, her residual anti-Catholicism lasted for the rest of her life. So I don't know what she thought when Pacelli walked through the door. But Franklin D. Roosevelt greeted him.

During the course of their conversation, Roosevelt said to Pacelli that he thought the greatest problem facing the United States was Fascism. Pacelli said that it was Communism. Roosevelt insisted it was Fascism. They went back and forth between Communism and Fascism. In the end, they agreed to disagree. But the account, recorded by a secretary (I found it online, in the Smithsonian Oral History Archives), is very interesting. It points to a continuity in his obsession with Bolshevism. America was going to fall to Communism.[33]

In 1937 he visited Lisieux. He spoke very openly there about a Neo-Paganism, a cross that is contrary to the cross of Christ, a broken cross, the *Hakenkreuz*—the swastika. It's very clear what he was saying.

Budapest, 1938: He attended the International Eucharistic Congress and the same themes came up over and over again. What is interesting about the speeches made from 1936 onwards, after the Nuremberg Laws, is that there was practically no direct mention of the persecution of the Jews. Now, even taking into account that it would have been diplomatically inappropriate for him to speak about matters relevant to another country, it still caused some concern, especially in Budapest, when he was there for the international congress. The first antisemitic law in Hungary had just been passed.[34] Miklós Horthy's Christian Principles had just been passed. Hungarian bishops sat in the Hungarian National Parliament and voted on these laws. That there was no public comment caused some concern.

I'll finish by adding just one final comment. Pius XI was greatly concerned about what he called *Il Terribile Triangolo* (The Terrible

33 www.aaa.si.edu/collections/interviews/oral-history-interview-florence-kerr-11700.

34 The April 1938 law restricted the number of Jews working in industrial and commercial enterprises and banks, as well as in professions such as law, medicine, engineering, and journalism, to 20 percent of the total number of employees.

Triangle): the persecution of the Church in Spain, Mexico, and Russia by leftist, anticlerical regimes.

In summary, Cardinal Pacelli, as Secretary of State, was attempting to meet the needs of the Catholic Church interpreted through the Holy Father—at the time Pius XI—in a world where the foundations in which he had grown up were changing and crumbling, and the means of responding to this, which had worked for centuries, were no longer feasible.

Discussion

Andrea Tornielli: I would like to underline again that concordats are not, in themselves, treaties of friendship and recognition. Legally speaking, they are defense treaties, and they were intended as such by the Catholic Church and the Holy See. For example, the concordat of 1933 was made with the German state, not the Third Reich, and is still in force today. It is still cited in the concordats the Holy See makes with different *Länder*. This shows that the text had nothing to do with the recognition of Nazism. Furthermore, without this example being considered provocative in any way whatsoever, I would like to remind you that in August 1933, before the concordat between the Catholic Church and Germany was approved, there was the Transfer Agreement[35] between the Zionist organizations and Germany, later backed up by the 1935 World Zionist Congress. Could this possibly mean that the Zionist organizations recognized an anti-Jewish regime? No. It was an agreement made in order to help persecuted people escape.

35 An agreement made in August 1933 between the Nazi regime and the German Zionist Federation that encouraged the immigration of German Jews to the Land of Israel, then Mandatory Palestine, by allowing them to transfer some of their funds from Germany to the Land of Israel through the purchase of German goods. The pact allowed would-be immigrants to place at least 1,000 pounds sterling—the amount the British charged for an immigration certificate to Palestine—in a German bank, and upon arrival in Mandatory Palestine, to collect either that same amount of money or its equivalent in goods. The Zionists were interested in the agreement because it enabled Jews to reach Palestine thanks to the "A" certificate granted by the British mandatory authorities to so-called wealthy immigrants. However, they were severely criticized by some Jews, who felt that the pact was a transgression of the anti-Nazi boycott and a rupture in Jewish unity. The Germans were interested in the agreement for those very reasons, and because it would help get rid of more Jews.

I don't want to make inappropriate comparisons; I'm only saying this in order to explain how the concordat was not a friendly agreement.

Finally, I would like to remind you all, with regard to anti-Communism, that in 1925 Pacelli himself tried to negotiate a concordat with the Soviet Union. He was following the instructions of Pius XI. He met Georgy Chicherin, Soviet Minister of Foreign Affairs, and tried to reach a concordat. So, even though it was anti-communist, the Church dealt with everybody, in an attempt to defend itself.

Thomas Brechenmacher: I found the remarks concerning the relationship with the bishops of particular significance. It is interesting that von Preysing's appointment as Bishop of Berlin in 1935 happened through his friend Pacelli. We have found an interesting exchange of letters concerning this appointment. Von Preysing was in charge of an idyllic diocese situated in Eichstätt, Bavaria, and was not in favor of leaving. He asked Pacelli if he really thought that a simple bishop like him, from this small diocese, was suitable for that, and if he was really fit to take over such a big and important diocese as Berlin. Pacelli answered that that was exactly what he thought and moreover, that he believed there were situations in which one had to do things one did not like. In this case, to move to the center of the new Reich.

We found a second letter, written a few months later, in which Pacelli wrote to von Preysing saying that he had not transferred von Preysing there to remain quiet but that he had transferred him because Pacelli believed he had to speak out more often and take a stand. Here we have very clear demands to von Preysing, who later became known as one of the bishops who spoke out. Pacelli's demands were to go and speak out. This fact is very important, because it shows us that these were not lone bishops acting individually. They always acted in close coordination with the Holy See.

Concerning the *Reichskonkordat*: You [Paul O'Shea] said he knew his enemy. Based on my research, I can't be sure of that. I, rather, have the impression that getting to know the enemy took him a longer time. You quoted the source that states that Hitler would not immediately break all the articles. But this assessment proved to be wrong, as Hitler basically broke all the articles. They believed that if they, in a civic environment, shaped by the legal traditions of the 19th century, negotiated a treaty, all of them would honor it. But that was a complete misconception of the National Socialists. The post-negotiations to the *Reichskonkordat* went on until 1935. It was not until 1934-35 that they recognized that they had the concordat, but the persecution of the Church continued and they were running into a big problem. The true face of National Socialism was becoming visible. In this context, it is interesting that in November 1936, Faulhaber was still traveling to Obersalzberg to meet with Hitler. Prior to his visit, he consulted with Pacelli who said that he was not convinced that this was leading anywhere. Faulhaber thought that it was worth a try, but Pacelli was already beginning to distance himself from this approach saying that basically, it was pointless to negotiate with those people. That it was not going to be successful.

Again, it is wrong to assume that what would happen later in Nazi Germany was clear from the beginning. Rather, we are dealing with a development that went on for several years.

Dina Porat: I'd like to mention briefly two thoughts. One is that all those present are learning a lot from each other. There are many facts and many documents that not everyone is aware of.

It seems to me that the more quotes we have of Pacelli as Nuncio and Secretary of State regarding his empathy and wishes—whether as his master's voice, or his own, he must have agreed one way or another—and the more documents revealed here, the greater the gap between these expressions and what was done or not done, said or not said, during the Holocaust, i.e., during the time of the Final Solution. The question asked in the first session—the difference or the discrepancy between the private and the public Pacelli, or even between the relations he had with those around him and his public face—is more striking. The more understanding we have of this, the weightier the question: Why didn't he speak, let's say in 1942, more openly?

A second remark: regarding the question of historians looking for Hitler's order for the Final Solution. Most historians today agree that no such explicit order existed. We are not looking for it, because the atmosphere was already created and they understood what Hitler's wish was without an order. The atmosphere was created through explicit expressions such as in Hitler's speech of January 1939, when he said that should international Jewry plunge the world into another war, the result would be the extermination of the Jewish race.

I'm not sure the comparison is appropriate; Pius XII did not speak openly. Had he said something really clear—we have to rescue the Jews—had he mentioned the word Jews, mentioned extermination, then of course there wouldn't have been any need for written documents. But it wasn't said, and so the comparison is not valid.

Susan Zuccotti: I have three questions. The first is for both of the presenters. In his very interesting book, Peter Godman wrote about information he was able to obtain by studying the secret archives of Pius XI.[36] These had been recently opened, and he found advice given to Pius XI by the Holy Office and also by a team of Jesuits, regarding the position the Pope might take in an encyclical about Nazism. This was in preparation for the encyclical of 1937, *Mit brennender Sorge*. The advice being given to Pius XI was much more forceful; it spelled out an anti-Nazi position that was in fact much stronger than the actual encyclical. In relation to that I have a couple of questions: Could you comment on that diversity, on the fact that you, Professor Durand, called the encyclical "very strong," but in fact Godman called it weak, much weaker than the advice he was being given?

An additional observation: From Godman's book we can see how much can be learned from open archives. Here, with this information, we are able to see debate and discussion within the Vatican on a particular issue. With the opening of the archives of Pius XII, will we not also be able to very much broaden our understanding of the diversity of opinion? That's my first question.

The second question is for Paul O'Shea, who commented on the fact that the concordat with Germany stipulated that the Pope could not comment on internal domestic affairs. That was also part of the concordat with Italy in 1929, but there was a stipulation in which the Pope

36 Peter Godman, *Hitler and the Vatican: Inside the Secret Archives That Reveal the New Story of the Nazis and the Church* (New York: Free Press, 2004).

reserved the right to comment on matters of moral import. I wonder if that stipulation existed in the German concordat as well.

And my final question is shorter. I was under the impression that when Pacelli went to Budapest in 1938, he did make some kind of a comment. I know for a fact, but again, I don't have the direct quotation, that in *La Civiltà Cattolica* there was an article supportive of the Hungarian [antisemitic] law. I wonder, Paul, if you could comment on that as well.

Sergio Minerbi: It seems to me, one: Secretary of State Pacelli considerably aided, through the Catholic Center Party in Germany, the election of Hitler as Chancellor.

Two: The concordat was the first international agreement signed with Nazi Germany and, as such, it implicitly gave a kind of recognition to Hitler and his government. This is rather important.

Three: In 1935 or 1936 Faulhaber delivered a very nice speech praising the contribution of the Jews to civilization, etc., so nice a speech that the secretary of the World Jewish Congress in Geneva immediately wrote him a letter of congratulations. Faulhaber answered through his secretary, not directly: "I was not speaking about the Jews of today, I was speaking of the Jews of the Bible."[37]

Four: The Transfer Agreement. It is a little difficult to compare this with the concordat for one simple reason: This was an agreement to allow Jewish people in Germany wanting to emigrate to Palestine to take out at least 1,000 pounds sterling with which one could then, according to the laws of the [British] Mandate, buy a so-called "capitalist" immigration-to-Palestine certificate, and avoid waiting in line for years until you got a certificate from the British Government. So it was a question of life or death, as it could have allowed Jews from Germany to come to then-Palestine.

Five: With all due respect to the excellent presentations we have heard, the civil war in Spain had a major influence on other people, as well as on the Vatican. The Spanish Civil War was preceded by the declaration of Cardinal August Hlond, primate of Poland, who

37 The reference is to the Advent sermon of 1933.

said in February 1936: "It is a fact that Jews are waging a war against the Catholic Church. They constitute the vanguard of atheism, the Bolshevik movement, and revolutionary activity,"[38] and so on and so forth. He came to the conclusion that the main enemies of the Church were in this order: the Jews, the freemasons, and the Bolsheviks. I wonder whether—this was more or less on the eve of the Spanish Civil War—the same idea was not also present inside the Vatican. The fact is, that while Pius XI wanted to maintain diplomatic contact with the legal government of Spain, his Secretary of State was maintaining contact with the cardinals working together with Franco against this government.

My final point: Budapest. As far as I remember, during this congress there was an antisemitic declaration by Pacelli, but I don't have the text here.

Dina Porat: Just a word about the Transfer Agreement. It was signed in August 1933. In August 1933, it was not yet a matter of life or death. And also, it was not just to acquire a certificate, there was also a financial agreement with Germany, according to which this money would buy German goods and machines. So there is a point of controversy, and here Dr. Tornielli is right in not comparing it, but pointing to a problem.

Matteo Napolitano: Just a few words on the concordat. I emphasize that it was not an agreement with the Nazi regime, but with the Nazi State. This was said at the time by the great historian Jacques Nobécourt. However, if you took the collection of concordats (*Enchiridion dei concordati*) and checked those from 1933 onwards, you would see that the 1933 Concordat is referred to in a series of concordats made by the Vatican with the various *Länder* of democratic Germany, the Federal Republic of Germany.

Both the popes that succeeded Pius XII and the governments that succeeded Hitler in the Federal Republic of Germany, including following the reunification of Germany, have referred to this concordat.

38 This was written in the Pastoral Letter of February 29, 1936, which was read in churches across Poland.

I absolutely do not mean it as a provocation, but perhaps we should open an historiographical trial against the SPD government in the Federal Republic of Germany for having recognized the concordat between the Vatican and Hitler.

Andrea Tornielli: In respect to something that Ambassador Minerbi said. I would like to remind you that prior to the concordat signed in July 1933 between Germany and the Holy See, the Four-Power Pact or Quadripartite Agreement was signed on June 15, 1933.[39] This was an agreement of collaboration and solidarity with Germany, signed by France, England, and Italy. Therefore, the concordat between the Holy See and Germany was not the first international agreement.

Jean-Dominique Durand: The issue of the concordat: I have never seen—but I may have not seen everything—any minutes of discussions or meetings around the concordat. I have never found such documents (for the time being, maybe other historians like Thomas Brechenmacher could answer this better than me), particularly of this renowned assembly at the beginning of January, with the German primates summoned to Rome.

As to the various drafts: It is obvious that an encyclical, even if prepared like this, in an extremely short span of time—between January and then published in March, right?—usually results in different drafts, out of which one is eventually chosen. I don't know whether we should dwell on the differences between these drafts, but Paul O'Shea clarified the situation perfectly when he clearly underlined the diplomatic issue. The fact is that it is always difficult for the Vatican to interfere with the internal affairs of another state, the Vatican being a state itself. Harsh diplomatic notes, very interesting for clarifying this encyclical, were exchanged with the German Ambassador in Rome, Diego von Bergen. The reply to the protest of the German Ambassador comprises only two pages, while Pacelli's reply comprises almost seven pages—six-and-a-half pages, to be precise. This

39 The Agreement between Fascist Italy, Nazi Germany, France, and England was reached on June 7, 1933, but was finally signed on July 15, 1933.

important document should be studied, but of course we don't have the time for that right now.

With regard to the concordat: Andrea Tornielli replied about the Four-Power Pact having been signed already in June. This point must be emphasized: The concordat was signed with the German State, and negotiations began before that, back in 1931. There were previous concordats with various *Länder*, Bavaria in particular. Of course, the concordat can be criticized, i.e., that it conveyed some kind of illusion. I've said it. Nevertheless, Vatican diplomacy always has the choice to seek concordats with various states in order to coordinate its relations with that state and defend whatever can be defended, primarily with regard to the totalitarian states. We are well aware of all the efforts invested by the Holy See to reach a concordat type of agreement with Soviet Russia.

A few months ago, last November, a doctorate thesis was submitted in France that is probably the first such thesis based on the open archives of Pius XI, on the relationship between the Holy See and Russia. The thesis revives this whole event and clearly demonstrates that the idea was to have a continued relationship with the Russian state and not the Communist regime. For that period, the relationship inevitably had to pass through the Communist regime. This rationale could also be applied to Germany.

Concerning the Civil War in Spain: This was unquestionably a very important moment in history, and it must be studied in depth. I'm planning to do this myself. I possess several documents by Jacques Maritain, the French philosopher, but we cannot dwell right now on this topic, since everything must be done based on documents from the archive, even if some Spanish colleagues have already begun doing so. Anyway, Cardinal August Hlond's letter binds Cardinal Hlond, but it does not bind either Pacelli or the Pope. Instead, I have found in Pacelli's notes—the renowned notes I cited earlier today—a segment about the Spanish War. If my memory serves me right, they are dated July 1936, taken during a dialogue between him and the Pope. In these documents Pacelli wrote that the Pope was everybody's Father. Everybody's Father—also of the anti-clericals. This document needs to be analyzed further. According to this document, the Pope was enraged with the Nuncio in Spain, because he had probably written a misleading report, but I did not have the time to investigate beyond this observation; I must go back to the archive.

Session Three: Pius XII, Orsenigo and the German Bishops

What role did Cesare Orsenigo play in Vatican diplomacy? Was he trusted? What instructions did Pius XII give the German bishops to deal with Nazi policy and antisemitism?

Presenter: Thomas Brechenmacher

The research project I have been working on for the past few years focuses on the reports of the Apostolic Nuncio in Germany, Cesare Orsenigo, during the period 1930-1939. The reports issued after 1939 are not open to the public yet, as the Vatican secret archives for this period are still sealed. However, all available nuncial reports are being analyzed, and after editing they will be released to the public on the Internet.[1] In the spring of 1930, the Lombardian priest Cesare Orsenigo succeeded Eugenio Pacelli as Apostolic Nuncio in Berlin. Compared to his predecessor, a well-qualified career diplomat of the Curia, Orsenigo brought with him no comparably high qualifications. However, he had held the office of Apostolic Internuncio in The Hague since 1922, and that of Nuncio in Hungary since 1925. Orsenigo is said to have been pushed towards a diplomatic career by his friend from Milan, Achille Ratti—Pope Pius XI himself.

Orsenigo's job in Berlin was doubly challenging. He could not duplicate, much less measure up to, the high diplomatic administrative level set by Pacelli in 1917, and he was immediately confronted with the intensifying political and economic situation in Germany. The final crisis of the Weimar Republic, as well as the extremist policy of the National Socialist dictatorship, put extremely high demands on the Nuncio, who was neither physically nor psychologically strong enough to deal with these events.

1 The reports of 1933 went online in the summer of 2009. www.dhi-roma.it/orsenigo.html.

It was not long before Orsenigo's relationships with the German bishops suffered; some bishops viewed him as weak, anxious, and diplomatically unskilled. However, Pius XI and Pius XII refused to act on the repeated requests to remove him. The fear that the German government might not accept a new envoy of the Holy See if Orsenigo were to be recalled might have played an important role in this decision. Nevertheless, after heavy bombardment in February 1945, Orsenigo was so badly affected psychologically that he fled from Berlin to Eichstätt, where he died on April 1, 1946.

The opinion of historians regarding Nuncio Cesare Orsenigo is predominantly negative, even while recognizing the difficulties of his task. This picture was basically determined by the portrayal of Orsenigo's activities as Nuncio by the Berliner Vicar General Walter Adolph, who considered Orsenigo's work a failure. According to Adolph, Orsenigo's political thinking must have been influenced by Italian Fascism, although one could not conclude that he sympathized with German National Socialism. The "failure" of Orsenigo's mission was rooted "not in his personal incapability, but in the strength of the anti-ecclesiastical policy relentlessly carried out by the party and the state, with Hitler at its head."[2] There exists today only one scientifically valid work about Orsenigo: Dieter Albrecht's 1980 edition of the exchanges of Orsenigo and the German government of the Reich.[3] While this work presents the "official" position of the Nuncio with regard to the government in Berlin, the ongoing internal communication between Orsenigo and the political headquarters of the Holy See in Rome remained murky. However, until recently this was the only material available with which one could make a legitimate judgment of Orsenigo—the principal source of his activities as Nuncio, i.e., his reports from Berlin to the Vatican Secretariat of State under Cardinals Pacelli and Maglione between 1930 and 1945, remained inaccessible.

Following the opening of the Vatican archives containing documentation from the period of the pontificate of Pius XI (1922-1939), this situation changed substantially. Now, for the first time, the bulk

2 Walter Adolph, *Sie sind nicht vergessen: Gestalten aus der jüngsten deutschen Kirchengeschichte* (Berlin: Eigenverl, 1972), p. 17.

3 Dieter Albrecht, *Der Notenwechsel zwischen dem Heiligen Stuhl und der deutschen Reichsregierung III: Der Notenwechsel und die Demarchen des Nuntius Orsenigo 1933-1945* (Mainz: Matthias Grünewald Verlag, 1980).

of Orsenigo's reports up to the spring of 1939 is fully accessible, and thus the complex development of information can be documented. Besides Orsenigo's reports, this material includes the instructions of the Secretariat of State, under Pacelli, to Orsenigo; the correspondences between the Nuncio and the Cardinal Secretary of State and other officials of the curia; and the Secretariat of State's internal papers.

The reporting from Germany is extremely dense, especially during the politically explosive phases—for example, the period of the "assumption of power" by the National Socialists between January and April 1933—during which Orsenigo wrote or telegraphed Rome often, and even several times a day. His reports document the end of the Weimar Republic and the history of the National Socialist dictatorship from the point of view of the interests and perceptions of a curial diplomat. The Nuncio discusses extensively not only topics immediately connected with the Church (the concordat with the Reich, the struggle between church and state, the question of schools, youth work, foreign currency, questions of morality, the occupation of bishops' sees, etc.), but also the bigger political questions of the time (National Socialism and Communism, the economic crisis, the establishment of the dictatorship, antisemitism and the persecution of Jews, German foreign affairs, and so on). In addition to the approximately 1,500 (up to now unknown) reports of Orsenigo between 1930 and 1939, the Vatican secret archives contain some 500 relevant documents, in particular letters from Pacelli to Orsenigo (as well as at least 2,000 other documents for the period until 1945).

Orsenigo's reports were decisive in determining the policy of the Holy See towards the German National Socialists. If we fail to take this essential source into account, we will be unable to make any academic judgment concerning the relations of the Holy See to National Socialist Germany later on. I am therefore currently preparing, in collaboration with the German Historical Institute in Rome and the Vatican secret archives, a digital edition of Nuncio Orsenigo's reports from Germany, which we intend to make freely accessible on the Internet. The digital edition will present the original Italian version of the texts, together with German translations, notes, and comments. The first year—1933—will be available shortly; preparation of the other years (1930-1932, as well as 1934) is already well advanced.

These previously inaccessible sources are decisive for making a fair judgment of Orsenigo, and with it a judgment of the policy of the Holy See towards the German National Socialists. They provide us with the following insights:

1. Neither Cardinal Secretary of State Pacelli nor Nuncio Orsenigo was a sympathizer of National Socialism. On the contrary, it was clear from the outset that a new pagan movement had taken power in Germany, one which was anticlerical and which would wage war against the Church (as opposed to Italian Fascism, which for a long time did not fight the Church). It was also clear that the National Socialists' understanding of man (including its antisemitism) could not be compatible with the Church's understanding of man and his natural rights.

2. There were certain illusions—particularly in the first months of National Socialist rule in Germany—that perhaps a way could be found for the Church to coexist alongside the regime. At the beginning, at least, there were uncertainties about how fiercely and for how long National Socialism would go forth in its fight against the Church.

3. Like in Rome, Church representatives in Germany differed in their views regarding how to deal with the anticlerical regime. Should one follow a policy of permanent negotiations, giving as much freedom as possible, or should one engage in direct confrontation through loud protests? Nuncio Orsenigo was certainly inclined towards the first position, but these were negotiations between two parties with incompatible, ideologically opposing worldviews.

Orsenigo's reports of the first years of National Socialist rule show how the illusion of some Vatican leaders of achieving an armistice with the National Socialists slowly evaporated. However, since the Nuncio was often obliged to deliver quick information and appraisals of situations to Rome, one must be careful to take all his reports into consideration. Besides, incorrect evaluations of the situation were often formed, especially in the rapidly developing events of 1933. An example of this is Orsenigo's report on the electoral behavior of the Catholics on March 5, 1933, when he overestimated by some 1.5 million the number of Catholic voters for the NSDAP (report from 07.03.1933). Only by taking the entire body of the reports into consideration can one see that in the early period of the Nazi regime, considerations were often made based both on facts and incorrect information. Pacelli, however, was apparently more sharp-sighted than Orsenigo in the early stages of the clash with National Socialism. Thus, for example, Pacelli advised Orsenigo to formulate his New Year address to the diplomatic corps in Berlin in 1934 in a less conciliatory manner and more sharply against the German government.

On the other hand, Orsenigo's reports also contain sharper insights, testifying that the Nuncio learned to understand and evaluate better the true character of National Socialism. This process of development is recognizable only by those who pursue the reports thoroughly. I'll give some examples:

On April 11, 1933, Pacelli wrote about the "antisemitism" of the German government: "Unfortunately, the antisemitic principle was accepted by the whole [German] government, and unfortunately this fact will stick like a disgrace of maliciousness on the first page of the history of German National Socialism [...]!"[4]

Regarding the anti-Bolshevism of the National Socialists, Orsenigo wrote in his September 14, 1935 report on the Nuremberg Party Congress: "This Congress [seems] to pursue the goal to incite a boundless war against Bolshevism in all nations by holding the Jews exclusively responsible for it. These [Party] talks, loaded with figures, names, and facts, cause a deep and terrible impression, whipping up feelings amongst the German people whom they appeal to with specifics about investigations, calculations, statistics. It will come as no surprise if, after the celebrations of the Party Congress, the antisemitic hunt will be renewed with still greater fervor. On the other hand, the criticism of Bolshevism is so cleverly presented as being fully justified in the eyes of the people that it is difficult to find here a non-Jewish German who dares to totally disapprove of these claims. The more tempered would

4 Orsenigo to Pacelli, Berlin, April 11, 1933, Prot. No. 6954. Thomas Brechenmacher, ed., *Die Berichte des Apostolischen Nuntius Cesare Orsenigo aus Deutschland, 1930-1939* (Teil I: Das Jahr 1933). See digital edition www.dhi-roma.it/orsenigo.html, doc. 96.

limit themselves to raising some doubts concerning the methods with which the fight is being carried out. [...]

"I do not know whether the whole of Russian Bolshevism is the exclusive work of the Jews; but here they found a way to make the people believe this assertion and, as a consequence, to move forward against the Jews. If the National Socialist government lasts long enough, as it appears, the Jews are condemned to disappear from this nation."[5]

Three days later, on September 17, 1935, Orsenigo characterized Hitler's Party Congress speech with the following words: "Hitler's [...] speech was an exhibition of a peculiar, not to say haughty, philosophy of history [...] also looking at his relationship to Christianity that unfortunately revealed the absence of any religious belief, be it Christian or otherwise. Any meaningful religious activity is prohibited or denied across the whole of Germany; Germany belongs only to National Socialism, and is guided exclusively by the party and the army."[6]

Exceedingly clear was his report on the events of November 9, 1938: "Concerning the antisemitic vandalism: Destructions began, as if ordered, at night, immediately after the news arrived of the death of a young diplomat in Paris [i.e. the murder of the secretary of the Legation, Ernst vom Rath, by Herschel Grynszpan] [...]. The blind vengeance of the people spread everywhere, in the same pattern: At night they smashed all the shop windows [of the Jews] and set the synagogues on fire; in the days that followed all their shops were looted—as they were defenseless—and their goods, even the most valuable ones, were destroyed in the wildest manner. Only on the afternoon of November 10, after the day when the mob, unhindered and with no opposition from the police, had satisfied its most barbaric desires, did Minister Goebbels give the order to stop, and called the incidents an expression of the 'anger of the German people.' This one order alone was sufficient to restore calm. All this leads one easily to conclude that the order, or the

5 Orsenigo to Pacelli, Berlin, September 14, 1935, Prot. No. 14482, Archivio Segreto Vaticano (ASV), Archivio della Congregazione degli Affari Ecclesiastici Straordinari (AES), Germany, B. 9a, fol. 32r–33r. It should be noted that during the Party Congress Hitler announced the introduction of two antisemitic measures, known later as the Nuremberg Laws. These laws were "The Law for the Protection of German Blood and German Honor" and "The Reich Citizenship Law," both depriving Jews of basic civil and social rights.

6 Orsenigo to Pacelli, Berlin, September 17, 1935, Prot. No. 14518; ASV, AES, Germany, B. 9a, fol. 60RV.

permission for the excesses, came from the very top. With his assertion that the so-called 'antisemitic reaction' was the 'work of the German people,' Goebbels did great injustice to the true and fair German people, who make up the absolute majority of the Germans."[7]

Thus, on the basis of the information now available, one must reconsider the prevalent opinion of Cesare Orsenigo, i.e., that he was a weak and overtaxed nuncio, and that he was too conciliatory in his relationship towards National Socialism. The presentation of the entire body of the reports calls for a new and more balanced judgment, focusing on the confrontation between National Socialism and the Catholic Church.

Respondent: Sergio Minerbi

First of all, regarding the character of Monsignor Cesare Orsenigo: Yes, he was indeed weak, but he was put in an impossible situation. Not that I have any sympathy for him, but to become an ambassador after someone who is now your superior as "prime minister," and who knows everything better than you can ever imagine knowing, i.e., Pacelli as Secretary of State while Orsenigo was in Berlin, is not an easy position to be in. Not only was it not easy, but there was also a constant clash, because the bishops of Germany constantly bypassed Orsenigo by writing straight to Pacelli who, when he became Pope, said he would "personally deal with Germany."[8] No doubt Pacelli wanted to be very present in Germany, so Orsenigo probably did not have many options. He could have gone home—that is always a possibility for a diplomat—but insofar as he wanted to remain in his post and do his job in the best way possible, he was handicapped from the very beginning. That's issue number one.

Orsenigo was handicapped further by another problem. On the one hand, there was no clear policy of the German bishops, since they were not united, and on the other hand, there was no clear policy of the Vatican towards Germany. So he had to represent a policy that did

7 Orsenigo to Pacelli, Berlin, November 15, 1938, Prot. No. 25341, ASV, AES, Germany, B. 742, file 356, fol. 40R–41R.

8 *Actes et Documents du Saint Siège relatifs à la Seconde Guerre Mondiale* (ADSS) (Vatican City: Libreria Editrice Vaticana, 1965-1980), vol. II, p. 419.

not exist, that had to be improvised daily. This was almost a "mission impossible" from a professional point of view. Let's see what happened. Orsenigo received instructions in March 1943 from Secretary of State Maglione to hand a letter to von Weizsäcker, then Under-Secretary of State for Foreign Affairs (before von Weizsäcker went to Rome later in 1943). He handed over the letter—a letter of complaint regarding how the Church was being treated in occupied Poland. Two days later von Weizsäcker called him, took the letter, and said: "The letter deals with Poland, which is outside the Vatican's jurisdiction and therefore is unacceptable."[9] What do you do? Do you take it back? What do you tell von Weizsäcker—that clearly he had already read it, otherwise he would not have known that it was "unacceptable"? There are no written instructions on diplomacy as to what to do in such a case.

It had to be someone much stronger—not only stronger, but also with a much more influential position inside the diplomatic service of the Vatican—that could have some bearing, place some weight on the German Foreign Office. (The German Foreign Office itself is a question to be debated, because Ribbentrop was a perfect Nazi and von Weizsäcker was not, or at least he claims that he was not sympathetic to Nazism.)

So here was a tragic situation in which both von Weizsäcker and Orsenigo had to undertake a policy not completely their own, a policy with which they did not identify. And then 60 to 70 years later people sit at a table—like we are now—and say, well, he was weak, he did not do his job. This is a little too easy. It was a difficult situation because the Vatican was still unclear about what to do with Germany.

This is especially visible in the period of Pope Pius XI and Secretary of State Pacelli. The policies of both of them may have been identical at the beginning, but they certainly were not at the end of the period. What could Orsenigo do? While protesting on behalf of the Church in Poland, immediately, before he even finished his sentence, his counterpart in the German Foreign Office tells him it is none of his business. It's out of his jurisdiction. The German Foreign Office did not recognize the

9 ADSS, vol. VII, pp. 268-270. Quoted by John F. Morley, *Vatican Diplomacy and the Jews during the Holocaust, 1939-1943* (New York: Ktav Publishing House, 1980), p. 122.

extension of Orsenigo's jurisdiction, now covering Poland. So Orsenigo was doomed to fail.

There is another point I would like to make, concerning Uditore Giuseppe Di Meglio. *Uditore*, as far as I understand, is a rather low diplomatic rank. It's less than an ambassador, even than a counselor; it is the lowest rank in the embassy. Di Meglio waited until he was called back to Rome, and when he went to the Secretariat of State in December 1942, he wrote an unbelievable report about antisemitic actions against Jews! Whoever claims that the Vatican did not know, was not informed, did not understand what was happening, is absolutely mistaken. Di Meglio proves: 1) that information was available in the Embassy of the Holy See in Berlin; 2) that this information was generally not conveyed to the Vatican; 3) that he had to leave his post in order to be able to write such a report, which means that Orsenigo would not let him send such a report. Perhaps, just to be on the safe side, they feared censorship. It is possible, but for reasons I do not know, he was unable to send the same report from Berlin.

This report is particularly interesting[10] because in 1941 a well-known Italian journalist, Curzio Malaparte, wrote, as far as I understand, the first pseudo-novel on the Shoah with amazing descriptions of the Iasi pogrom.[11] The precision of his work was absolutely astonishing. He published it in *Corriere della Sera* in 1941, and after the war, in 1945, in his book *Kaputt*,[12] and he went around telling people what he had seen. The words of Di Meglio are identical to the words in *Kaputt*. I compared them. Which means that an Italian journalist in 1941 could see with his own eyes how Jews were locked in wagons, to such a point that there was no air to breathe, and how, three days later (after these trains had traveled around), the doors were opened, and all the bodies fell out. It was terrible. Di Meglio wrote, without mentioning Malaparte, that an Italian journalist came to the Nunciature, and this was what he reported.

10 Uditore Di Meglio's report to the Secretary of State, December 9, 1942, ADSS, vol. VIII, pp. 738-742.

11 More than 10,000 Jews were killed in the Romanian city of Iasi in a pogrom that began on June 27, 1941.

12 Curzio Malaparte, *Kaputt* (Florence: Vallecchi, 1964), pp. 164-174.

By the way, Malaparte also went to Mussolini in 1942, telling him exactly the same things. So I am full of appreciation for Malaparte, but I am also full of appreciation for Di Meglio, who had the courage, when it was possible, to present a truly amazing report, which was later published in the *Actes et Documents du Saint Siège* (ADSS). The fact that he was not able to send his report while Orsenigo was still there speaks for itself.

There was another, similar problem: Kurt Gerstein, a Nazi officer who made a point of visiting concentration camps, came to the Nunciature wishing to talk with the Nuncio, Orsenigo, but he was rebuffed. I am unsure as to why nobody would receive him. Maybe they felt it was a trap by the Gestapo, or perhaps they did not believe that Gerstein had come in good faith, and therefore refused even to receive the written paper he wanted to leave there. It was only some years later that the Gerstein Report became known. But again, it *was* possible to receive unbelievable news at the Nunciature of Berlin.

One more point: On January 23, 1943, Konrad von Preysing, the Bishop of Berlin, wrote a letter to the Pope. (By the way, there are 18 letters from the Pope to von Preysing; to no other bishop did he ever write so many letters.) Von Preysing wrote, "It would be much better to recall Orsenigo home, because here he is only carrying out the policy of the Gestapo."[13] This is astonishing! In the middle of the war, under the nose of the Nazis, the Bishop of Berlin did not hesitate to ask Pius XII what he was doing and to express his opinion that Orsenigo was doing nothing.[14] (By the way, von Preysing paid for his stand because unlike many of his colleagues who were appointed cardinal during the war, he was not appointed cardinal until the liberation.) Pius XII had a special, personal relationship with him, and he evidently not only sympathized with him, he also believed him. So it *was* known, even then, that Orsenigo couldn't represent the policy of the Holy See, if such a policy existed.

I am not sure such a policy existed. There is conflicting evidence. The letter that Maglione sent on March 15, 1943 is a letter of protest, but this

13 ADSS, vol. VII, pp. 392-396.

14 Letter of von Preysing to Pius XII of January 23, 1943, ADSS, vol. II, pp. 36-37. Von Preysing accused Orsenigo of greater loyalty to the Gestapo than to his fellow Catholics.

protest was not heard in Rome. On October 16, 1943,[15] when Maglione received von Weizsäcker, there was no protest. Von Weizsäcker told Maglione that he should know that he would not forward their conversation to Berlin, and Maglione agreed.

Discussion

Andrea Tornielli: I would like to remark on the report written by Monsignor Di Meglio, whom I was lucky to get to know during the last years of his life. The report, written in Italian, talks about the concentration camps, as follows: "They say such concentration camps have been set up so far in Poland, which makes one think that the Eastern regions, and Poland in particular, have been established, in the German Government's plans, as the final **place of residence** for the Jewish populations of Europe."[16] **Place of residence**. In other words, although Di Meglio spoke about deportation in locked wagons and the fact that Jews had been left to die inside those trains, he did not speak about the Final Solution and the extermination of the Jews. Instead, he maintained that the Germans decided to relocate the Jews to Poland. That is what was written. I certainly have no intention of belittling the magnitude of the matter—this was not the only report made public by Di Meglio—but in this detailed report he's not speaking about the Final Solution as mass extermination, rather as the transfer and relocation of the Jews.

Michael Phayer: I'm hoping that Thomas Brechenmacher can clarify the relationship between Orsenigo and von Preysing. I would also like to come back to a point that Sergio Minerbi made repeatedly, that he's not sure if there was any Vatican policy with regard to the Nuremberg Laws and the copycat laws that followed, such as those in Hungary in 1938 and later in France, when the Vatican was actually given an invitation to comment on the antisemitic laws. At what stage—and maybe other people can clarify this—did the Vatican shift its position with regard to

15 On October 16, 1943 the Germans carried out a roundup in Rome, arresting more than 1,000 Jews and deporting them to Auschwitz.

16 As noted in the Introduction, quotations represent the essence and not always the precise formulation of what can be found in the original document. Emphasis added.

the antisemitic laws? Was it at Nuremberg, or was it later? I would like to hear Thomas Brechenmacher clarify the relationship if possible.

Matteo Napolitano: I have a few comments concerning the relationship between Orsenigo and Pacelli from the moment Orsenigo became the official speaker for both the Holy See and the diplomatic corps at various official events such as celebrations, parties, etc.

Orsenigo sent the text of the speech he intended to deliver ahead of time, evidently for approval. The corrections made by the Secretariat of State are often adjustments that tend to somewhat moderate the effect the local environment has on any diplomat, because a diplomat must always maintain a fair balance between the instructions—the orders he must obey—and the local environment, such as the friendships he establishes with local people.

And so the Holy See instructed him, or rather told him, to attenuate these tones a little, which were—not always of course, but sometimes—a little too favorable with respect to the regime. At a certain point, Pacelli said, the Holy Father, to whom he submitted the text of the speech he intended to make before Hitler, told him to leave out the poetry and concentrate on the substance, without "fluttering around" (*svolazzi*) too much.

My second point is regarding the summoning of Ambassador von Weizsäcker following the roundup of October 16, 1943: I believe this issue should be better defined. There is a controversy in the historiography concerning the "silence" of the Vatican with respect to the raid, because the only source we had was that of the German Ambassador at the Vatican, who very much wanted to demonstrate, with excessive optimism, how successful the outcome of his mission had been. He sent two messages to the Minister of Foreign Affairs in Berlin, but not the minutes of his meeting with Maglione. Professor Minerbi explained that he asked permission not to report to Berlin the essence of his dialogue with the Secretary of State [Maglione]. Maglione agreed provided that action would be taken. And the closing paragraph, which I'm quoting almost literally, reads as follows: "The Ambassador asks, 'And if things should not turn out exactly as the Holy See wishes?' 'The Holy See,' says Maglione, 'does not wish to be faced with the need to protest. Should it be forced to protest, the Holy See shall have to rely on

Providence for the consequences.'" Therefore, we need to investigate the silence of von Weizsäcker, rather than that of the Holy See, in this delicate matter—the raid on the Jews of Rome.

With regard to what was known and why, I would like to point out that in some American documents there is a remark, I think by the Secretary of State, that he did not believe in the existence of the crematorium furnaces. We are talking, if I'm not mistaken, about 1943, when this fact had been published in the *Foreign Relations of the United States,* the official documentary record of major U.S. foreign policy decisions.

Dina Porat: Both presentations point quite clearly to the fact that Orsenigo was circumvented by the German bishops, and he was in a difficult position because his predecessor, now his superior, had been in Germany for 12 years and had all the connections and therefore didn't need him—he could continue them directly. Therefore, Orsenigo did not formulate, and certainly did not dictate, any policy. Rather, the policy of the Vatican towards Germany was definitely Pacelli's or Pius XII's. This places Orsenigo's role as a decision maker out of consideration, more or less. Moreover, it only adds to the questions surrounding Pius XII, his policy, and its results.

One small clarification: Earlier we spoke about 1933—the Transfer Agreement on the one hand and the concordat on the other—as well as other events. During 1933, there was a general feeling that the Nazi regime might be transitory and would fall in a number of months. Did this feeling that perhaps it would be a short-lived regime play a part in the considerations of the Vatican during 1933? The concordat was very hastily drawn up, from January to March, though negotiations started way before, and then it was concluded. Was this feeling a motivation for action on the part of the Vatican?

Susan Zuccotti: Sergio [Minerbi], did I misunderstand you? Was Malaparte's article about Iasi printed in *Corriere della Sera* in 1941? Namely, was it public knowledge throughout Italy in 1941?

My second question concerns the diplomatic pouch. There was an implication that Orsenigo was constrained in his reports because they might have been intercepted. Was there not a secure diplomatic pouch?

My third question is about Kurt Gerstein's report. It's generally known that he was not able to deliver it to the office of Orsenigo, but he did deliver it, did he not, to von Preysing? Do we know for a fact that von Preysing relayed that report to the Vatican?

Thomas Brechenmacher: We are dealing with several problematic issues here. Regarding von Preysing and Orsenigo: I would avoid referring to the bishops in general. The German episcopacy was already divided in the 1930s. One faction tried to reach a consensus in negotiations. The other argued that negotiations did not work and they had to stand up and voice their position in public. Von Preysing's comment on Orsenigo, cited by Sergio Minerbi, has to be understood in that context. I am not sure that his exact words were: "Orsenigo's work is helping the Gestapo." But it is a fact that von Preysing distanced himself considerably from Orsenigo. He wanted Orsenigo to leave. The comment was voiced in the specific situation of the 1940s, when Orsenigo was running out of options. He still followed his old strategy of sending in notes of protest. As you know, the exchange of letters between Orsenigo and the government of the Reich was published in three heavy volumes. In 1943, von Preysing declared that Orsenigo's approach had failed. Therefore, he sent this request to the Pope: Shouldn't we dismiss this nuncio, who is not achieving anything anymore?

But we should also remember that the consensus had not always been to dismiss the nuncio. The matter had already been discussed in 1936. At the Holy See, the opinion was that they knew Orsenigo was not the most suitable candidate for this position. Nevertheless, in 1936, a congregation of cardinals came to the conclusion that it was better to keep Orsenigo in place. First of all, they didn't know if a new nuncio would be accredited. That remained uncertain. The second argument was that they needed a nuncio as a channel of information. We know this from the sources. In 1939, Pius XII discussed this matter with the German bishops. They concluded that they knew that Orsenigo was not the most suitable candidate for that position. But they asked that he be kept in place, for he was an important channel of information. There had certainly been a development. Later, in 1943, we see different positions, with that of von Preysing documented in the sources.

The German bishops are the first problematic issue. The second, of course, is that under normal circumstances, a nuncio does not make policies by himself. He is the representative of the Pope in a foreign country, and he has to represent Papal policy. He is not supposed to act on his own. The only exception to this rule was Pacelli himself, during his term as Nuncio in Germany in the 1920s. He did something that nuncios usually never do. He was active in shaping Church policy. Orsenigo could not do that, and he was not supposed to. He was not a decision maker, or a person that would press for a decision. To judge his behavior in this context raises the question, what role did Orsenigo play? The conclusion is that Orsenigo did in fact deliver valuable information, for example, on the persecution and murder of the Jews. Orsenigo reported on July 4, 1942 that there were rumors circulating in Berlin about mass deportations and mass killings happening in the East. This was prior to Di Meglio's report.

Another point: There was an encryption in use. We can see that in the original texts. Passages classified as "dangerous" or "delicate" were encrypted. My judgment is limited, as I am not an expert in that field, but I was told by someone with an interest in these passages that the code was fairly easy to decipher.

So, Di Meglio actually went to Rome to report directly. The fact that Di Meglio wrote his report in Rome leads me to conclude that this was not happening against the will of the Nuncio. Or perhaps it was done that way because the Nuncio did not want it to be sent from Berlin.

Sergio Minerbi: First of all, to the question of what exactly von Preysing wrote. In his letter of January 23, 1943 to Pius XII, von Preysing accused the Nuncio of being more loyal to the Gestapo than to Catholicism. I quote:

> His almost instinctive position against groups loyal to the faith, who have come into conflict with the Gestapo have robbed him of any sympathy and trust in the eyes of the Catholics in Germany. [...] Perhaps it would be possible to [have him] replace[d by] Monsignor Colli, by someone with a brain and a heart as *chargé d'affaires*, while His Eminence the Nuncio would step out for a prolonged vacation.[17]

17 ADSS, vol. IX, doc. 26, pp. 93-94.

Mr. Tornielli said that they were not speaking about the Final Solution. This may be true, but the Vatican was already aware of it from other sources, as well as from Pirro Scavizzi, a military chaplain who went to Russia with the hospital trains of the Order of Malta. Scavizzi sent four reports to the Pontiff, and had seen him twice, personally. So whether they did or did not take action was not due to a lack of information.

To Susan Zuccotti: In the edition I have of *Kaputt*, which is a very early edition—1945-1946, I believe—Malaparte wrote that certain parts are based on his own reports in *Corriere della Sera*. He was a war correspondent for *Corriere della Sera*, stationed first in Croatia and then in Romania. He was a Fascist, but he was also a Communist, he was everything, but this was the first time, as far as I know, during the Shoah, that somebody had written such things in a newspaper and then in a book.

Regarding diplomatic pouches: Yes, they could be intercepted. Yesterday, I was reading a book about Orsenigo written by a lady in Milan, possibly a relative, in which she describes the camps set up in Germany after 1943 for 800,000 Italians. Between 1943 and 1945, soldiers and other Italians—non-Jewish—were concentrated and interned in Germany. Orsenigo was not allowed to go to the camp. He could not send a letter to the camp. However, a clever Italian, a military chaplain, managed to send registered letters regularly to Orsenigo in Berlin with a stamp that it had passed military censorship. It cost him one box of cigarettes. So even when there are problems of communication, with Italian wit you could overcome them.

To the question of the Gerstein Report: It was delivered to the legal assistant of von Preysing. I am not aware that it arrived at the Vatican, because we have no reaction from that side. Maybe it was sent; maybe not. It was published after the liberation.

Session Four: Pius XII's Messages to European Bishops, Leaders and Governments

Pope Pius could have communicated secretly with European bishops to tell them to encourage Catholics confidentially to protect Jews or to protest publicly against Nazi atrocities. Did he do so? Do we have any knowledge about papal appeals to local authorities, on behalf of Jews, besides the known exceptions of Slovakia and Hungary? To what extent did Pius XII influence government policies towards the Jewish populations in Catholic countries?

Presenter I: Matteo Napolitano

When we speak about the Holy See, we speak about a *sui generis* state, a state that has no territory and, consequently, according to classic diplomatic codes, does not have a temporal power capable of making people respect it [the Holy See]. Thus, what kind of diplomacy can the Holy See exercise, considering these objective limitations? The Holy See, in its effectiveness, in its diplomatic action, and in its spiritual action often depends upon the temporal power of others. In other words, how are its actions perceived and acknowledged by other states with territories, populations, and laws of their own, as well as superior political powers?

When Stalin asked at the Teheran Conference[1] how many divisions the Pope had, the answer appeared in *Time,*[2] and Stalin received it through Churchill. Stalin was told that he would meet the Pope's divisions in heaven. This is just to give you an idea of how aware Pius XII was that this type of diplomacy, classic diplomacy, had its limits in terms of overall power.

1 The Teheran Conference was held between November 28 and December 1, 1943. The participants were Joseph Stalin, Franklin D. Roosevelt and Winston Churchill.

2 "Urbi et Orbi," *Time*, December 14, 1953.

This is where alternative research stems from. Throughout World War II, the diplomatic action of the Holy See had objective limitations. The first of these was that World War II did not manifest itself exactly like World War I. It contained a significant ideological conflict, where the war between powers, as commonly defined, became a war between contrasting ideological systems. As was rightly mentioned this morning, even in 1942 it was not guaranteed that the democratic system—meaning the allied countries (if we add the Soviet Union, we would have a bit of difficulty talking in these terms, but just for the sake of synthesis)—would be able to defeat Hitler and the new Hitlerian order.

The second limitation was that after January 1942, the Shoah represented a new, unprecedented phenomenon. The project of exterminating all European Jewry was something that connected all the states. We can see this in the actions of the other democratic powers, as documented by the American OSS [Office of Strategic Services] papers. There was a problem of priorities: The democratic powers did not always consider the destruction of the extermination camps a major priority in the war.[3]

So classic diplomacy had to be abandoned. And, in fact, this was what happened. The Holy See's political power could only be successful if other entities listened to it [the Holy See]. Otherwise, the situation reverted to the quite antiquated concept of *Res Publica sub Deo*,[4] where the Pope appeared to have a political power capable of applying his rules and making others respect them. Whoever was of this opinion in 1940, in a generally secular and laicized world, naturally made reference somehow to a rather old, temporal, concept of papacy.

I've mentioned an alternative diplomacy: keeping alive the entire network of nunciatures or dioceses. However, in Poland there was no nunciature. Further, the Primate of Poland escaped when the Soviets and the Germans divided the country among themselves, a joint dominance that in fact brought about the extinction of Poland.

So what alternative was there? One I would call "catacomb diplomacy," namely, a diplomacy that had to be conveyed underground,

3 Richard Breitman, *Official Secrets: What the Nazis Planned, What the British and Americans Knew* (New York: Hill and Wang, 1998).

4 Literally, "public affairs, under God," meaning the primacy of religious power over civil power.

through the delicate network of nunciatures and dioceses that still existed, in order to act as much as possible on behalf of the Jews and all those who were suffering. One piece of evidence that we have of the success of this kind of diplomacy is what happened after the war. From what I've seen, the Jews who survived the Shoah considered Pius XII a great friend. The manifestations of gratitude are innumerable, but I shall not dwell on this data, of which we are all aware.[5]

Let us now analyze the intermediary interpretive filters that shape or guide the way we see Pius XII.

1. Anti-communism. In my opinion, Pius XII's anti-communism does not account for everything, for one simple reason: Pius XII's model of anti-communism is not Hitler, but rather a "Western branded," pro-American, anti-communism. Thus, I am somewhat hesitant to accept the theory that anti-communism affected Pius XII's actions in favor of the Jews.

2. The relationship with Hitler. Let us not forget that Hitler was considered an acceptable statesman for a long time. No one broke off their diplomatic relationship with Nazi Germany when Hitler enacted a series of antisemitic laws.

3. Pius XII's attitude towards Zionism. This topic can be interpreted in different ways, some of which present favorable viewpoints. It is true that there were some reservations, to a certain extent, with respect to the planned establishment of a Jewish state in Palestine, but this did not prevent the transfer of Jews to Palestine through a rescue network, which also passed through Monsignor Roncalli, then apostolic delegate in Istanbul and the future Pope John XXIII.[6]

Another topic I would like to discuss is the existence of any documents that can prove concrete assistance on behalf of the Jews. Information gathered on the situation in the Baltic countries, in Poland, and elsewhere demonstrates that a network operated by the Vatican did indeed work to

5 Even during the war there was a similar pattern of gratitude from Jews. See, for example, *Actes et Documents du Saint Siège relatifs à la Seconde Guerre Mondiale* (ADSS) (Vatican City: Libreria Editrice Vaticana, 1965-1980), vol. X, doc. 10.

6 Uri Bialer, *Cross on the Star of David: The Christian World in Israel's Foreign Policy, 1948-1967* (Indiana: Indiana University Press, 2005). The Vatican officially recognized the State of Israel in December 1993.

the benefit of the Jews. We could argue about Scavizzi's report, which is a little problematic in this regard, but we don't have time for that now.[7] We can argue about what was known. We can obviously debate why the American secret services blocked Riegner's telegram[8] from the World Jewish Congress of Geneva. We can certainly discuss all of these points, but one thing must be mentioned: This network of assistance was indeed put into effect—albeit in quite an intricate and complicated manner that depended upon the conditions and circumstances of the moment in different fields, such as visa applications. It must also be emphasized that no distinction whatsoever was made—maybe because there was not enough time to do so—between non-baptized and baptized Jews.

One could claim that they accepted non-baptized Jews in the vague hope that they would be baptized later. Anything can be inserted within a certain context. But the main thing is that work had been done in this respect, to the point that they wanted to get in touch with and support the existing rescue agencies, and the American Jews wanted to cooperate with the Holy See in this endeavor (this is documented).[9] I don't believe these Jews were baptized American Jews.

Pius XII accepted this collaboration with American Jewry and even declined the proposal made by the associations of American Jews to pay the Holy See money for its help on behalf of the European Jews. This collaboration, however, did not start right away, but only from 1940, when Jews began to be interned. There are three documents, not published in the *Actes et Documents du Saint Siège* (ADSS), in which the Secretary of State offers financial assistance to the detainees of a concentration camp in the south of Italy. Thirteen thou-

7 Don Pirro Scavizzi was a Catholic priest who was sent as military chaplain to the Eastern Front. He wrote four secret reports for Pius XII, which included descriptions of things he witnessed at the front.

8 Gerhart Riegner, representative of the World Jewish Congress in Geneva, sent a telegram in August 1942, informing the Allies of the German plan to exterminate the European Jews. He received this information from German industrialist Eduard Schulte.

9 For the contacts with the World Jewish Congress, see, for example, M. Easterman to Monsignor Godfrey, July 19, 1943, ADSS, vol. IX, annexed to doc. 271, pp. 406-408; Easterman to Pius XII, August 2, 1943, ibid., pp. 417-418; Easterman to the apostolic delegate in London, Monsignor Godfrey, September 24, 1943, ibid., pp. 488-489. See also Godfrey's reply in note number 2, p. 489.

sand lire were given in two separate checks, each attached to a letter from the Secretariat of State. One of these letters is signed, if I'm not mistaken, by Montini.[10] I have here a copy of these documents. Anyone who wishes to review them is welcome to do so; they are not confidential.[11]

So the checks were sent and a list was composed detailing precisely how this money was distributed. The Archbishop of the Campania Region, Giovanni Palatucci's[12] uncle, made a list of items that shows that some of this money was spent on visas. I forgot to mention that in the first letter, the Secretariat of State demanded the money be spent above all "to benefit those who suffered persecution for reasons of race." This was the exact wording used in that letter, a private letter. Palatucci obviously understood what this meant, and although Jews were not specifically indicated, I don't think there could have been any possible misunderstanding. And afterwards, we see in the list an item regarding the purchase of passports.

Another example of help given to Jews is when the British delegation applied to the Holy See for help with the transfer of Polish Jews to Palestine. In this case, the Holy See was criticized because Maglione's message (or perhaps it was Domenico Tardini's) to wait was unequivocal. He was engaged in a waiting game, while the Jews were in a hurry to escape.

What was the proposal made by the British? They suggested helping heads of Polish Jewish families get to Palestine, offering Hitler in exchange Germans who resided in Palestine. So I ask myself: Those Germans residing in Palestine, were they not Jews who had already moved there?

10 Giovanni Battista Montini (later Pope Paul VI) became, with Domenico Tardini, the closest confidants of Pius XII. When Secretary of State Maglione died in 1944, Pacelli appointed Montini and Tardini heads of the State Department.

11 Archivio Centrale dello Stato (ACS), Ministero dell'Interno, Direzione Generale di Pubblica Sicurezza. The documents are published in *Giovanni Palatucci: il poliziotto che salvò migliaia di Ebrei*, Dipartimento della Pubblica Sicurezza del Ministero dell'Interno (a cura di) (Rome: Laurus Robuffo, 2002). These documents include the correspondence between the Vatican, the Apostolic Nuncio in Italy, and the Bishop of Campania, Monsignor Palatucci, as a response to the requests for help presented by Palatucci on behalf of the internees.

12 Giovanni Palatucci was recognized as a Righteous Among the Nations in 1990.

Interjection from the audience: No, they were Templers.[13]

Matteo Napolitano: That's not what the documents say.

Interjection from the audience: Maybe not, but it was the Templers.

Matteo Napolitano: My doubt is justified based on the reading of the Vatican documents.

My last point concerns the famous "silence." Was it a culpable silence, or rather operative reserve? What was it all about? On September 29, 1939 (Professor Minerbi will correct me if I'm mistaken), the French Prime Minister Édouard Daladier, who was trying to make Pius XII talk both for internal political reasons and also because of the general conditions of the time, asked Pius XII to speak out openly on the war situation in Poland. A short time later, on October 20, 1939, there was the first encyclical on Poland. So what did Daladier ask for? He asked him, for understandable reasons, not to speak against Germany, but against the Soviet Union. What Daladier was actually asking Pius XII to do was to speak against a state with which France was not even engaged in war, while keeping silent with regard to a state with which France was at that moment at war, albeit for less than a month.[14]

This shows that the issue of silence should be analyzed more thoroughly, when talking about what he should have done.

How was the first encyclical on Poland received by Great Britain? Extremely favorably, according to the war cabinet's report, dated October 30, 1939 and found in Britain's national archives. This leads us to ask ourselves whether the question of silence should be considered not from the viewpoint of the Vatican documents (because it's only natural for an historian to demand that all possible archives be opened), but from the

13 Templers are members of the Temple Society (in German: *Tempelgesellschaft*), a German Protestant sect with roots in the Pietist movement of the Lutheran Church. During World War II, the British Mandate considered the Templers residing in the Land of Israel to be enemy aliens and they were subjected to different degrees of segregation. Around 1,000 Templers were exchanged for 550 Jews who were under German occupation.

14 *Documents Diplomatiques Français, 1939 (3 septembre-31 décembre)*, Ministère des affaires étrangèries, France, Commission de publication des documents diplomatiques français (Brussels: PIE–Peter Lang, 2002), doc. 164. This document was reproduced in ADSS, vol. III, doc. 18.

point of view of those who had read the words of Pius XII. This is valid with respect to the 1939 encyclical and, it seems to me, with respect to the famous radio broadcast in December 1942 where the word "race" was mentioned and not the word "Jews."[15] Nevertheless, *The New York Times* widely reported about the encyclical, claiming that the Pope had finally expressed himself clearly about what was happening.

In conclusion, there are many complex questions that need to be studied. Above all, an attentive comparison must be carried out between the documents already available to us and those concerning the pontificate of Pius XII, to which we hope the Vatican will allow access (in the near future).

Presenter II: Paul O'Shea

The first point I want to make, which is at the heart of what we're meeting about over these two days, is, as Matteo Napolitano has already alluded to, that it is wrong to take Pius out of context. He did not act alone; he was the head of an institution, in whatever way you wish to describe that—political, theological, religious, etc. He worked with a team, in whatever way you understand that. He was also the sovereign of the Vatican State. He was not alone. He worked with other people.

Having said that, to use U.S. President Harry Truman's line, "The buck stops here." The buck did stop at Pacelli's desk. He was a micromanager, so everything crossed his desk, just about. Certainly everything to do with Germany, and definitely anything that he considered of serious importance.

So the question about whether he knew what was happening throughout the war and beforehand—the six months before the war—is a bit of a non-question, because he knew. He knew as much as any other well-informed head of state anywhere in Europe or the United States.

Second, the Pope was, as is the case today, as powerful as the Church, i.e., as the entire Christian or Catholic people allows him to be. If it suits a government to listen to papal policy, then great. If it suits a govern-

15 The term used by Pius XII was *stirpe*, which can be translated as "race" or "ethnicity."

ment not to listen to papal policy, then there's nothing that can be done. It was as real back in the 1930s and 1940s as it is today.

Third, he knew from as early as 1935 that there would be no martyrs in Germany. The Catholics in Germany were not prepared to die for their faith; they were certainly not prepared to put their lives on the line to save Jews. I believe this caused him great distress, and he heard that from the German bishops.

Fourth, there were watershed moments throughout the years of the war, and hindsight is a valuable tool to the historian, but it's dangerous to read into it—looking at the history as we're doing today—because it leads to the possibility of creating false statements.

The world of 1939 was a vastly different world to that of 1942. The world before Stalingrad was a different world to the world afterwards, for the Allies as much as for the Axis nations.

In that context, looking at the questions posed, could the Pope have communicated secretly? That's a problematic question, as Thomas Brechenmacher alluded earlier; the Vatican's secret codes were little more than schoolboy "lemon juice on paper" exercises that could have been read by anybody with the slightest knowledge of secret communications. The Vatican knew that material sent out of Rome to anywhere was likely to be intercepted by the Italians, who then carefully resealed it; when it crossed the border into Switzerland *they* read it; and when it crossed the border into Germany *they* read it; so by the time it got to Berlin it had probably been handled by about three or four different secret services. The Pope knew that everybody read his mail. And it was the same with correspondence going to Rome.

Did this stop communication? No, it didn't. The published record in the ADSS shows that even with the use of some circumspect language, the Pope communicated clearly with the bishops. The letters to von Preysing is one example.

Following on from that, the evidence provided in the ADSS points to continual communication from the Pope, Secretary of State Luigi Maglione, and others to the nuncios, apostolic delegates, and *chargés d'affaires* throughout Europe, occupied and unoccupied, as well as to local bishops. And there were more than a few frank disclosures made in letters sent to the Pope. One example is the letter of the Ukrainian Bishop of Lvov [Lemberg], Andrey Sheptyts'kyi. His letter, written somewhere between August 29 and 31, 1942, describes in enough detail a massacre of Jews in Kiev, possibly Babi Yar,[16] to suggest that the bishop had been given first-hand information from a witness, and this information was forwarded on, uncensored, to Rome.[17] There's no response to that letter in the ADSS.

As I said, the Pope used circumspective language in writing to the bishops, and in particular to von Preysing: "The decisions concerning the Jews [and by that I understand the Pope to mean decisions relating to rescue operations, etc.] were best left to the judgment of the local bishops."[18] This appears to be the pattern that Pacelli followed with the German bishops in particular.

The next issue is the appeals to local authorities. There is some data on this, but not enough at this point to provide a satisfactory answer.

There is one huge area that remains largely unexplored: care for prisoners of war, refugees, and displaced persons, in which Pius undertook his most visible pastoral and public initiative. Within a few weeks of the outbreak of war in September 1939, the Pope reorganized the Vatican Information Office (VIO) with the mandate to offer "universal and impartial" service to all who asked for help. He placed this office under the supervision of Giovanni Montini and the Congregation of Extraordinary Ecclesiastical Affairs; it was directed by Russian-born Bishop Alexander Evreinoff.

Between September 1939 and October 31, 1947, over 21 million letters and telegrams passed through the VIO. Vatican Radio broadcast over 1.25 million messages between June 1940 and May 1945. It became an international clearinghouse for families of prisoners of every culture, religious tradition, and political background, seeking news of other family members, including Jews.[19]

During the war years, the Vatican received and acted upon thousands of letters requesting help to locate Jewish families caught in German-occupied Europe. The collection of selected documents in *Inter Arma*

16 A ravine located in northwestern Kiev, the capital of the Ukraine, where many tens of thousands of Jews were murdered from September 1941 onwards.

17 Andrei Sheptytsky to Pius XII, August 29-31, 1942, ADSS, vol. IIIb, doc. 406.

18 ADSS, vol. II, doc. 105.

19 *Inter Arma Caritas: l'Ufficio informazioni vaticano per i prigionieri di guerra istituito da Pio XII, 1939-1947*, two volumes (Vatican City: Archivio Segreto Vaticano, 2004).

Caritas, published in 2004, demonstrates the efforts undertaken by the staff of the Vatican Information Office.[20] The sheer scale of the work pointed to the most energetic and consistent attempt undertaken by any government or non-government agency during the war years to locate and find Jews across Europe.

I now move to the next point: observing political neutrality. This was one aspect of Vatican diplomacy during the war. Another was addressing the moral questions that arose because of the war. Broadly speaking, papal protest at German Nazi atrocities can be classified under four headings:

1. Instructions and reminders of Christian doctrine. The abuse and killing of defenseless people is wrong, it violates Divine Law, and these crimes cry out to God for vengeance. He says that explicitly in the Christmas address of 1939.

2. Exhortations and direct admonitions to the clergy and the Church faithful. The Pope's letters to the German bishops throughout the war pointed at this in a general way. Now, it is unthinkable that the Pope would say to the bishops—please remind the Faithful of the Divine Law, that it's wrong to kill people, or it's wrong to sleep with your neighbor's wife, or it's wrong to covet his donkey—the bishop should be doing that anyway. The record shows, for example, that when it came to the euthanasia campaign, von Galen in Münster certainly did.[21] I have, however, yet to see any documentary evidence that says he protested to the deportation of the Jews from Münster.

So, while there were occasional mentions of specific issues related to the prosecution of the war, these were few and far between. The most famous occurred in the 1943 letter to von Preysing in Berlin. It's the one that I've already cited of April 30, 1943.

3. Exhortations and direct admonitions to responsible authorities. There is ample evidence in the ADSS of the activity of the nuncios, Secretary of State Maglione, and Pius himself writing and appealing to heads of state on behalf of hostages, prisoners of war, refugees, etc.

20 Ibid.

21 Clemens August Graf von Galen was the Bishop of Műnster. He was a known critic of the Nazi regime and he issued public denunciations of the Nazi euthanasia program.

Volumes 6, 8, and 10 of the ADSS are devoted exclusively to the victims of the war.

The concern of the Pope covered an enormous range of people, situations, and war zones. One strange little example from the Australian perspective: There were a lot of Italian prisoners of war in Australia. The apostolic delegate in Australia, Bishop Giovanni (John/Jack) Panico (the locals called him "Panicky Jack"), wrote to Rome to say they needed help looking after the Italian prisoners of war. Rome responded.

Limited resources, as Napolitano pointed out, meant Vatican responses were often restricted to Italy. Outside of Italy, the Pope had to rely on the good will and the good faith of Catholic and other people.

4. Diplomatic actions by the nuncios and the Secretariat of State. The most limiting disability of the Holy See was its inability to enforce its will. Stalin's "How many divisions has the Pope got?" is a good example. The Vatican was totally dependent on the willingness of governments and local leaders to accept moral responsibility for their actions. As an officially neutral state, the Vatican constantly balanced its statements between all warring parties and, I would suggest, satisfied none. Consequently, the major diplomatic statements were couched in archaic diplomatic terms designed to express a general moral point, but not to make any particular judgment of the party concerned.

Applying the same categories to what was possible for the Jews of Europe, building on what's gone before, what I call "a pattern of possibilities" emerges.

First: Instructions and reminders of Christian doctrine. The public addresses that the Pope made at Easter, on his name day on June 2, and at Christmas made frequent mention of the immorality of killing the defenseless. Jews certainly came under this heading, but were never named, apart from general references to the innocent and those persecuted for reasons of race.

Second: Exhortations and direct admonitions to the clergy and the faithful of the Church. The Christmas address of 1942 was the closest Pius ever got to making an unequivocal public statement condemning the murder of the Jews. The message was not lost on those prepared to read and listen carefully. Moreover, according to the popular news reports of the day, the Pope's reference to the Jews was recognized without ambiguity. It made headlines in *The New York Times* and *The*

Times of London. It was reported extensively throughout the press in Australia, in *The Sydney Morning Herald*. The Germans, of course, listened to every single word he said. Ribbentropp said that this was a thorough condemnation of everything National Socialism stood for; as far as the German Foreign Office was concerned, the 1942 Christmas address showed the Jew-loving Pope defending the Jews. However, the address was largely read and listened to outside occupied Europe.

Of greater potency was the communication Pius maintained with the bishops of Germany and throughout occupied Europe. As has been mentioned before, in the third volume of the ADSS, a two-part volume that deals with Poland and the Baltic States, there is a plethora of documentation on communication between Rome and the bishops of the Baltic States and Poland. It may have been disrupted many, many times, but the mail still got through.

Third: Exhortations and direct admonitions to responsible government authorities. There's ample evidence of the activity of the nuncios, Secretary of State Luigi Maglione, and Pius himself writing and appealing to people such as the renegade priest, President Tiso in Slovakia, Regent Horthy in Hungary, Premier Antonescu in Romania, Minister Laval and Marshal Pétain in Vichy, as well as Mussolini and Hitler, pleading for a halt to transports to the East, for the provision of basic healthcare and adequate food, and for permission for the inhabitants of the ghettos and camps to practice their religion.[22]

The results of these direct admonitions varied according to the nature of the country, local antisemitism, that country's relationship with Nazi Germany, and the stage of the war. Despite some success in halting aspects of the Final Solution, the appeals of the Pope and his legates were largely unsuccessful. Certainly, most of the admonitions sent to Berlin were ignored. At his trial, Ribbentropp said the top drawer of his desk was stuffed with letters from Rome.

22 Pius's communications with heads of state were usually determined by the nature of his relationship with that person. Since Hitler and Mussolini required delicate and tactful approaches, Pius communicated with them through the nuncios, and then it was often done in the form of appeals in "the name of the Holy Father," see, for example, ADSS vol. VIII, doc. 182, note 5, p. 326. While Mussolini was prepared to make some pretense at considering papal requests, Hitler usually ignored them, preferring to leave it to Ribbentrop to deal with the Vatican. As for other Axis or Axis-allied heads of state, the Pope's appeals to them are found scattered throughout the ADSS, written by the Secretary of State.

Finally under this heading: diplomatic action. The published record demonstrates a constant level of activity of information being received and responses communicated. This area of Vatican activity will remain largely speculative while the archives relevant to the war remain closed. This area remains the single greatest lacuna facing historians.

Until the archives of the Secretariat of State are opened for the period 1939-1945, it is impossible to compile a complete picture of what the Pope and his coworkers did or did not do for the Jews of Europe. The published documents are a valuable source, but only give the end result, not the details or the processes that led to the result, and the earlier discussion we had about *Mit brennender Sorge* and some of the related issues about the Reich's concordat point to that. The opening of the archives concerning Germany up to 1939 have now given us a far better picture of the tensions within the Vatican and how they came to produce the documents they did. The International Catholic Jewish Historical Commission came to grief on precisely this point in July 2001.[23] In their 47 questions arising from the ADSS, the Commission repeatedly asked for access to more documentation that would illuminate and explain particular points.

Historians need to see the memoranda that flowed between the different offices of the secretariat, the Pope's notes, etc. Until then, the most that can be said based on the evidence primarily from the ADSS and the few scraps that have come through from diocesan archives, the work that Susan Zuccotti has done in *Under His Very Windows,*[24] and other testimonies that have begun to surface over the last 10 to 20 years give us hints of what happened.

Until we have the opening of the official archives, all I can say is that from the evidence available, Pius XII had a highly accurate picture of the Nazi killing process from at least the middle of 1941, and the Vatican, in his name, was engaged in a series of protests to heads of states in an attempt to halt the deportations. With the exception of Vichy,

23 In 1999, the Vatican appointed a commission of three Jewish and three Catholic scholars to assess the wartime behavior of the Vatican. In October 2000, the commission issued a preliminary report with 47 questions on Pius's behavior during the Holocaust. After failing to gain access to the Vatican archives, the commission resigned in 2001.

24 Susan Zuccotti, *Under His Very Windows: The Vatican and the Holocaust in Italy* (New Haven: Yale University Press, 2000).

which was a whole other case, and particularly the torturous logic of the marriage laws and the attempts to engage in rescue, the evidence seems to be that they were directed primarily at baptized Jews because of local circumstances and that most of the rescue work operating throughout Europe was done on local and private initiatives.

The argument that the Pope ordered the convents and monasteries of Rome to take in Jews is, I think, suspicious. I would be very surprised if such a written order exists, despite recent reports in the media that such documentation has been found. Likewise, it would be extremely silly to think that the Pope would say, "Don't rescue them."

So at the end of my reflection on the papal response, on the Pope, and the Holocaust, if the Pope is to be blamed for not speaking clearly enough (and I think there is an argument for that), then responsibility for that blame must rest upon the whole of the Catholic world too. It wasn't just the Pope.

Yes, he had a moral obligation to speak the truth without fear, as he says in his first encyclical, *Summi Pontificatus*,[25] and as he repeated throughout the war in his public addresses.

Did he agonize over what he did and didn't do? I think he did. But—and this is speaking as a Catholic and as an historian—as the visible head of Christ's Church on Earth, who believed that this temporal organization served the higher purpose of preparing the people of God to enter into eternity, I believe he placed that position as his foremost concern and there is a logic to that. He placed it on such a level that nothing could be allowed to impede that final objective. Because at the end of the day, Pius XII was a late Tridentine Catholic,[26] a man shaped in the ecclesiology of the late Tridentine period, who believed that ultimately the Church was the vehicle of salvation and that human history would be judged not by the Hitlers, Mussolinis, Roosevelts or Churchills of the world, but as taught in the Christian scriptures, "By the God and Father of our Lord Jesus Christ."

And so I repeat: If the Pope is to be said to have been negligent in his duty, then that negligence must also be shared by the rest of the Church,

25 The encyclical was issued on October 20, 1939.

26 The term "Tridentine" refers to the Ecumenical Council of Trent, held in the 16th century, and to the teaching and legislation decided during that council.

because the evidence is absolutely unequivocal that the European Catholic Church did not rise up to save the Jews of Europe.

Respondent: Michael Phayer

A preparatory remark: Not only will we know far more when the archives from 1939 until the end of the war are opened, we also lag far behind. We, those people interested in Christianity and the Holocaust, lag far behind other Holocaust historians who have researched the archives in Eastern Europe, digested much of that material, and incorporated it into Holocaust literature, thanks to Yad Vashem and the United States Holocaust Memorial Museum. So we have a long way to go.

In general, I agree with Paul O'Shea that the responsibility [for not speaking out enough concerning the Jews] is a shared responsibility. Underlying that, and this is my general conclusion, is that there was no way Pope Pius XII could have spoken out publicly, because the entire Christian world was immersed in antisemitism. But certainly he could have spoken secretly to any number of European bishops sympathetic to the Jews' suffering. There were some who were not antisemitic, who would listen with open ears, and many others who would not. At the end of the day, the Church was divided at the very time it was coming under the heel of the Communist regime.

Specifically, did letters get to Pope Pius XII? Did he know what was going on? Just read the letters the Polish bishops and others wrote to the Pope about what the Germans were doing to the Polish Catholics. It was terrible persecution. He certainly got that information. Then things turned around, as I explained earlier, and the Polish Catholics supplanted Polish Jews at the work places and they stopped writing to Pius XII. They didn't tell him what was happening to the Polish Jews. The Polish bishops later apologized for this, on the 50th anniversary of the end of World War II.

And now, after not speaking out on behalf of Polish Catholics, the Pope had basically backed himself into a corner. Had he then spoken on behalf of the Jews, Polish Catholics would have criticized him relentlessly.

Czechoslovakia was out of control, as Paul O'Shea mentioned, because of Monsignor Tiso. There was no way the Vatican could deal with him—you all know the famous quote by Tardini[27]—and so they turned to the civil officials, and they made a decent effort in that regard.

The case of Hungary is particularly acute. Nuncio Angelo Rotta was willing to go out of his way personally and officially for the Jewish people. The relationship between Rotta and the Cardinal Primate of Hungary Justinian Seredi, however, was totally shredded, because the antisemitic Seredi would not take the lead in defending the Jews in Hungary late in the war. And so Pope Pius could only communicate about the Hungarian Jews through civil channels, not through the Church. And he did, but very late, and only in a limited way. When half of Hungarian Jewry had already been shipped off to Auschwitz, an appeal was made to Pope Pius XII by the Jews, by Roosevelt, by Churchill, to address the Hungarian people over the radio and save who was left. But Pope Pius did not do that. He was not willing to push Justinian Seredi any further than he already had, which was not very far.

A sideline: Franklin Gowen, assistant to Myron Taylor, President Roosevelt's personal envoy to the Vatican, claimed that the reason Pius XII refused to give the radio address was his fear of Communism.[28] He knew that at that point in the war, the Communists were going to take over Hungary; they would occupy all of Eastern Europe, and he did not want to divide the Hungarian people on the question of what to do with the Jews. However, there were at least three, if not four, Hungarian bishops who were more than ready to speak out on behalf of the Jews in Hungary. There's a division between them and the majority of bishops under Justinian Seredi. The case of Hungary does not show the Vatican in a very strong light. Or rather, it shows it in too strong a light.

In Austria, as we know, Cardinal Innitzer got into great trouble at the Vatican for welcoming the Nazis at the time of the *Anschluss*. Later on though, Innitzer actually did quite a lot to help save Jews. Whether or not this was under direction from the Vatican remains unknown.

27 The quotation is: "The problem is that the president of Slovakia is a priest. Everybody understands that the Holy See cannot control Hitler. But who will understand that it cannot restrain a priest?" Notes of Tardini, July 13, 1942, ADSS, vol. XIII, p. 598.

28 F. Gowen, Vatican City, to Myron C. Taylor, November 7, 1944, U.S. National Archives and Records Administration (NARA), Entry 1069, Box 4, Location 250/48/29/05.

Another case that puts the Vatican in a very poor light is Croatia. We have an expert on Croatia here who wrote his MA thesis on the Catholic Church and the Holocaust in Croatia, which was, as you know, the remnant state of Yugoslavia.[29] Could Pope Pius XII have communicated with the government and bishops of Croatia? Of course he could have! He personally held discussions with the murderer Ante Pavelić,[30] one of the top killers of World War II, before and during the Holocaust.

He was also in constant contact with Archbishop Aloysius Stepinac. He knew what was going on; Stepinac knew what was going on! Stepinac was a strong supporter, as was Pius XII, of the Catholic State of Croatia, but not of the murders. While this issue is unclear, I'm coming down strongly in favor of Stepinac and against the Vatican. They didn't back up Stepinac, either then or later on.[31]

We must remember that the genocide in Croatia was largely against Orthodox Christians. 60,000 Jews were killed out of more than 400,000.[32]

Germany is another case that needs special attention. Thomas Brechenmacher was absolutely correct in what he said this morning. The reason that von Preysing and Orsenigo did not get along is that they had two different agendas: Von Preysing had had enough of the concordat; he wanted the Pope to speak out. He wanted the end of it. Orsenigo wanted to play the same game the Vatican and Pius XII were

29 Jovan Ćulibrk, *Holocaust Historiography in Yugoslavia and its Successor Countries*, unpublished MA thesis, Rothberg International School, The Hebrew University of Jerusalem, 2009.

30 Croatian Fascist leader who headed the Ustashe nationalistic group, and from April 1941 headed the Ustashe Independent State of Croatia, which collaborated fully with Nazi Germany.

31 Menachem Shelah, "'Christian Confrontations with the Holocaust': The Catholic Church in Croatia, the Vatican and the Murder of the Croatian Jews," *Holocaust and Genocide Studies* 4, no. 3 (1989), pp. 323–339; Norman J.W. Goda, "The Ustaša: Murder and Espionage," *U.S. Intelligence and the Nazis,* edited by Richard Breitman, Norman J.W. Goda, Timothy Naftali and Robert Wolfe (Washington, D.C.: National Archives Trust Fund Board for Nazi War Crimes and Japanese Imperial Government Records Interagency Working Groups, 2004), pp. 206 ff.

32 Vinko Nikolić, "Genocide in Satellite Croatia during the Second World War," in Michael Berenbaum, ed., *A Mosaic of Victims: Non-Jews Persecuted and Murdered by the Nazis* (New York: New York University Press, 1990), pp.74–79; Jonathan Steinberg, "Types of Genocide? Croatians, Serbs and Jews, 1941-45," in David Cesarani, ed., *The Final Solution: Origins and Implementation* (London and New York: Routledge, 1994), pp. 176-177.

playing. This was clearly going to be a point of tension between the two.

I will now look at the 1942 Christmas address in three different cases: Germany, France, and the Netherlands.

In Germany, the Vatican surely knew what was going on. 1941 may have been a bit early, but according to Maglione's own notes, by the spring of 1943, they knew. They knew exactly what was taking place; they knew about the gassings. They didn't know exactly where, but they knew.

At this point, Cardinal Bertram, the titular head of the German bishops, wrote to Maglione asking if there was anything he could do to make sure that the sacraments were distributed to those in the concentration camps. He meant, of course, converted Jews. Maglione wrote back: "We're doing everything we can to see that this is done."[33] He didn't write back that these people were being murdered by the tens of thousands. This was a critical point in time, because Bertram was the number one opponent of the von Preysing position. If Bertram could have been won over, then von Preysing might have been more successful during the 1943 Fulda Conference at convincing the German bishops to speak out against the Holocaust.

Returning to the Christmas address of 1942 and the new position of the Vatican in 1943: Pope Pius told the German bishops in 1943 that what they said in 1942, along the lines of "murder is wrong," was enough. They didn't have to go beyond that. Von Preysing wanted to go further; he wanted to send people to the concentration camps. He wanted a correspondent to go back and forth between them and the concentration camps. But at that point, in 1943, Pope Pius said no.

The one clear case proving that people understood what Pius XII said in the Christmas message of 1942 is the Netherlands. The great difference between the Netherlands and the other European countries is that in the former there were seven bishops all on the same page. They were all ready to oppose the actions of the German administration in their country under Arthur Seyss-Inquart. Following the 1942

33 Ludwig Volk and Bernhard Stasiewski, eds., *Akten deutscher Bischöfe über die Lage der Kirche 1933-1945* (Mainz: Matthias-Grünewald-Verlag, 1972), Series A, vol. 38, pp. 269-272. Maglione's reply is in the footnote.

Christmas address, the Dutch Redemptorist priest De Witte wrote a letter to Pius XII, telling him that what was happening to the Jews was extraordinary and he had to take extraordinary action. The letter was accompanied by a cover letter from the Cardinal Bishop of Utrecht, Johannes de Jong.[34] He got no reply. They wrote the letter because after the address they thought Pope Pius XII wanted to do something; three months later they found out that he didn't intend to do anything. The reply they got from Tardini was that he had sent their message on to the Dean of the Dutch Seminary in Rome, because he was "interested in these questions."

The last case I wish to mention is France. As you know, a handful of French bishops spoke out in 1942 regarding what was happening to the Jews.[35] At the end of the year, Pius XII gave his Christmas address, in which he seemed to say it was time to take some sort of action against what was happening to the Jews. Did this handful of French bishops get any encouragement to proceed? No. There were two dozen other French bishops who didn't want to say anything. Just a handful were ready to go ahead.

In a recent French book, the author claims that the reason the French bishops—those six at least—did not speak out in 1943 based on what Pius XII said at Christmas of 1942 was because of a meeting between Cardinal Emmanuel Suhard and Pope Pius. Aware of the position of his Dutch counterparts, Suhard argued that since they were under a legitimate government (as opposed to the imposed government of Seyss-Inquart in the Netherlands), the French bishops should not do the same thing.[36] Pius XII agreed with Suhard and thus told the Dutch, the Germans, and the French that enough was enough!

Dina Porat: Could you please repeat what you said about the Pope's chances of being heard if he had spoken out clearly, when most of Europe was antisemitic anyway?

34 ADSS, vol. IX, pp. 287-289.

35 Serge Klarsfeld, *Vichy-Auschwitz,* two volumes (Paris: Fayard, 1983 and 1985), pp. 353-355, 369, 405, 412-413.

36 Jacques Duquesne, *Les Catholiques Francais sous l'Occupation*, new edition (Paris: Grasset, 1996), pp. 295 ff., 306 ff.

Michael Phayer: The point is that he would have run the risk, and he knew this, of dividing the Catholic world between those who were rabid antisemites and those who were not. This point is similar to that which Paul O'Shea was making—it was a shared responsibility.

Discussion

Jean-Dominique Durand: I would like to begin with Professor Napolitano's report, in particular what he said about Communism. To reduce the Pope's position to anti-communism alone seems to me a little too reductive. On the other hand, the important papers, reports, and diary of Myron Taylor (well conserved and accessible at the Library of Congress in Washington) clearly demonstrate the very firm relationship between Pius XII and the United States through his extraordinary friendship with President Roosevelt. There is a great deal of correspondence (published letters) between Pius XII and Roosevelt that proves Pacelli's—later Pius XII's—anti-communism, similar to that of all Catholics of that period and afterwards, due to obvious reasons which I will not elaborate upon now.

But this anti-communism does not make them lose sight of the importance of the United States' role—above all, with respect to the final victory—on the Western Front. I don't think we could ever say that Pius XII's position was favorable towards Germany, despite the fact that the United States was allied with the Soviet Union.

His anti-communism did not deter him when, in 1941, the U.S. authorities asked the Pope to assist them in convincing the American Catholics to become engaged in the war effort. This was some time before the U.S. entered World War II. The Pope accepted and he let the American Catholics know that the right front was naturally the Western Front, that is to say, the one that would be led by the Americans.

My second point concerns the statements that may be viewed as insufficient on Pius XII's part. One cannot speak about *silence*, because the Pope had spoken out several times, in his own way. One may argue about the effectiveness of his words, but he had spoken out at least three times.

The problem was addressed in almost the same terms by other "moral" authorities. I speak in particular about the Red Cross of Geneva, an organization of Protestant origin, which confers upon it a very spiritual way of viewing things.

I have here, for example, a document dated February 18, 1943. It is the minutes of a meeting with various representatives of organizations, as well as of the nunciature, the YMCA, the Ecumenical Council, and the International Union of Aid for Children. During this meeting they said that they understood the need to proceed with caution. Above all, they approved the committee's decision not to make a big public statement deploring the persecution of the Jews, since it would not be effective. The final choice of the Red Cross—on which studies have already been written[37] due to the complete opening of their archives—demonstrates that the question of an intervention, of a statement, was a problem for many other moral authorities in the world. If a comparison were made, it could help us understand the position of the Holy See.

A third point is Michael Phayer's words regarding the French bishops. Perhaps I did not understand you properly, but I do not believe a meeting was held between Cardinal Suhard and Pius XII during the war. And also, could you please tell me which book you referred to in your speech? In France there is a current discussion on this topic, and some books are known to be problematic.

Finally, there are various problems with regard to France that should not be forgotten: First of all, the separation between the so-called "free zone" and the "occupied zone," at least until November 1942; second, the Vichy Government and the personality of Marshall Pétain, who was highly regarded and admired by the bishop veterans of World War I; third, the bishops who did speak out. Although they were few, many others committed themselves (to help Jews). I am thinking about several bishops who were conservatives, of the right, admirers of Pétain, but eventually became involved [in rescue activities]. One example is the Bishop of Clermont-Ferrand, Gabriel Piguet, who was deported despite his close connection with the Vichy regime. In secret, he saved many people.

37 See, for example, Jean-Claude Favez, *The Red Cross and the Holocaust* (Cambridge: Cambridge University Press, 1999).

Grazia Loparco: Paul O'Shea mentioned the pieces of evidence we have regarding Pius XII's deeds by means of convents, by means of the Religious.[38]

Since 2002, a group of scholars of the history of the religious institutions has been engaged in retrieving documents relating what took place in the religious houses of Rome (and let us hope in the whole of Italy) regarding Jews and other people in need of help. This research is not directly motivated by an interest in Pius XII, rather by an historical interest in collecting documents that, as we have heard, are getting lost. In addition, not much was recorded on paper in the religious homes, and the verbal witnesses are gradually dying off. So it is important to collect whatever can be found, even though a critical assessment of these documents is necessary. This research shows that of the approximately 750 religious homes that existed in Rome in 1943, some 220—150 for women and 70 for men—hid Jews.

Tomorrow, in my short address, we will try to understand—in the absence of a written order, which we have not found and which we probably shouldn't even expect to find—what happened in these religious homes. Was it due to a spontaneous initiative, or was there also some kind of a message given? The testimonies we have managed to gather show examples of both. In some cases there was a spontaneous action, while in others the superiors (men or women) were hesitant at the beginning, but subsequently opened their religious homes upon instructions transmitted orally by priests or people connected to the Holy See. We must remember that many Vatican employees celebrated daily masses in the religious communities of Rome. So we should also keep in mind the informal communication channels, those networks naturally overlooked by the diplomatic channels, but which were as real as the official ones.

38 The term "Religious" refers here to a person, lay or cleric, who professes the three evangelical counsels (chastity, poverty, and obedience) by means of solemn or simple vows and is a member of an institute of consecrated life either within a religious order or religious congregation. The person lives a common life following a rule or constitution under a religious superior. The term "religious house" refers to those institutions where religious men or women live a common life, following a common rule under the leadership of a religious superior.

Susan Zuccotti: I wish to make a similar point to that of Sister Grazia Loparco. I believe we did not thoroughly address the question of the Pope's ability to transmit instructions to bishops and priests in other countries, aside from Italy. Certainly, the diplomatic pouch was not the only way; there were traveling priests who could carry letters; there were all kinds of envoys going back and forth. There were ways to transmit papal preferences and I suspect that that was done more than we know, but probably not enough.

One example: In the ADSS there is a document referring to a letter from the bishop of Timişoara in Transylvania, in which he complained that many German Catholics in his diocese or parish were complaining that the Vatican Information Office was doing too much to address the letters and requests for information from Jews; what should he do about this? The answer that came back to him from some official was: "The Vatican Information Office serves the needs of all the populations in each geographic area. It just so happens that in your parish or diocese, many of those making the requests are Jewish. We will serve them as well."[39] So far, so good. The problem was that he then went on to say: "Tell those who are handling this correspondence to do so discretely." He could have said: Make it known. Make it known to your population that these people are dying in deportation. Or at least make it known that these are persecuted people and that we at the Vatican have mercy and compassion and concern for them too. Make it known. Make it known discretely. You don't have to make positive statements, but make it known."

It seems to me that this was a lost opportunity to convey these kinds of instructions. It's easy for us to claim that the Pope didn't really have to say "don't kill people," everybody knew that. But, unfortunately, he did have to say it. This is just one small example of thousands of opportunities on a very small scale that seemed to have been lost over and over again.

Another matter: I'm surprised that nobody raised the question of the many diplomatic overtures and initiatives made by Italian officials in the nunciature of Borgongini Duca regarding the deportation of Jews

39 The Apostolic Nuncio Monsignor Andrea Cassulo to Cardinal Maglione, July 21, 1943, ADSS, vol. IX, pp. 410-411; Cardinal Maglione to Monsignor Cassulo, August 20, 1943, ibid., p. 436.

from the Italian-occupied territories, particularly Croatia. Those diplomatic initiatives by the Secretariat of State deserve to be remembered.

On the other hand, in the case of Slovakia, I believe that the diplomatic initiatives have been slightly overstated here today. This is a very difficult subject. The initiatives made by the Vatican Secretariat of State regarding Slovakia were much weaker in the beginning, in 1942, during the first major deportations of Jews. These were primarily Jews by religion [Jews who did not convert to Christianity], and the protests were mild; they became much stronger in 1944, when Jews who had converted began to be deported.

The only other point I would make is on the question of instructions. Cardinal Tisserant wrote to Cardinal Suhard in Paris at the end of 1939, along the lines of: I have repeatedly suggested to His Holiness that he issue an encyclical in which he reminds Catholics throughout Europe that they should act according to their consciences. I fear that the failure to do so will be a black mark on the Catholic Church. This was early—December of 1939—but the idea here was of issuing a strong message, a single instruction, not like the Christmas message of 1942, buried in 26 pages of very difficult language. This did not have to be an attack on Germany; it did not have to be an attack on National Socialism; it did not even have to mention Jews. Rather, a clear message: Obey your consciences and remember your Christian teachings.

Dina Porat: I would first like to comment on what Loparco and Zuccotti said about Jews hiding in monasteries and all over Europe. Professor Napolitano mentioned the many thank you letters the Pope got after the war. But most of them were written by people who were very young when they were hidden. After the war, they had no idea who to thank. They did not remember where they were exactly, the name of the person who took care of them, and therefore whom they should thank. So they thanked the Pope. When he passed away in 1958, many letters of condolence were sent from Israel to Rome stating their thanks, but with no details, just thanking him in general. It wasn't him personally; it was a general thank you to the monasteries, churches, etc. Even if they were not that young during the war, they didn't know exactly whom to thank.

This was also 1958, which in Israeli terms was before the Eichmann trial,[40] and in general terms, before Rolf Hochhuth's play *The Deputy*, both of which led to a lot of research that criticized the Pope.

My second point—already made, especially by Professor Phayer—is that according to the material in Barlas's archive, Roncalli had a bad feeling and he expressed it. While he didn't say Pius XII, he spoke about superiors whose power and influence were great, but who refrained from action and lacked resourcefulness in extending concrete help. There was plenty of correspondence, mainly about children, in which Roncalli told Barlas that he had had no response from Rome. So it wasn't just action, it was also *in*action.

A last point: I asked you, Professor Phayer, to repeat what you said, because it really struck me as an awful thing to say. Not on your part, but as an analysis of an awful situation. What you said was that even if Pope Pius XII had spoken out clearly, there was rabid antisemitism among much of the Catholic and European populations. What does that mean? That the Jews were doomed anyway? So what are we sitting here for? Even if, more or less, having spoken openly would have affected a small part, just a small part? I believe we must differentiate between antisemitism and the wish to murder Jews. You can be an antisemite but not wish to murder Jews. These are two different things. There are other motivations for murder. This is a very major—and painful—point that you have made.

Thomas Brechenmacher: Allow me to build on this very topic. The statement concerning the widespread antisemitism amongst Catholics cannot, in my opinion, be left unchallenged. I would beg to differentiate between a religiously motivated anti-Judaism, which, without a doubt, could be found in many Catholics, especially Catholics at the grassroots level. It was fueled by the known judgments on Jews, as well as the racist antisemitism, from which the Church distanced itself in the decree of the Holy Breviary in March 1928. We know from the sources that this was the will of Pope Pius XI. They said they rejected this modern

40 Adolf Eichmann was a Lieutenant Colonel in the SS. He was appointed by Reinhard Heydrich to be in charge of the logistic organization of the mass deportation of Jews to the death camps. After the war he escaped to Argentina, where he was caught in 1960 and brought secretly to Israel. His trial began in 1961 and he received the death sentence.

antisemitism with its racist background. Naturally, that doesn't mean that the roots of the older anti-Judaism had vanished. But I think it is shortsighted to conclude that all Catholics had been potential Jew-murderers from the start, and that they would have continued with the killing, unimpressed even by a papal statement. In my opinion, that is too superficial.

This mindset was rejected sharply, even in 1938, when Pope Pius XI addressed a group of Belgian pilgrims, declaring that antisemitism had nothing to do with civilization, with the Christian idea of humanity, and they should not identify with that in any way.

By the way, in reference to the theology that was made very clear by Cardinal Faulhaber: In his advent sermons, which were cited earlier, he spoke about the Jews of the Old Testament, not about those living in present times.[41] By talking about them at the advent of 1934, which was a very brave thing, he made a clear point, referring to the theology: These are the people of the First Covenant, and we are connected like two sides of the same coin. (Faulhaber used the image of a second medal, which makes no sense.) That means: From a theological standpoint Jews and Christians belong together. On that basis, it is impossible to develop a legitimization for Catholics to abuse and murder Jews.

Dan Michman: We are coming to the end of this session, and I wish to raise two aspects that we have still not paid attention to. One relates to the issue, already raised, of rescue and conveying messages, hidden messages—Professor Napolitano called it "catacomb diplomacy." We also have sources from another side, from the grassroots: the Yad Vashem files of the Righteous Among the Nations. I bring here the Belgian case because that is the one I have studied more in depth.

In 1980, the Center for Research on World War II in Brussels (which has since been renamed, the acronym of which is CEGES/SOMA) carried out a survey among all priests of the Catholic Church in Belgium concerning their actions regarding several issues during World War II.

Quite a clear pattern emerged: The majority of Jews were rescued by Catholic institutions or individuals. We must emphasize, of course, that Belgium was almost entirely Catholic; 98% of its population was

41 The reference is to the Advent sermon of 1933.

Catholic (although many were secular). But the survey shows a clear difference between parishes. In one parish there was a rescue network, and in the neighboring one—not. What does that mean? Was there any directive coming from above? The actual pattern of behavior apparently refutes this. We know that Cardinal Jozef-Ernest van Roey did hardly anything to promote rescue, in spite of what was written in a book published shortly after World War II.

It was actually a lower echelon of bishops and other activists like Kerkhofs, Reynders, and the like who quite clearly took the initiative. When you read (in the 1980 survey and in the Yad Vashem Righteous Among the Nations files) the testimonies of the simple people in the parish, they said—well, he (i.e., that bishop or priest) came to me and asked me to provide refuge [to a Jew], and of course I had to do what he said (because he was my spiritual and moral authority). We have a similar example in Holland. We talked about Monsignor De Jong in Utrecht. In a recent Ph.D.,[42] we found that, on the personal level, most of the Jews rescued in the Netherlands were rescued in the south, in the Catholic regions of the country, and not, as was presumed before, by the Reform Protestant Church (the *Gereformeerden*). Once again, we have testimonies that show that people who had clear anti-Jewish views, anti-Judaistic views, rescued Jews due to an order given by the local church authority. It was given from above in that country, but there is no sign that it was an order given from Rome. Many books have been written about De Jong; nobody found directives given by the Pope; only *post factum*, later on, in 1943, was there some message from the Pope that he approved of what had been done, but not beforehand, not on the spot.

This is one thing we can learn regarding rescue initiatives, and it relates also to the Church Orders. It is very interesting—we have talked about this at Yad Vashem—that one of the things that should be researched is the religious orders, because that is another channel where we can learn about the involvement of the Pope. In Belgium, for instance, one religious order—the Don Bosco order—was very active

42 Marnix Croes & Peter Tammes, *'Gif laten wij niet voortbestaan': Een onderzoek naar de overlevingskansen van joden in de Nederlandse gemeenten, 1940-1945* (Amsterdam: Aksant, 2004).

in rescuing, but other orders were not. So what made the difference? Who decided? This is an open question, but it is very important to understand what came from the Vatican, and what was a local decision. The pattern I see is that at a certain moment, a certain middle echelon of the Church leadership—people who have a clear standing and say at the top of a network (a parish, a religious order, a convent, a seminary, etc.)—decides to act and then the whole network acts, because that is the character of the Catholic Church. Because of its hierarchical structure and its tradition of loyalty and obedience to a higher authority, when one person who can decide indeed decides, then the whole group or network joins in. Moreover, and this is very important, sometimes the rescuers said: It's the word of God (that we have to save the Jews or the persecuted); they didn't say: It's the word of the Pope; we have to do so because he ordered us to.

This brings me to another, major issue, and with this I will finish: I once had a correspondence with Professor Ian Kershaw, the author of the masterly biography of Hitler, and concerning a certain issue he said he was profoundly ignorant. I'm also profoundly ignorant regarding issues of Catholic Church doctrine. But in order to be ignorant, you still have to know something. And I know that in the idea of *Historia Sacra* there is a role ascribed to the Jews in the future, at the end of days: The final recognition of Christ by the Jews is the necessary link to the apocalypse. So the Jews have to survive for that purpose. From this point of view, i.e., the internal point of view of Church doctrine (and not because of external factors), at the moment that it became clear that a systematic murder of the Jews was taking place, this had to affect Catholic doctrine deeply, because it shatters the foundations of Catholic theology.

So in December 1942, the Allies made their joint statement. They lagged behind regarding the numbers, they didn't know how many Jews had been killed already, but one week before the Pope's declaration of December 1942, on December 17, they issued a declaration in which they openly and clearly stated that a systematic murder of Jews was taking place. What does a "systematic murder of Jews" mean for Catholic theology? This is clearly an issue at the center, at the heart, of Catholic theology, and which, I believe, should be researched. However,

I have yet to find any discussion of this in any of the correspondences relating to rescue, or elsewhere in internal Church correspondence.

Andrea Tornielli: Certainly in the debate on what to do and what to say, the Catholic Church demonstrated itself to be inadequate with respect to the tragedy of the Shoah. But then the whole world was inadequate with respect to this tragic event, an event whose scope was, in certain terms, unimaginable.

However, I believe that there was an internal debate in the Catholic Church, and that the decision—I'm referring to the question raised by Professor Zuccotti in the case of Timişoara—to be discrete in public declarations, of making known to the public that help should be extended, was considered necessary in order for this help to be able to persist (although everyone can judge the consequences). The caution displayed in the declarations was, in the minds of the Secretary of State and the Pope, what allowed the help to be extended, as the Red Cross has claimed.

I would also like to recall the interesting testimony of the Bishop of Luxembourg, Jean Bernard. Bernard spent two years in Dachau. In his memoirs, published in 1962,[43] he said that the Christian prisoners in the camp were so afraid of the words of the Vatican religious authorities that every time a protest was made they would say no, you have to keep quiet, because every time you protest, our conditions here get worse.

Therefore there is, in my view, one legitimate issue: The Catholic Church knew that the Jews—and not only the Jews but all those who were persecuted—needed concrete help, but it retained that this help should not derive from public statements or declarations. This is a focal point: Anyone can discuss what should have been done, but this was at the heart of the Church's motivation; this is why it acted as it did.

David Bankier: I would like to respond to Dina Porat and Michael Phayer, and also add a few comments.

If we concentrate on the activities of the different church organizations, this symposium will go in a direction we do not currently wish

43 Jean Bernard, *Priestblock 25487: A Memoir of Dachau* (Bethesda, MD: Zaccheus Press, 2007).

to develop. This, for example, would be taking up Dan Michman's suggestion to see why the Don Bosco Order was different from the Benedictine Order, or other orders.

So I suggest we stick to what we intended from the beginning: the Pope and his attitude. The major question this afternoon is: At what point did the Pope understand that his response was not proportionate with what was happening? At a certain stage in the war, not only non-Jews, but also Jews and Jewish organizations needed no further information to know what was happening to the Jews. There's no point in discussing whether he had to read in the *Corriere della Sera* about the Iasi pogrom in which the Romanians killed 13,000 Jews. The crucial question is: At what point does an event become a precipitator that leads to a change of awareness of reality?

Have a look at the Jewish underground in the Warsaw Ghetto. There they knew that the Germans were murdering Jews; they knew that Treblinka was not a settlement as the Nazis said, but a place where Jews were gassed. At what point did the underground say: Enough is enough. We are not going to wait any longer to do something? Or the situation in another ghetto, Bialystok; here there was a Jewish underground as well. They knew that deportation to Belzec meant extermination. Nevertheless, they didn't respond appropriately to what they knew, until a certain moment when they said: Enough is enough! We cannot continue giving the same old responses.

Regarding the non-Jewish responses: At what moment do people or governments say: We have enough knowledge; we don't need another example from another witness that the Nazis are killing Jews; we must change our response? And indeed, at a certain moment, in December 1942, the Allies said: Enough is enough! We must make a declaration. We don't know if it will affect Hitler, if it will change his policy, but we must do something. Let's broadcast it on the BBC. We cannot continue with the same discourse as before. Enough is enough.

Take Roosevelt's declaration in 1944, that whoever collaborates with the Nazis will be punished. I am not concerned with why he made this statement at this late stage; I am more interested in his decision to say, at a certain point, enough is enough!

Consider those who tried to assassinate Hitler in July 1944. They didn't need any more data on what was happening to the Jews in the

East. Some of them were members of killing squads themselves. But at a certain moment in 1944, some of the conspirators said: Maybe we will not succeed in killing Hitler, but enough is enough! The history of World War II should mention that there were some Germans who dared to do something against the Nazis' mass murders.

So my question is: At what moment did the Church reach the conclusion: We must change our response?

When the Nuremberg Laws were issued, were they sufficient to provoke the German bishops or clergymen to say: Enough is enough? Definitely not. When the *Kristallnacht*[44] was perpetrated, was this a matter to trigger a response of: Enough is enough? Of course not. When the deportations began, was it a reason to say: Enough is enough? Also not. The critical question is, for Pius XII, what was the issue that would spur him to say: Enough is enough? To say: The previous discourse isn't working. If I do something surreptitiously, I might save 2,000 Jews. But if I make a public declaration to the world media I'll save 4,000.

Every day of the summer of 1944, the Nazis pushed 12,000 Jews into the gas chambers. Did this impel Pius to reflect: At this stage there are no longer two options but only one—to issue a public statement, even considering the risks involved, because enough is enough!

Maybe Michael Phayer is right; the Pope might have pondered: What is the point in issuing a declaration that condemns the Holocaust? The large majority of European Catholics would not back it anyhow. That's a terrible conclusion because it means that, for the large majority of Christians, the unprecedented extermination of their Jewish neighbors was not sufficient reason to say: Enough is enough.

44 The pogrom of November 1938.

Session Five A: Pius XII and Hiding in Italy

Did the Pope give instructions to help or hide Jews in Italy? What documentation do we have in this regard?

Presenter: Grazia Loparco

I would first like to say that I owe my understanding of the importance of testimonials to Primo Levi. I wrote my first graduate thesis on Levi in 1984, and I am fortunate to have known him personally. He communicated to me a very strong sense of memory, which I hope can educate us all.

As an associate of the Coordination of Religious Historians,[1] I represent a group of religious scholars, men and women who, since 2002, have been conducting research on the shelter offered to Jews in the religious houses of Rome.[2] Although it is a difficult task, we hope to be able to reconstruct a map of all such houses in Italy, region by region.[3]

1 www.storicireligiosi.it.

2 Grazia Loparco, "Gli Ebrei negli istituti religiosi a Roma (1943-1944). Dall'arrivo alla partenza," in *Rivista di Storia della Chiesa in Italia* 58, *1,* 2004, pp. 107-210; idem, "L'assistenza prestata dalle religiose di Roma agli ebrei durante la seconda guerra mondiale," in Luigi Mezzadri and Maurizio Tagliaferri, eds., *Le donne nella Chiesa e in Italia. Atti del XIV Convegno di studio dell'Associazione Italiana dei Professori di Storia della Chiesa: Roma, 12-15 settembre 2006, Storia del cristianesimo Saggi* (Cinisello Balsamo, MI: San Paolo, 2007), pp. 245-285; Francesco Motto, *Non abbiamo fatto che il nostro dovere: Salesiani di Roma e del Lazio durante l'occupazione tedesca* (1943-1944) (Rome: LAS, 2000); Andrea Riccardi, *L'inverno più lungo 1943-1944: Pio XII, gli ebrei e i nazisti a Roma* (Rome: Laterza, 2008).

3 As mentioned, the term "Religious" refers here to a person, lay or cleric, who professes the three evangelical counsels (chastity, poverty and obedience) by means of solemn or simple vows and is a member of an institute of consecrated life in either a religious order or religious congregation. The person lives a common life following a rule or constitution under a religious superior. The term "religious house" refers to those institutions where religious men or women live a common life, following a common rule under the leadership of a religious superior.

I begin my presentation with a number of premises.

The first one concerns the search for an explicit document, one explicit intervention of Pius XII, which would prove his interest—or lack there of—in the Jews. In my opinion, such a search is quite futile. If there had been an official and explicit document, it would have been published in *L'Osservatore Romano* or in *Acta Apostolicae Sedis*.[4] Since no such documentation exists, studies conducted on whether it does or does not exist should, I believe, be abandoned.

Nonetheless, this does not mean that the Pontiff did not intervene in various ways. Not officially, but through the regular channels, namely the Secretariat of State, various offices of the Vatican, and the nuncios. I therefore believe that the search efforts should be focused in this direction.

With regard to individual religious houses, the time they were living in did not lend itself to written communications or proclamations. There were, however, the institutional channels, i.e., the internal network of the Holy See's organization—the Vicariate of Rome, the Parish priests, and the prelates who had contact with the religious communities—as well as the various contacts with churchmen who brought messages from higher echelons and who could not risk exposing themselves or others to reprisals as a result of imprudent acts. Again, I maintain that it is improbable that the Pope gave any written order, official or secret, to help Jews, and it is out of place to consider it a necessary proof. (Besides, it seems that no written document exists stating that Hitler ordered the extermination of the Jews.)

I would now like to make an historiographical observation. In some books, the case of Rome is not represented as being unique, as if things would have unfolded there similarly as in any other city. However, the number of Jews that were saved—at least 4,500 of a total of 10,000-12,000 living in the city in 1943—and the number of religious houses involved in rescue and the methods they employed require particular consideration. So too with regard to a possibly direct, namely, oral communication, thanks to the Vatican ministers in the offices of the Holy See who celebrated daily Mass in the female communities. Alternatively,

4 *Acta Apostolicae Sedis* is the official gazette of the Holy See, which publishes the official decrees, laws, encyclicals and decisions.

they could have received indications and then conveyed them to their superiors. So this particular feature of the city of Rome must be taken into account.

Finally, we must also remember that the sheltering of Jews in these religious houses, though very relevant to the experience of Rome and Italy, cannot be separated from the help granted to politicians and their families, draft dodgers, evacuees, orphans, soldiers or partisans. This was done as a charitable act, displaying their unyielding love for every human being.

In my research, I used sources already indicated in my previous works, as well as others found in the archives of religious houses.[5] Recently, I added verified documents from the archives of the Congregation for Institutes of Consecrated Life and Societies of Apostolic Life. In particular, I was able to peruse 107 reports sent by as many female religious institutes—not religious houses, religious *institutes*—each of which included several houses or just a few. These reports were sent in May-June 1944, in response to a circular sent out on April 14 by the Congregation of the Religious, asking for information on the charity activities being carried out with respect to refugees, evacuees, and war victims. While we know from other sources that many of these institutes were hiding Jews, out of the 107 reports released, only a few expressly mentioned Jews. One example is the extraordinary case of the Sisters of Notre Dame of Sion, which hosted many Jews. The report of the Mother General mentions refugees in general, but fails to cite any Jews. The silence of many indicates, I believe, prudence. The explicitness of others, on the other hand, shows that declaring their presence would have amazed no one. Moreover, none of the institutions that admitted to having hidden Jews added any particular justification, indicating that it was considered normal that Jews should be counted among those seeking refuge.

Another source I recently found concerns the requests of bishops or cloistered nuns addressed to the Pope. These requests were conveyed either to the Congregation of Religious or presented in an audience with Pius XII. What I found particularly striking is that the questions were

5 For more details and full quotations, see the written version presented for the workshop, "Pio XII, gli ebrei e le case religiose in Italia. Sulle tracce dei documenti."

often answered within 24-48 hours. Sometimes it would take longer, but in several cases an indication of the response was ready within 24 hours, even if it was just to say that the response would be given orally.

I turn now to some points regarding the city of Rome and, more generally, Italy.

First, what proof do we have that the Pope had in fact conveyed an instruction of his own? Remember, we are talking about *indirect* interventions of the Pontiff. I would first mention those made prior to October 16, 1943. At the beginning of the 1939 academic year, the female religious congregations of teachers received encouragement from the Congregation of the Institutes of Studies and Seminaries to grant economical advantages to baptized Jewish students wishing to study at Catholic schools. This was a result of the racial laws, in which Jews had been forbidden to attend public schools. Consequently, the Congregation invited the nuns to help these Jewish families, many of which were in dire financial straits.

In October 1943, an elderly Jew asked to be hosted in a female monastery, together with his wife, a housemaid, and a niece. This request was conveyed to Monsignor Montini. The case highlighted to the Pope the need to respond through the Vicariate to the religious institutes. A note indicated the Pope's readiness to help the refugees, and so the next day, on October 2, Montini wrote that he had spoken to Cardinal Luigi Traglia, the deputy manager (*vicegerente*) in Rome.[6]

Another element we must examine is the declarations and protection notices distributed in the religious institutes prior to October 16. Some of the documents found in religious houses indicate a number of actions undertaken by the Holy See to protect them. For example, on September 28, 1943, the Servants of Mary received a declaration from the General Secretary of the Congregation for the Propagation of the Faith, Monsignor Celso Costantini. The declaration certified that the College of St. Alexis Falconieri was built by the congregation,

6 "Mr. X, with his wife (aged 76), an old maid, and a niece, asks to be hosted in the convent of the Oblate Sisters of Via Garibaldi, in Gianicolo. They are ready to accept the wife but not him. He is 84 and cannot be separated from his wife, who is sick and needs his help. He would like the nuns to obtain the permission to accept him as well. He is of the Jewish religion [...]." *Actes et Documents du Saint Siège relatifs à la Seconde Guerre Mondiale* (ADSS) (Vatican City: Libreria Editrice Vaticana, 1965-1980), vol IX, doc. 356, p. 496.

depended upon it, and enjoyed the same rights and privileges as the Pontifical Urban College of "Propaganda Fide."

Nonetheless, by the beginning of October they most probably realized that a declaration given by the Holy See was insufficient to protect the building.

From September[7] until the beginning of October 1943, many religious houses had been equipped with bilingual (Italian and German) placards signed by Rome's Military Commander Rainer Stahel, protecting the buildings from being searched.[8]

Furthermore, various institutes were provided with a declaration of their dependence upon the Vatican City State. Consequently, it was forbidden to search or appropriate them without previous agreement with the superior officers. For example, the Servants of Mary received a declaration dated September 25, 1943, attesting that the order was at the dependence of the Saint Congregation for the Religious and therefore not liable for search or requisition without a previous agreement with the Congregation.[9] The Ursuline Sisters and the Missionary Sisters of the Immaculate Conception kept an identical document, dated October 1943.[10] These letters made use of specific institutional connections; they were signed by the Governor of the Vatican City State on behalf of the Secretary of State, as well as by General Stahel. All these declarations were distributed prior to the ghetto roundup of October 16 and were used as a basis to grant secure refuge to the persecuted.

On October 25, following the ghetto roundup, the Secretariat of State issued a letter to the religious institutes advising them to exercise prudence in posting those signs, in order to avoid over exposure and attracting too much attention.[11]

7 The Missionaries of the Immaculate Conception wrote in their chronicle that they received such a placard from the Vicariate on July 20, 1943, but we can assume that the date is wrong. Grazia Loparco, "Gli Ebrei negli istituti," p. 184.

8 For the quotation see ibid., pp. 117-119. Monsignor Hudal declared that more than 500 placards were distributed in Rome and other cities.

9 For the full quotation see ibid., pp. 166-167.

10 For the full quotation see ibid., pp. 156-157. For the Missionaries of the Immaculate Conception the information appears in the Chronicle. They mention that the letter arrived via an envoy of the Vatican.

11 Ibid., pp. 157-158. We also found copies at the institutes of the Servants of Mary and the Ursuline Sisters.

This seems confusing. First they were given a declaration intended to protect the building, and thereafter they were told: Be careful not to expose yourself too much. This indication seems to have been motivated by two facts. On October 22, the Germans tried to carry out a search at the Institute of the Sisters of the Holy Child Mary, near St. Peter's Square. The day after, Father Aquilino Reichard warned the superior officers to be cautious. He was close to German circles and said that, according to General Stahel, the SS did not respect the extraterritorial buildings and convents as the commander himself did. In fact, Stahel argued that the vicariate's approach—and I quote—"that helped Jews, deserters, etc." was imprudent with respect to the SS to such an extent as to compromise with misunderstood charity both the Church and the refugees themselves.[12] Stahel, as Military Commander of Rome, was well known to the soldiers and such a personalized document could not have been agreed upon with any office of the Holy See, except the Secretariat of State. And in fact, as Stahel was considered too pro-Italian-Catholic and was not particularly trusted by the Nazis and the Fascists, he was replaced in November on account of his favorable attitude to the operations of the Church, which included helping Jews.

The cited documents provide evidence of the intervention of the various offices and institutions of the Holy See, while the specific document signed by Stahel can be attributed directly to the Secretariat of State.

Upon the replacement of Stahel, all the placards signed by him naturally lost authority. Thus, from November onwards, the risk and even fear of many religious institutes being searched increased. Indeed, there were some cases of raids.

Then there were some articles on the first page of *L'Osservatore Romano*, expressing "charity choices, with no exception." Due to lack of time, I will not cite them all, but you can read the transcripts. I would like to recall, however, two of them. On October 25-26, 1943, an article was published on the first page, talking about the Pope's charity:

> With the growth of so much evil, the universally paternal charity of the Supreme Pontiff has become, one could say, even more

12 *Notes de la Secrétairerie d'Etat*, October 23, 1943, ADSS, vol. IX, doc. 382, p. 518.

> active for all people; it does not pause before boundaries of nationality, religion or descent [*stirpe*]. This manifold and incessant activity of Pius XII has been greatly intensified recently by the increased sufferings of so many unfortunate people.[13]

This was one week after the raid in the ghetto and many knew how to understand the hint. Another article was published immediately following the raid of the Pontifical Lombard Seminary. There, a priest from Rome wrote: "... it was impossible to prevent a Roman priest from taking in anyone in need, because that is where the discernment between good and bad occurred."[14]

Further proof regarding the Pope's indirect intervention stems from the religious houses. The documents convey the conviction of the Religious to respond to the Pope's appeal, or to act in harmony with him. We have many testimonies—both contemporary, as well as others given later. Since the latter may alter the facts, I have tried to distinguish between those that were written at the time (like the chronicles), and the memoirs and testimonies that were published 30, 40 or 50 years after the actual events.

From the approximately 750 religious houses in Rome, we have information about more than 148 for women and at least 72 for men that hid Jews. In February 1944, after the raid on the Papal Basilica of St. Paul Outside-the-Walls, the safety of the religious houses was thrown into doubt: If St. Paul, which was extraterritorial, was raided, what might happen to the other houses? There was no more security. Uncertainty reigned over all parties; both Jews and the Religious felt unsafe. Nevertheless, the Holy See encouraged them to continue their actions, while avoiding imprudence.

At the beginning of February, immediately after the raid on the Basilica of St. Paul Outside-the-Walls,[15] the secretary of the Congregation of the Institutes of Studies and Seminaries Monsignor

13 The article was originally published in italics, in order to emphasize its content. "La carità del Santo Padre," *L'Osservatore Romano*, October 25-26, 1943, p. 1.

14 Sergio Pignedoli, "Carità cristiana," ibid., December 30, 1943, p. 1.

15 On the night between February 3 and 4, the Fascist police entered the Papal Basilica of St. Paul Outside-the-Walls, violating the status of extraterritoriality, and arrested several hidden persons, among them Jews.

Ruffini held a conference in the religious house of the Ursuline Sisters, speaking to the women's division of *Azione Cattolica*. The author of the house chronicle communicated that Ruffini had said in the name of the Pope that hosting refugees may continue.[16] We have other similar statements from that period.

The Missionaries of the Immaculate Conception mention in their chronicle as early as July 9, 1943 that at the "request" of the Pope, the religious communities had shared their food and lodging with refugees, among them, Jews. [17]

The Sisters of Perpetual Succour note in their chronicle of 1943 a large influx of women, children, and elderly people in the General House. The Mother General was absent and the Mother substituting for her did not feel she could refuse: "Moreover, the Holy Father Pius XII appealed to the charity of all Religious Communities to help the population by all possible means. The community of Sisters of Perpetual Succour was one of the first to respond to the vibrant message of the Holy Father."[18]

The Sisters of the Holy Child Mary, very close to the Vatican, wrote:

> From time to time there was a phone call for the Mother Provincial from the Secretary of State. The reason was always the same: someone on the run, a persecuted family needing refuge, protection, help. One could not refuse the representatives of the Pope; when every space in the house was filled, we also opened the rural cottage in Via della Camilluccia, where about 30 people found refuge.[19]

As the emergency ended, the Camaldolese monks, who hid Jews in the monastery of St. Gregorio al Celio, wrote in their chronicle:

16 Grazia Loparco, "Gli Ebrei negli istituti," p. 163.

17 Ibid., p. 184.

18 *Chronique générale de la Congregation des Soeurs de Charité de Notre Dame du bon et Perpetuel Secours*, Année 1935, Archivio della Casa Generalizia, Rome.

19 Chronicle of the Community of Via del S. Uffizio in Rome, Archivio Generale delle Suore di Caritá delle Sante Bartolomea Capitanio e Vincenza Gerosa, Milan.

> This is the time when people knock on the doors and our Religious Institutes open their friendly gates. Even the nuns open the cloisters for this deed of charity. As always, during these months the Church writes fresh pages of charity and fraternity. [Description of the raid of St. Paul, G.L.] All the newspapers wrote and gossipped about it [...], distorting the truth. People shout against the Holy See, which hosts in its extraterritorial religious houses men and others saved from the German plunder. The souls of our guests lose tranquility [...] The press deliberately publishes a decree of the Congregation for the Religious that forbids dressing those who do not belong to the community in religious clothes, or to host strangers. The Father Superior goes personally to the Congregation that denies the decree. When the local police officer cares to notify the Father Superior that he should act according to the promulgated decree, he receives the gentle answer: "Orders will be received only from the superiors."[20]

Yesterday, someone mentioned anti-Judaism—antisemitism—manifested in various forms. Frankly, the nuns did not study theology, so I believe they knew little about anti-Judaism. Except for the prayer of Good Friday and some homily, what could they have known about it?

However, the fact that many religious houses hosted Jews makes me think that had the faithful and the common religious people been prejudiced by anti-Judaism, how could they have hosted so many Jews without an indication from above? The answer is that being human prevailed; it was an instinctive resistance to the injustice being carried out against fellow human beings.

Further, the distribution of rations as well as financial help by the Vatican could only have taken place if the elevated number of hidden people had not been known. In Rome, particularly in the spring of 1944 (it was a very cold winter), there was famine. There are factual testimonies to this fact, including strategies of procurement on the

20 *Cronaca dal 1934 al 1948*, Congregation of the Camaldolesi, S. Gregorio al Celio, Rome, in Archivio Generale a Camaldoli, ms. 44, pp. 88-90.

black market, and stories of begging in the streets in order to be able to provide food for those in the house.

Another element to consider is the presence of men in female religious houses. The above-mentioned case was not the only one. In Rome alone, we have certain testimonies that offer proof of several female religious institutes in which whole families were hidden. In most cases they were separated, i.e., the women and the children stayed in female houses and the men in male houses. However, there were also cases in which the situation was different. Without the explicit permission of the Ecclesiastic Superiors, the Religious, especially the cloister nuns, could not have let men stay in the house.[21]

With regard to Italy: In a bibliographical review I am trying to complete, we have so far found 102 towns and villages with approximately 500 houses in which Jews were hidden. It would be very interesting to produce a map of these rescue stories.

Just one word with regard to the cloistered monasteries: We have a few letters from superiors, addressed to the Holy Father, with responses conveyed by means of the Congregation, requesting that women from the outside stay in a cloister. There are no further details. Permission was granted, subject to taking necessary cautions and according to the "special faculty" granted by the Pope. The papal cloistered monasteries needed special permits—I have one here with me that talks about a bishop from Montefeltro who wrote to the Prefect of the Congregation for the Religious in February 1944 that he may have gone too far in using the faculties at his disposal. He requested legitimization of what he had done and permission to continue in the future.

These letters speak of "recent declarations." What were the "recent declarations" of the Pope and the Holy See? It was at the beginning of 1944, so I believe they were talking about the radio message, about oral indications, about powers awarded to bishops. Whether we will find out more regarding the correspondence between the Pope and the bishops

21 For example, the Augustinian nuns of the Santi Quattro Coronati, the Sisters of our Lady of Sion, the Brigidine Sisters, the Ursulines of the Roman Union, the Daughters of Mary Help of Christians, the Sisters of St. Joseph of Chambéry, the Sisters of St. Mary of the Garden, the Sisters of Charity of the Immaculate Conception of Ivrea, the Handmaids of Charity of Brescia, and the Adorers of the Blood of Christ.

when the secret archive of the Vatican opens, I don't know. Of course, in order to understand the essence of some requests—especially in relation to the female monasteries, where the cloister was kept according to the rigid canon law of 1917—we must be familiar with the ordinary and extraordinary faculties and their administration, the frequency of the audiences of the Congregation's representatives with the Pope, as well as the issues presented to him.

All these elements, although indirect, demonstrate that most Religious would not have acted spontaneously. Although many did act spontaneously, many others did not because they were afraid. Certain nuns have told us that they decided to act after a certain monsignor, the Holy See, or some other religious authority told them to do so. The reality is therefore multifaceted. While there are voices that still talk about a direct involvement of the Pope,[22] since we are talking about high risk, the Pope couldn't have given a peremptory order.

The number of institutes involved, with different levels of autonomy in the decisions regarding strangers, shows that it couldn't have been only simply a spontaneous movement, without the knowledge of the Pope. Moreover, oral transmission was so efficient that I believe there was no need for a written document, but rather encouragement and confirmation, depending on the situation.

The fact that many Jews felt the need to thank the Pope shows that those who experienced these actions perceived his personal engagement. An example of this is the letter from a French rabbi who, on June 22, 1944, thanked the Pope, not only for having visited the Pius XI Salesian Institute, which had hidden 70 Jewish boys, but also for what he had done for the Italian Jews, in particular in Rome.

22 For example, a superior of the Daughters of the Sacred Heart of Jesus wrote to her superior residing in Bergamo in April 1944: "It is not true that the Holy Father wants to and works in order to evacuate the Religious; I was in the Vatican and talked to Monsignor Ottaviano [sic: Ottaviani, the councillor of the Holy Office, accused by Colonel Mario Battistelli of producing baptism certificates for Jews and hosting them in the Lateranese palace] who is involved in everything, in order to get his advice on whether to let the nuns leave. He dissuaded me and told me that the Holy Father had declared that even if persecution came he would not move, and he would like the religious institutes to do the same [...]." Letter of Mother Ignazia Pessina to the Mother General [Luisa Martorelli], Rome, April 23, 1944, in the Archivio Generale delle Figlie del S. Cuore, Rome.

Respondent: Susan Zuccotti

The question of a possible papal order to Italians to hide Jews during the Holocaust must be addressed in two parts: First, all of Italy with the exception of its capital, and then specifically the city of Rome. The Pope, after all, was the bishop of Rome. The guidance he gave to Bishop Konrad von Preysing in Berlin on April 30, 1943, and to other bishops elsewhere at different times, to the effect that each bishop should decide on responses to the persecution of the Jews in his own diocese, depending on local conditions and problems, applied equally to himself as the Bishop of Rome.[23] Rome was also, of course, the Eternal City, the center of the Catholic world, a unique and special place arguably requiring unique and special responses. Finally, what occurred in Rome was "under the Pope's very windows," in his own backyard. An attack on "the Pope's Jews" represented a special challenge to his position and prestige as a moral leader of the world. There is every reason to suspect that the Pope acted differently when the fate of Rome was in question.

Let us then look first at Italy as a whole. Like Catholics elsewhere, Italians received guidance from the Pope's Christmas and Name Day messages, as well as from his encyclicals and speeches printed in *L'Osservatore Romano* and conveyed to the people, if not directly by that newspaper, then by their priests in Sunday services and weekly bulletins. Italians learned that the Pope spoke of universal brotherhood, the unity of man, the need for compassion and love, and the condemnation of needless violence. Like Catholics everywhere, they interpreted these messages in conformity with their own tendencies. In Italy, where antisemitism certainly existed—especially within the Church—but where it did not impact deeply on the daily life of the population, papal appeals for compassion, however vague and imprecise, may have had some influence on the treatment of the Jews. Indeed, many priests and nuns who helped Jews spoke of the teachings—wishes—of Pius XII as a factor explaining their behavior.

More specific, however, is the question not of papal teachings but of a papal *order* to men and women of the Church to open their doors to

23 For Pius XII's message to von Preysing, see ADSS, vol. II, doc. 105, April 30, 1943, pp. 318-327.

Jews. It has been suggested that the coordinated effort between several archbishops and bishops, particularly in Turin, Milan, Florence, and Genoa, to hide Jews could only have occurred as the result of a papal order. I have argued, and I argue here again today, that this theory is false. It is perfectly clear that the efforts of prelates in those cities to help Jews began when individual representatives of the Italian Jewish assistance organization Delasem (Delegazione Assistenza Emigranti Ebrei) went to individual archbishops and bishops to ask for help. When those prelates agreed, the Delasem representatives turned over their lists of clients and financial resources to them. Each bishop then recruited a local coordinator, usually a priest who was already acting as his secretary, who called on other priests and parishioners and made contacts in surrounding towns and villages. Rescue networks were then set up and, finally, contact was made with colleagues in other dioceses. The rescue effort was often remarkable and the Pope may have had some knowledge of it, but it was not the result of a papal order.[24]

Apart from the Delasem initiative, why else have I come to this conclusion? First, because not all bishops, archbishops and priests were so cooperative. The priest Don Leto Casini wrote of his experience in Perugia one cold winter day, when the local bishop, on hearing that Casini was in the city to bring Delasem rescue funds to a nearby parish, literally threw him out of his office. After making his delivery, Casini was forced to spend the night on the street, waiting for his train.[25] Another witness, a Jewish fugitive, wrote of a local bishop in the Val d'Aosta, not far from the active rescue area around Turin, who strongly disapproved when one of his priests, Don Giuseppe Peaquin, hid him and his wife as well as an entire family of Yugoslavian Jews, none of whom spoke Italian.[26] If the Pope had given general instructions to

24 I have examined in detail the relationship between Delasem and several Italian archbishops and bishops who helped Jews. Zuccotti, *Under His Very Windows*, pp. 233-290.

25 Don Leto Casini, *Ricordi di un vecchio prete* (Florence: Editrice La Giuntina, 1986), p. 61. Don Casini assisted Cardinal Elia Dalla Costa, Archbishop of Florence, in hiding Delasem-sponsored refugees in Florence. He received the honor of Righteous Among the Nations at Yad Vashem in 1965.

26 Statement of Davide Nissim, December 13, 1954, Archivio Centro di Documentazione Ebraica Contemporanea [CDEC], Milan, 9/1, f. Biella.

bishops to help Jews, would he have given them only to some and not to others?

Second, as already mentioned in the case of Bishop von Preysing, Pius XII seems to have instructed his bishops to respond in these matters as they saw fit, depending on local circumstances. Would he then have ordered them to act in a specific way? This does not make sense. Or, bypassing the local bishops, would the Pope have ordered the directors of religious congregations throughout Italy to open the doors of their monasteries and convents to Jews? It would have certainly been highly irregular and unnecessary. The heads of religious houses, in most cases, might have sought permission from the directors of their orders to shelter outsiders on a long-term basis, or to accept guests of the opposite gender, or to break rules of cloister, and the directors of the orders might have informed the appropriate person at the Vatican of their decisions, but that is not the same as a papal order.

There is also the question of evidence. No bishop or archbishop—and no priest working for them—ever suggested after the war that they acted as they did because of a papal order, with one exception. The exception, as is well known, was Don Aldo Brunacci, Dean of Assisi, who claimed to have seen a written order from the Pope in the hands of his bishop, Giuseppe Placido Nicolini, in September 1943.[27] I would suggest that Brunacci may well have been mistaken. If such a written order ever existed, why would it not have been preserved, especially at a time when the Pope was being criticized for his reticence regarding condemnation of the Holocaust? Hiding a single piece of paper would not have been difficult. The Bishop of Assisi is known to have hidden the documents and valuables of some of the Jews he was helping.[28] He would have done the same with a written papal order to save Jews, had it existed.

There is also the much-debated issue of a possible oral order from the Pope to save Jews. Spokesmen for Pius XII often cite two very impor-

27 For Brunacci's claim, see his "Giornata degli ebrei d'Italia: Ricordi di un protagonista," public lecture, Assisi, March 15, 1982, printed in full in Don Aldo Brunacci, *Ebrei in Assisi durante la guerra: Ricordi di un protagonista* (Assisi: Libreria Fonteviva, 1985), pp. 7-15. Don Aldo Brunacci was honored as a Righteous Among the Nations at Yad Vashem in 1977.

28 See the testimony of Graziella Viterbi, in Zuccotti, *Under His Very Windows*, p. 263.

tant witnesses who allegedly testified to an oral order. One of these was Monsignor Giovanni Battista Montini, the future Pope Paul VI, who allegedly told Italian Jews who wanted to honor him for helping Jews that he had "only acted upon orders from the Holy Father." But this quotation comes from the notoriously unreliable writer Pinchas Lapide, who provided no source for his claim.[29] The second witness was another future pope, Monsignor Angelo Roncalli, later Pope John XXIII, who allegedly said that in helping endangered Jews, he had simply carried out the Pope's orders—first and foremost to save Jewish lives. This claim comes from the American papal spokesman Ronald Rychlak, who obtained it from Pinchas Lapide. Lapide explained that Roncalli made that statement to him personally in 1956 or 1957, when Roncalli was patriarch of Venice and Lapide was the Israeli consul there.[30] But Lapide actually wrote that Roncalli said that he simply carried out the Pope's orders: First and foremost to save **human** lives, not Jewish lives, as Rychlak wrote.[31] Furthermore, if Roncalli did in fact say so, he would have been referring to his activities in Turkey and Eastern Europe, where he served as Apostolic Delegate during the war. He would not have been discussing the opening of Church institutions in Italy.

Let us now turn to the much more complicated and subtle question of papal instructions in the city of Rome. There is no question that thousands of Jews survived in hiding in religious houses in the Eternal City, and sometimes even in Vatican properties. The story is impressive and moving, and deserves great respect. But why did it happen, or how did it begin? I have suggested, and continue to maintain, that the role—the

29 Pinchas E. Lapide, *The Last Three Popes and the Jews* (London: Souvenir Press, 1967), p. 137; also published as *Three Popes and the Jews* (New York: Hawthorn Books, 1967). Montini never made such a claim elsewhere. In his well-known letter to *The Tablet*, for example, written in response to condemnations of Pius XII's silence by Rolf Hochhuth in *The Deputy* in 1963, Montini wrote about the Pope's goodness and courage and penned the famous phrase, "An attitude of protest and condemnation [of the Holocaust] would have been not only futile but harmful." But Montini never claimed that the Pope had issued a directive to save Jews. This would have been the moment. For the letter, see G.B. Cardinal Montini, "Pius XII and the Jews," *The Tablet*, received on June 21, 1963, and published on July 6; reprinted in Eric Bentley, ed., *The Storm Over "The Deputy"* (New York: Grove Press, 1964), pp. 66-69, and in *Commonweal*, February 28, 1964, pp. 651-652.

30 Lapide, *The Last Three Popes*, p. 181.

31 Ronald J. Rychlak, *Hitler, the War and the Pope* (Columbus, MS: Genesis Press, 2000), p. 242. (Emphasis added.)

initiative—of Pius XII in the sheltering of Jews in religious houses and even in Vatican properties in Rome was minimal. I based this position originally on what seemed like a significant lack of evidence of a papal order in both the written and oral testimonies of rescuers. For example, even Cardinal Pietro Palazzini, who as a young priest helped Jews hiding at the Pontifical Roman Seminary at the Lateran during the occupation, said nothing in his 1995 memoirs about a papal order. What he did say about the Pope was apt. He made it clear that Vatican officials, especially Montini, the vicar of Rome Francesco Marchetti Selvaggiani and the vice-vicar Luigi Traglia, knew what was going on at the seminary. He also wrote that "the guidelines provided by Pope Pius XII were to save human lives, on whatever side they may be." He then said:

> Under the pressure of events, although so very tragic, men rediscovered the Christian message, that is, the sense of reciprocal charity, according to which it is a duty to charge oneself with the salvation of others. To rediscover it, one voice was often raised among the din of arms: the voice of Pius XII. The refuge offered to so many people would not have been possible without his moral support, which was much more than a tacit consent.

As evidence of the "voice of Pius XII," Palazzini cited his various Christmas and Name Day messages.[32]

Cardinal Palazzini's words describe the situation in Rome well. We know that some prelates and priests at the Vatican, including Secretary of State Cardinal Luigi Maglione, as well as some of their non-clerical friends and advisors, occasionally asked the Pontifical Roman Seminary and other Vatican properties and religious houses to accept individuals, both Jews and non-Jews, who were in danger. We know that Vatican officials sometimes sent extra provisions to religious houses, like the convent of the Sisters of Notre Dame de Sion, in full knowledge that those houses were sheltering extra "guests." We know that some priests from northern Italy travelled to Rome for Church business and observed

32 Pietro Palazzini, *Il Clero e l'occupazione tedesca di Roma: Il ruolo del Seminario romano maggiore* (Rome: APES, 1995), pp. 17-35.

that Jews and others were being hidden in some religious houses.[33] They may well have assumed that the rescue effort was consistent with the papal will and used that information to justify their own rescue efforts. But we also know that Roberto Ronca, the rector of the Pontifical Roman Seminary, received some kind of reprimand in December 1943 for accepting too many fugitives, and wrote a letter to the Holy Father apologizing for his excessive zeal.[34] According to Andrea Riccardi, Ronca explained that he had acted under his own responsibility in order not to compromise the Holy See, but that he always believed he was interpreting the will of the Holy Father.[35]

Other prelates hiding Jews and other fugitives seemed to have acted similarly to Ronca, i.e., they acted independently, in order not to compromise the Holy See. Monsignor Elio Venier, active in and a writer about the Resistance, told me that he did exactly that.[36] A close study of the documents in the *Actes et Documents du Saint Siège* (ADSS) indicates that the Pope did not know how many fugitives of all types were hiding within the Vatican City, and had to ask for a special inquiry in February 1944.[37]

In fact, reflecting the discord on the subject among priests and prelates at the Holy See, Pius XII seems to have been conflicted, uncertain, and highly ambiguous about the question of hiding fugitives in Church institutions. On the one hand, he sent general messages urging compassion and charity. On the other, we know from documents recently found in the archives of *La Civiltà Cattolica* that after the German-Fascist raid on the extraterritorial Vatican property of the Papal Basilica of St. Paul

33 See, for example, the visit of Don Francesco Repetto to the Pontifical Lombard Seminary, entries for December 9 and 13, 1943, recorded in the archives of the Lombard Seminary, b.7.A.73, *Diario*. Don Repetto was honored as a Righteous Among the Nations at Yad Vashem in 1976.

34 Ronca's letter, handwritten, signed, and dated, is reproduced in Carlo Badalá, "Il Coraggio di accogliere," *Sursum Cordo*, anno LXXVII, note 1, 1994, pp. 43-46, esp. p. 44. For details on this case, see Zuccotti, *Under His Very Windows*, pp. 202-210.

35 Andrea Riccardi, *L'Inverno più lungo*, p. 34.

36 Monsignor Elio Venier, interview with this author, Rome, November 13, 1996.

37 See, for example, Monsignor Guido Anichini, head of the Canonica di San Pietro, to the Pope, February 13, 1944, ADSS, vol. X, doc. 53, p. 129. The document informed the Pope that about 50 fugitives, most of them men, were being sheltered in that building. Of these, roughly 24 were non-Jews and 17 were Jews who had converted to Catholicism. The status of the others is not clear.

Outside-the-Walls in February 1944, when at least one fugitive was arrested in clerical garb, the Pope expressed his extreme displeasure that laymen and women be permitted to disguise themselves as such. He also directed that fugitives in religious houses not be provided with false documents—a directive that, had it been carried out, would have made hiding and rescue virtually impossible.[38] At this same time, after the raid on St. Paul, orders went out to many Vatican institutions that fugitives hiding there had to leave. To the distress of their rescuers, many fugitives did in fact leave the Pontifical Roman Seminary, the Pontifical Lombard Seminary, the Pontifical College of Priests for Emigrating Italians, and an unknown number of other places at this time, although their rescuers helped them find other hiding places, sometimes in other Church institutions.[39] In fact, many fugitives eventually returned when it seemed safe again. But even within the Vatican City, an expulsion order was issued, although it was rescinded when individual prelates hosting fugitives protested vigorously.[40] None of this is consistent with the claim of a papal order to open Church institutions to fugitives.

Along these same lines is the case of a Jesuit who, a month or so after the raid on St. Paul and the papal order to remove fugitives from certain Church institutions, asked the Vatican Secretariat of State if he could accept Jewish fugitives again. An existing document shows that the Pope was consulted, and the answer was, "He will be acting on his own responsibility."[41] This is also inconsistent with a papal *order* to open Church institutions.

38 From Padre G. Martegani, *Diario delle consulte di Civiltà Cattolica*, in the Archivio della Civiltà Cattolica, cited by the Jesuit Padre Giovanni Sale, "Roma 1943: Occupazione nazista e deportazione degli ebrei romani," *La Civiltà Cattolica*, vol. IV, quad. 3683, December 6, 2003, pp. 417-429, esp. p. 426.

39 I discuss this issue at length in *Under His Very Windows*, pp. 215-232. The best evidence for the expulsion order may be found in the archives of the Lombard Seminary, b.7.A.73, *Diario*, "Appendice," pp. 17-18.

40 ADSS, vol. X, note by Tardini attached to doc. 53, p. 129. Tardini stated that the expulsion order was issued by the Pontifical Commission for the Vatican City State, one of whose members, Cardinal Rossi, declared that it had been requested by his superiors, or, in other words, by the Pope. Prelates who objected then asked Cardinal Maglione to relay their concerns to the Pope. Tardini concluded, "In reality, those who wanted …left [*uscì...chi volle*]."

41 Ibid., doc. 93, notes of the Secretariat of State, March 7, 1944, and attached note, p. 171.

I would now like to consider some of the cases Grazia Loparco described in her article about convents and monasteries that hid Jews and other fugitives.[42] In many cases, witnesses from the period wrote that they took in certain fugitives on the specific recommendation of priests and prelates. I have no problem with that. I am sure that it happened often. An account from the Sisters of Notre Dame de Sion declares that the Vicariate gave permission to accept men. That too is credible; witnesses from other institutions also declared that the Vicariate knew that fugitives were present. Other witnesses wrote of their awareness that the Pope had called upon them to exercise charity and compassion. But only three witnesses testified that they had received a direct papal order to open their doors to all fugitives—and a direct papal order is what we are talking about here today. These claims must be examined carefully. In one, apparently written as a diary on a daily basis at the time, the writer recorded that on February 11, 1944, the secretary of the Congregation of the Institutes of Studies and Seminaries, addressing the heads of several religious institutions, relayed an appeal from the Pope that "wherever they could receive refugees, it would be well to do so."[43] By that date, the writer's convent was already receiving many fugitives. But the Vatican representative did not mention Jews.

A second case is equally problematic. In what is ostensibly a chronicle, written at the time, of a particular convent, the author wrote that "at the request of His Holiness Pope Pius XII, the religious communities have shared their food and lodging with the refugees who are filling the city of Rome. The persecuted Jews find asylum and comfort among us."[44] But the date of this entry is July 9, 1943, before Rome was filled with refugees and well before Jews were leaving their homes and trying to hide. The entry makes no sense.

The third case is problematic for another reason. It seems to be the testimony of a sister of the Sisters of St. Joseph of Chambéry, but it was written in 1996, one year before she was designated as a Righteous Among the Nations at Yad Vashem. Sister Ferdinanda Corsetti wrote: "In those terrible days, the Holy Father Pius XII... asked all the reli-

42 Loparco, "Gli Ebrei negli istituti" pp. 107-210.

43 Ibid., diary of the Communauté du Généralat, Rome, by Mère Marie Vianney Boschet, p. 161.

44 Ibid., chronicle of the Missionary Nuns of the Immaculate Conception, p. 184.

gious communities of Rome to open their doors to these persecuted brothers."[45] This is indeed a testimony, but the date renders it subject to the suspicion that it could have been a deliberate papal defense. Why would that information have been withheld for decades? Also, how could Sister Ferdinanda have known that the Pope asked "all the religious communities of Rome" to open their doors?

Much has been made recently of another unpublished document, ostensibly a hand-written memoir by an Augustinian nun in a convent in Rome known as the Santi Quattro Coronati. The author wrote in November 1943: "The Holy Father wants to save his children, including the Jews, and orders that hospitality be given to these persecuted people in the monasteries, and the cloistered houses must also adhere to the wish of the Holy Father..." She goes on to say, "And so, from November 4, we hosted the following people until the following June 6...." So this is not a day-to-day account, but rather a document written later. Further on, under the rubric "6 June [1944]," she wrote of taking in, in October, an Italian general who had been condemned to death "who stayed for five years."[46] Again, this cannot be a daily report but an ex-post-facto description that could easily have been written with ulterior motives.

It is clear that in examining testimonies about a papal directive, many questions must be asked: Who is the writer and how is he or she in a position to know? Was he or she a leader of the religious community, or was he or she told of a papal order by the superior in the house, perhaps to convince him or her to accept the great risks involved in hiding fugitives? When was the testimony given? Was it at the time, or years later, after Pius XII had been subjected to much criticism, making many men and women of the Church anxious to defend him? If the testimony is recent, we should ask why it was not given years ago. In addition, we need to ask what exactly is being claimed. Is the claim that the Pope ordered all religious communities to open their doors to refugees in general, or is there a specific mention of Jews? Is the reference to explicit referrals by higher clergy, which is not the same thing as a papal order? Is the statement to the effect that officials at the Vicariate or the

45 Ibid., testimony of Sister Ferdinanda Corsetti, p. 176.

46 Pina Baglioni, "Il Santo Padre ordina...," *30 Giorni*, July-August 2006, n. 7/8, pp. 32-46; and *Memoriale delle Religiose Agostiniane del Monastero dei Santi Quattro Coronati,* Rome, pages for 1943 and 1944.

Vatican knew what was going on? Or is it simply, "We were doing the will of the Holy Father"? These nuances are essential in evaluating the testimony, and as historians, we must consider them just as we would when examining any other document.

Discussion

Andrea Tornielli: I would like to say a word defending the memory of the esteemed Israeli diplomat, Pinchas Lapide. It is impossible to say today that everything Lapide said is unfounded. Pinchas Lapide spoke about the testimonies of Montini and Roncalli. Professor Zuccotti said that since Pinchas Lapide said it, it is worthless. I would like to remind you that Montini later became Pope Paul VI, and on two different important public occasions, he defended, with words written by Lapide, the memory of Pius XII. The first time was in an article published in the Catholic international weekly *The Tablet*, just before his election; the second time was when he met the President of the State of Israel at the end of a one-day visit to Israel in January 1964. So Pinchas Lapide is confirmed by the words of the Pope himself.

As far as Roncalli is concerned, again the claim is that this was entirely invented by Lapide. I would like to remind you that Roncalli's statement to Lapide was confirmed by his secretary, Monsignor Loris Capovilla, who is well over 90 (he was born in 1915) but still alive. Therefore, I hope that not everything said by Lapide will be dismissed just because he said it.

Secondly, as to the Pope's knowledge or lack of knowledge or support, I would like to remind you of the case of Ronca cited here. Monsignor Montini was the Deputy Secretary of State. He was the person who collaborated most closely with Pius XII. There was also Tardini, but there is no doubt that Pius XII got on better with Montini. There was a harmony of characters; they worked better together. Montini made a personal visit to the Pontifical Roman Seminary of Ronca, where refugees were hiding. It's impossible to imagine that all this was done secretly, as a spontaneous move. To argue such a thing demonstrates an ignorance regarding how the Catholic Church works! Montini, the main collaborator of the Pope, visited the convents!

In relation to the testimonies not being made immediately, and thus may be blemished by apologetic intents, I would like to remind you of two things. Apart from the idea that the Germans knew full well that the convents were hiding Jewish refugees—for example, this SS newspaper in Italian accuses the Capuchin monks of Milan for having filled the convents with Jews and helping them escape—yesterday I presented the document from the consult diary of *La Civiltà Cattolica*, which says that the Pope was interested in the welfare of Jews, etc. In yet another document found four years ago—the diary of the sisters of the Santi Quattro Coronati convent—in November 1943, they wrote about having hosted Jews, and that they did so following a papal order.

Now, it's pretty difficult to imagine that all this had occurred in Rome without encouragement from the Pope. Whoever helped, whoever hosted, knew they were backed up by the Pope.

And with this I'll finish: Regarding the testimonies, some of which are belated, it must also be pointed out that even after extending help, those religious institutions had no intention of making public the fact that they helped anyone at all and, in particular, Jews. This was also mentioned by Sister Grazia Loparco: Jews were just part of all the refugees being helped. There was certainly no awareness of the existence of a specific Jewish problem among those who hosted the refugees at that time. They had simply escaped together with political refugees, and no differentiation was made.

Thomas Brechenmacher: I would like to start by commenting on Andrea's remarks. First, the book by Pinchas Lapide is wrong on many points, but that doesn't mean that it is wrong on every point. There are those two statements, by Montini, issued in June 1963 and January 1964. (By the way, they were also issued here in Jerusalem, at the Mandelbaum Gate, during the first visit of the Pope to the Holy Land, where he defended Pius XII against allegations, especially by Rolf Hochhuth.)

But other documents exist that contradict the argument that there were many uncoordinated or individual actions, for example, the testimony of Margarete Sommer, Managing Director of the Welfare Office of the Berlin Diocesan Authority. In a reaction to Hochhuth, she said that they acted knowing that everything they did was not on their own behalf, but on behalf of the Holy Father. Further, there is another remarkable statement by Robert Leiber, the private secretary of Pius XII—someone who knew him very well and had worked closely with him since 1917—as early as 1961, before Hochhuth's *The Deputy* raised the discussion stating that Pacelli was always fully informed and asked to be informed about everything. Leiber emphasized that everything passed over his desk.

Finally, from my personal findings in the archives: From 1935, the St. Raphael Organization, which was organized by the bishops, worked in Germany. We have already mentioned the baptized Jews. According to the racial terminology of the National Socialists, baptized Jews were Jews as well. The St. Raphael Organization reported this fact to Rome; they sent very detailed reports. These files can be accessed. Their help to the Jews was therefore coordinated, recognized, and approved by Rome.

Michael Phayer: Sister Loparco, maybe I missed something. Did you mention whether or not Bishop Alois Hudal[47] or Ambassador Weizsäcker participated in giving notices to the convents and monasteries?

Matteo Napolitano: I would like to comment on Professor Zuccotti's presentation. Are we talking about the same issue? When using certain terms, are we referring to the same thing?

Firstly, I will comment on Delasem by citing something from Cantoni, which certainly will not be to Professor Minerbi's liking but could be useful. Delasem was in contact with the Vatican. Cantoni, who, as Professor Minerbi wrote, was certainly not in favor of the Vatican, wrote quite nice things about Pius XII. We may argue, Professor Minerbi and I, as to the reasons for doing so, or about the instrumental use of what he wrote, but let's go back to our subject matter. On the one hand, we speak about Pius XII's church as being a centralized church, where nothing could be done without his wish. On the other, we see

47 The Austrian Bishop Alois Hudal was the rector of the ecclesiastical college at the Church of Santa Maria dell'Anima in Rome. He was a very controversial person, known for being pro-Nazi.

an anarchic situation, where everyone saves whomever he wishes, in whatever way he wishes. This seems peculiar.

Concerning Brunacci, I had two long registered dialogues. I do believe that the question of a written order is an issue that, as Sister Grazia said, is useless to study. Nevertheless, Brunacci is said to have seen the order. It was a circular, he said, sent on the third Thursday of 1943 or, actually, which he saw on the third Thursday of 1943. So it must have been September 9 or 16, that is, after September 8, the armistice and the occupation of Rome by the Germans. Now, while I agree that this question is not that important, crucial, or decisive, why would he have been mistaken? I would like to remind Professor Zuccotti that Brunacci did not speak about these events at an advanced age, but rather the moment the war was over. He remembered them well; he was still young. So why would he have been mistaken? And why wouldn't he have told the truth? According to Brunacci,[48] he also insisted that the title of Righteous Among the Nations be awarded to Bishop Nicolini, and specified that this title should have been awarded as a moral merit, say, to the directives of Pius XII.[49]

Regarding Cardinal Pietro Palazzini: When he heard he was also being awarded the title of Righteous Among the Nations, he stated: "The merit is entirely of Pius XII, who ordered us to do anything to save Jews." Here my source is not Yad Vashem, but Martin Gilbert's book *The Righteous*;[50] it would be interesting to carry out an analytic comparison of the various sources of reference. Gilbert, however, is not talking about Brunacci. He only cites another Righteous, Father Ruffino Nicacci; he had actually forgotten Brunacci.

One last point: According to the ADSS published by the Holy See, many Jews found refuge in the Pope's very own house. So how does one explain that the Pope's home is opened to Jews without him having any knowledge of it?

48 Interview with the author, May 30, 2004.

49 In Brunacci's file in the Righteous Among the Nations Department there is no testimony to such a request.

50 Martin Gilbert, *The Righteous: The Unsung Heroes of the Holocaust* (New York: Henry Holt, 2003).

Sergio Minerbi: I must confess I'm a bit perplexed. While strenuously defending Pius XII, assuming and not admitting that he merits it, you are denigrating the enormous spirit of solidarity that motivated the religious people, the Catholics, in the various convents. I don't understand your objective.

At the age of 14 I found refuge at San Leone Magno in Rome. Though I understand now it was only *carità cristiana* (Christian charity), they were trying to change my identity and convert me to a Roman Apostolic Catholic. After many years—too many years, though fortunately he was still alive—I went to look up the head of the institution, Don Alessandro di Pietro. He was in a retirement home of the Marist Brothers, near Turin. He still had a lively, agile, wonderful mind. I asked him: "Don Alessandro, you saw the Pope every month as the legal representative of the Marists. Did you receive any order, any request, any appeal from the Pope to save Jews?" He said, "No." Then, understanding he was in dire straits, he added, "But there was a general example given by the Vatican..."

I wrote exactly what he told me, just as I wrote exactly what Cantoni said, even though I did not like it. Professor Loparco may or may not agree with me, but I don't think they ever asked themselves if they had or had not received an order from Pius XII. There wasn't time for contemplating such things. When I arrived on November 1, it was absolutely impossible to make any political reflection of this kind. It was unrealistic.

My second point: I interviewed Don Leto Casini, cited earlier. He spoke a lot about Archbishop Dalla Costa of Florence: "It was him who inspired me," he said. "It was him who ordered me, it was him who sent me. He did not say a word about Pius XII!"

Earlier Professor Zuccotti mentioned Padre Benedetto, or Benoit, in Rome; she's been writing his biography. But in *La Civiltà Cattolica* there is an article written by Sale, if I'm not mistaken, about a December 1943 meeting. The article says (I'm citing from memory) that Father Benoit did things that were unheard of and, above all, falsified identification documents. This must have been absolutely prohibited. But without false identification documents, who could have been saved? This was really incredible.

Regarding Montini's visit to Jerusalem: Since I was present, I can still exploit my memory. Upon leaving Israel, when he was the last speaker at the Mandelbaum Gate, he began denigrating the State of Israel for having, he said, accepted the theses of Hochhuth, while in fact Israel was one of the very few countries in which his play had been banned! By the Government! Because it was considered to be offensive to the head of a foreign country. So we are mixing things together that have nothing to do with each other.

Interjection from the audience: But he did speak.

Sergio Minerbi: He spoke in favor of Pius XII, attacking those who denigrated him, like Hochhuth. This was an attack on the State of Israel with no justification.

Jean-Dominique Durand: I would like to say a couple of words on how the Holy See functioned. Obviously, many official documents were published through *L'Osservatore Romano*, or in the official acts, etc., but many others were only transmitted orally. Why? Because, as Professor Loparco rightly said, everyone lived together in the city of Rome. One should take into account not only the operation of Rome in the framework of its connection with the Vatican, but also Italy as a whole. That is, everybody knows everybody, especially given that almost all of the Vatican's officers are Italian. There's a kind of Italian unanimity within the Holy See. Everybody knows everybody; they went to the seminary together, they had so many shared experiences together. It may seem a little difficult to put into words, but this operation was not always rational, but rather based on personal acquaintance. It was, I would say, a capillary system, allowing a great deal of information to circulate.

As an example, I have researched the succeeding period, when the Holy See followed intensely the political affairs of the Christian Democracy during the 1950s, 1960s, and onward. I realized that many things came from above, for example, the order that one must be listed with the Christian Democracy Party. The idea always came from above, namely from the Vatican, from Montini, and the Pope, particularly at the time of Pius XII, who closely followed Italy's political affairs. I could give many examples of political careers that were either encouraged or halted from above.

One must be aware of this capillary system. However, there are moments when a written order is simply unfeasible. In the case we are dealing with today—to require, to look for a papal order—I completely agree with what Professor Loparco said and I apologize, but I do not agree with Professor Zuccotti's research on the papal order. Was the papal order feasible at that moment, when there were so many risks? Could something that was so hazardous for everybody have been written down? It was risky for the Holy See, for the convents, and above all for the refugees, Jewish or non-Jewish.

The idea of issuing a written order seems utopian.

Paul O'Shea: Thank you very much for the wealth of information, especially Sister Grazia Loparco for reminding us of the value of oral testimony, particularly of the witnesses that add so much to the record. I have one question regarding what appears to be a recurring theme.

I remain unconvinced that Pinchas Lapide is as valid a source as some speakers would suggest. With all due respect Andrea [Tornielli], being quoted by the Pope is hardly a validation that what he said was necessarily true and accurate. The bottom line is: Where did he get this information from, and why is it not footnoted in his work? This also leads us back to the mysterious figure of 860,000.[51]

More to the point though, is what both speakers said: This brings us once more to the bottom line of the whole presentation, i.e., that despite everything else that was going on in Rome and Italy at the time, Italians saved human lives. Italians saved Jews, Italians saved partisans on the run, Italians saved escapees and prisoners of war, Italians saved people. And if we are looking for a Christian theological perspective, it's got to be Matthew 25:40: "...whatever you did for one of the least of these brothers of mine, you did for me." And that is really the only way I can understand why people did what they did, from a Christian perspective.

51 In some publications it is stated that 860,000 Jews were saved by the Catholic Church. This number appeared in Lapide's book.

Grazia Loparco: I agree with this last statement: The motivation was unrelated to other characteristics; it was mainly about people. I believe the urgency to save human lives prevailed over any other consideration—religious, political or otherwise. So much so, that in the religious houses, they would hide the antifascists at first and, when necessary, also the fascists. Politics did not matter. In most instances, they were just people.

Then to Professor Zuccotti's question: If there was an order from above why did so many bishops do nothing? I am convinced that there was no order. It was an example that became an indication, which was then perceived as an order. Here, one must not only understand the structure of the Holy See, but also how an indication by the Pope was interpreted by the Religious. In their eyes, it was authoritative, especially since there was a personal example.

Could such a high risk have been imposed from above? On many occasions, for example, when the Jesuits' Provincial turned to Montini in March 1944 asking him what to do with the mothers begging them to hide their children, the reply, given on the same day (March 8, 1944—Montini spoke with the Pope) was that it was at their own responsibility. A further reply followed with a thank you from the Father. It was obvious: It could not be ordered, because there were certain risks involved. They were encouraged, but no *order* could have been given. This is very clear.

Regarding Ronca and the letter that was mentioned: The letter was published in 1994 by the scholar Carlo Badalá whose in-depth research on documentary sources in the archive of the Pontifical Roman Seminary is now in print. We must look at the entire letter, not only that specific phrase. The letter said that Ronca wrote to the Pope referring to the first group of refugees that his Holiness kindly deigned to address to him. In other words, Ronca was saying: I did not ask for permission on each and every occasion to hide other people, because I supposed I was in line with you. Thereafter, he clarified and said that he would continue to host people.

Regarding Monsignor Alois Hudal, in the ADSS: He himself claims to have received these placards, more than 550 declarations he could distribute among the religious houses in Rome and other Italian towns. He did not hide people directly, but rather acted as a go-between for distributing these declarations, which arrived, at least according to him, at many religious houses. We have collected some of these testimonies.

Susan Zuccotti: I believe Sister Loparco and I are basically very much in agreement. I would remind you again, I never said that there was no papal encouragement, approval or knowledge. There were times when he advised cautious prudence. I didn't have time to go into all of these examples, but of course he would advise prudence, that is only reasonable.

We're now getting down to a few details. I would like to say to Andrea Tornielli that I'm very much aware of Montini's statements, if not least from reading them in your book. I knew of course about what he wrote in *The Tablet* before, and I read your excellent summary of what he said, which I found very helpful. But I did not see in your book any reference that Montini had actually mentioned a papal order to open convents and monasteries.

As far as Ronca is concerned, I never said that there was no knowledge. Of course there was knowledge. Montini went twice a week—not only Montini, but also Traglia and others. I never said there was no knowledge or awareness, or at times even encouragement. He was reprimanded, again, on the grounds of prudence, and some refugees had to leave his institution for a short time.

Regarding the testimony of the nuns of the Santi Quattro Coronati: If you read the testimony very closely, it was not written in November 1943, it was written later, although we don't know how much later. There are two sentences in the testimony that make that very clear. It's a beautiful, fascinating testimony, and historically very valuable. But it was not written daily, and it would be useful to know exactly when.

Several panelists in this symposium have claimed that the Pope knew everything that was going on. It is quite clear however, when you read the ADSS that he did not know what was going on in Vatican City itself, in terms of how many refugees were being hidden there.

Regarding Professor Napolitano's comment on the Palazzini quotation: It was made in 1985 when Palazzini was honored by Yad Vashem as a Righteous Among the Nations. I looked in his Yad Vashem file; there is nothing there. As to the original source: I found it first mentioned by the American historian Rabbi David Dalin. Martin Gilbert picked it up from him. Where it came from originally I do not know, and that's important. As historians, we need to know what our sources are.

The same thing goes for the Jews hiding in the home of the Pope: I have never seen any reference to that, and I would ask for the source. The same goes for the allegations about Castel Gandolfo, which are very confusing and which we can discuss later.[52]

I would like to say to Professor Durand that I'm certainly not looking for a written order and by no means am I basing my conclusions on the absence of one. I know that orders were conveyed informally and orally, I understand that very well, but I have not seen much evidence for a specific order *before* the fact, which is, I believe, what we are talking about.

52 It is sustained that many fugitives, among them several Jews, hid in Castel Gandolfo, the summer residence of the pontiff, located in a town close to Rome.

Session Five B: Pius XII and German Diplomats

How should we understand the relations between the Vatican and the German diplomats in Rome?
An important meeting took place on October 9, 1943 between Pius XII and the German Ambassador to the Holy See, Baron Ernst von Weizsäcker. At that time, ongoing negotiations were taking place between the Pope and the German Foreign Minister Joachim von Ribbentrop. What was the outcome?
Many American historians agree that the Maglione-Weizsäcker discussion of October 16, i.e., the day of the razzia *[raid] in Rome, did not constitute a papal or Vatican protest regarding the events of that day. Is there agreement or disagreement on this point among European historians?*

Presenter I: Susan Zuccotti

I have decided to leave the first part of this question for my colleague, Sergio Minerbi, and address the second part myself. In addition to dealing with interpretations by American and European historians of the Maglione-Weizsäcker meeting on October 16, 1943, I will also look at their interpretations of other papal responses to the German roundup of Roman Jews that same day.

First, some historical context.

When Pope Pius XII learned from Princess Enza Pignatelli Aragona of the ongoing roundup early in the morning of Saturday, October 16, 1943, he immediately made a telephone call in the presence of his informant. The apparent result was that Vatican Secretary of State Cardinal Luigi Maglione summoned Weizsäcker to a meeting that same morning. Maglione left an account of the meeting, which is published in the *Actes et Documents du Saint Siège* (ADSS). It said, in part:

> I [...] asked him to intervene in favor of those unfortunate people. I spoke the best I could in the name of humanity and Christian charity. [I said]: "His Excellency, who is so warm and tender hearted, please try to save these many innocent people. It is painful for the Holy Father, painful beyond words, that in Rome of all places, under the eyes of the Common Father, so many people are destined to suffering only because they belong to a certain race..." After a few seconds of contemplation, the Ambassador asked me: "What would the Holy See do if such things were to continue?" I replied: "The Holy See would not like to be put in a position of having to express words of disapproval."[1]

After further discussion, during which Weizsäcker said that a papal protest at that time would "put everything at risk" regarding relations between Germany and the Holy See, Weizsäcker asked Maglione, "Will Your Eminence leave me free not to report this official conversation?" Maglione wrote that he "begged him to intervene, appealing to his sentiments of humanity. I left it to his judgment whether or not to mention our conversation, which had been so friendly."[2]

It is very clear from Maglione's own description of his meeting with Weizsäcker that the Pope did not issue a *protest* to the October roundup. Instead, he resorted to discrete diplomatic intervention, as was his custom. Weizsäcker did not even ask Maglione what the Pope would do if those arrested were deported; he asked instead what he would do "if these things continued," meaning the arrests themselves. In addition, Maglione did not say that the Pope *would* protest; he said instead that the Holy See "would not want to be obliged [*essere messa nella necessità*] to express its disapproval."[3] Not surprisingly then, very few historians, American or European, have interpreted this event as a papal protest. Robert Graham, the American Jesuit historian and one of four official editors of the ADSS, did refer to it as a protest,[4] but even

1 Notes of Cardinal Maglione, October 16, 1943, *Actes et Documents du Saint Siège relatifs à la Seconde Guerre Mondiale* (ADSS) (Vatican City: Libreria Editrice Vaticana, 1965-1980), vol. IX, doc. 368, pp. 505-506.

2 Ibid.

3 Notes of Cardinal Maglione, October 16, 1943, ADSS, vol. 9, p. 506.

4 Robert A. Graham, S. J., "La strana condotta di E. von Weizsäcker ambasciatore del Reich in Vaticano," *La Civiltà Cattolica*, anno 121, quad. 2879, June 6, 1970, pp. 455-471, esp. pp. 456, 457 and 464.

the adamant French papal defender Jean Chelini called it a *threat* of a public protest rather than an actual protest.[5] The French Jesuit historian and ADSS editor Pierre Blet agreed with that description, as did the esteemed Italian Church historian Andrea Riccardi.[6] The equally esteemed Italian Church historian Giovanni Miccoli also agreed, writing that Maglione's step should be seen not in terms of a protest, but rather as a humanitarian step. Miccoli pointed out that Maglione did not even mention a possible protest until Weizsäcker asked him directly what the Vatican would do "if these things continued." The whole meeting, Miccoli declared, demonstrated "the extreme reluctance of the Holy See to make a public protest."[7]

The real question, then, is not whether the Maglione-Weizsäcker meeting constituted a papal protest, but whether it and certain subsequent events constituted a *threat* of a papal protest significant enough to influence German behavior. Thus, it is crucial to look at what happened next. Sometime between noon and 5 p.m. on October 16, a letter from Bishop Alois Hudal, rector of the German ecclesiastical college at the Church of Santa Maria dell'Anima, was delivered by Father Pancrazio Pfeiffer to General Rainer Stahel, the German army commander in Rome.[8] The letter was then forwarded to the Ministry of Foreign Affairs in Berlin, probably that same evening. The letter said, in part:

5 Jean Chelini, *L'Église sous Pie XII: La tourmente (1939-1945)* (Paris: Fayard, 1983), p. 285.

6 Pierre Blet, S. J., *Pius XII and the Second World War: According to the Archives of the Vatican* (New York: Paulist Press, 1999), p. 216; Andrea Riccardi, *L'Inverno più lungo 1943-1944: Pio XII, gli ebrei e i nazisti a Roma* (Rome: Laterza, 2008), p. 126. Riccardi added that Maglione was ingenuous and naïve in trusting Weizsäcker.

7 Giovanni Miccoli, *I dilemmi e i silenzi di Pio XII: Vaticano, Seconda Guerra mondiale e Shoah* (Milan: Rizzoli, 2000), p. 252. Carrying the theme of the Vatican's reluctance to protest further, Sergio Minerbi wrote of the Maglione-Weizsäcker meeting, "Far from condemning the Germans, what mattered most to Maglione was to assure the ambassador that the Holy See was not taking any action against Germany." See Minerbi in Carol Rittner and John K. Roth, eds. *Pope Pius XII and the Holocaust* (London: Leicester University Press, 2002), p. 93.

8 Leonidas E. Hill, "The Vatican Embassy of Ernst von Weizsäcker, 1943-1945," *The Journal of Modern History*, vol. 39, no. 2, March 1967, pp. 138-159. On p. 148, he put the time at noon, from the Gumpert testimony (discussed below). Robert Katz, *The Battle for Rome: The Germans, the Allies, the Partisans and the Pope, September 1943-June 1944* (New York: Simon and Schuster, 2003), p. 107, stated that the time was 5 p.m.

> A senior Vatican source in the immediate entourage of the Holy Father has just reported to me that the arrests of Jews of Italian nationality began this morning. In the interests of the good understanding existing hitherto between the Vatican and the High Command of the German Forces [...] I earnestly request you to order the immediate cessation of these arrests in Rome and its environs. I fear that if this is not done, the Pope will make a public stand against it, which could not fail to serve anti-German propaganda as a weapon against us.[9]

The initiative and impact of the Hudal letter is the subject of disagreement among historians, both American and European. Pierre Blet suggested that Hudal wrote the letter following a visit from Prince Carlo Pacelli, the Pope's nephew, but he provided no evidence.[10] Andrea Tornielli repeated that claim, also without indicating his source.[11] Miccoli also believed that the writing of the letter was initiated by the Vatican—pointing out that Carlo Pacelli had visited Hudal that morning—but his evidence was weak.[12] Others who have claimed a papal initiative for the Hudal letter include Pinchas Lapide and the Italian Jesuit Angelo Martini.[13] Blet went on to say that Stahel sent the Hudal letter to Himmler, "who gave the order to suspend the arrests," an allegation that is virtually unsustainable since we know from a report by SS Lieutenant Colonel Herbert Kappler, chief of the German security police in Rome and overall commander of the roundup operation, that the roundup had already ended at 2 p.m. on October 16, before Hudal's letter could have gone to Stahel and then to Berlin and then to

9 Hudal to Stahel, October 16, 1943. This document from the archives of the German Ministry of Foreign Affairs was printed in full by Saul Friedländer, *Pius XII and the Third Reich: A Documentation* (New York: Alfred A. Knopf, 1966), pp. 205-206. Hudal sent a copy to the Holy See, also printed in ADSS, vol. IX, doc. 373, pp. 509-510.

10 Blet, *Pius XII and the Second World War*, p. 216.

11 Andrea Tornielli, *Pio XII: Il Papa degli Ebrei* (Casale Monferrato: Piemme, 2001), pp. 285-286.

12 Miccoli, *I dilemma e i silenzi di Pio XII*, p. 255. The source, ADSS, vol. IX, doc. 3, p. 510, identifies Carlo Pacelli as Hudal's informant, but gives no clear evidence for the claim.

13 Pinchas Lapide, *Three Popes and the Jews* (New York, Hawthorn Books, 1967), p. 259; Angelo Martini, S. J., "La Vera Storia e 'Il Vicario' di Rolf Hochhuth" *La Civiltà Cattolica*, anno 115, quad. 2735, June 6, 1964, pp. 437-454, esp. p. 444.

Himmler, who then contacted Rome.[14] The roundup ended at 2 p.m. not because Himmler stopped it, but because all the addresses of Jews on the German police list had already been visited.

Attributing the Hudal letter to a visit from Carlo Pacelli, of course, suggests that the Pope, following the Maglione-Weizsäcker meeting, made a second, unrelated attempt to threaten the Germans with a public protest. This flies in the face of Maglione's statement to Weizsäcker during that interview that he would leave matters to Weizsäcker's judgment. It seems reasonable to conclude from Maglione's statement that he would not have wanted to do anything that might jeopardize something Weizsäcker was doing. More to the point, however, is that several witnesses—and, as a result, many historians—believe that the Pope played little or no part in the Hudal letter. Those historians, both American and European, cover a wide spectrum of opinions regarding Pius XII. They include Owen Chadwick (British), Robert Katz (American), and Sergio Minerbi (Israeli).[15] The Canadian historian Leonidas Hill, the Israeli historian Meir Michaelis, and the Italian historian Andrea Riccardi also stated that the initiative for the Hudal letter came from the German diplomats, but added that the Pope or Carlo Pacelli may have played a role.[16] Robert Graham wrote simply: "Who the real author was and what the genesis of the Hudal letter actually was is not clear."[17] The conclusions of all these historians were based primarily on the testimony of Gerhard Gumpert, a young legation secretary in the financial division of the German Embassy to Italy who, when the embassy moved north after the armistice, attached himself to Stahel. Gumpert later testified

14 Blet, *Pius XII and the Second World War*, p. 216. Kappler's report stating the time the roundup ended is printed in Liliana Picciotto Fargion, ed., *L'occupazione tedesca e gli ebrei di Roma: Documenti e fatti* (Rome: Carucci, 1979), p. 19; and Meir Michaelis, *Mussolini and the Jews: German-Italian Relations and the Jewish Question in Italy, 1922-1945* (Oxford: Clarendon Press, 1978), pp. 367-368. Blet's source was probably Hudal, who noted that Stahel told him by telephone on October 17 that he had sent the letter to Himmler, and that Himmler had called off the raid because of the special character of Rome. ADSS, vol. IX, doc. 4, p. 510. Stahel and Hudal were claiming credit that was not due them.

15 Owen Chadwick, "Weizsäcker, the Vatican, and the Jews of Rome," *Journal of Ecclesiastical History*, vol. 28, no. 2, April 1977, pp. 179-199, esp. p. 192; Katz, *The Battle for Rome*, p. 107; Minerbi in Rittner and Roth, *Pope Pius XII and the Holocaust*, p. 93.

16 Hill, "The Vatican Embassy of Ernst von Weizsäcker," p. 148; Michaelis, *Mussolini and the Jews*, p. 366; Riccardi, *L'Inverno più lungo*, p. 132.

17 Graham, "La strana condotta di E. von Weizsäcker," p. 465.

that he had arranged with Weizsäcker's assistant Albrecht von Kessel and with Weizsäcker himself to have a letter prepared, signed by Hudal, and presented to Stahel by Father Pfeiffer. Gumpert also claimed that he, not Stahel, sent the Hudal letter to Berlin.

The next step in the complex drama was made by Weizsäcker, who sent a telegram to the German Ministry of Foreign Affairs the following day, Sunday, October 17, elaborating on the Hudal letter. Weizsäcker wrote, in part: "I can confirm the reaction of the Vatican to the removal of Jews from Rome, as given by Bishop Hudal [...]. The Curia is dumbfounded, particularly as the action took place under the very windows of the Pope, as it were. The reaction could perhaps be muffled if the Jews were employed in work in Italy itself. Circles hostile to us in Rome are turning the action to their own advantage to force the Vatican to drop its reserve. It is being said that in French cities, where similar things happened, the bishops took up a clear position. The Pope, as supreme head of the Church and Bishop of Rome, cannot lag behind them. Comparisons are also being made between Pius XI, a much more impulsive person, and the present pope."[18]

Some defenders of Pius XII, especially Robert Graham, resented Weizsäcker's telegram to Berlin on the grounds that it did not mention that Weizsäcker had actually met with Maglione and that the latter had spoken to him of a possible papal protest of the roundup.[19] This seems, however, to be taking the telegram out of context. Weizsäcker's goal in sending the telegram was not to record for posterity Maglione's threat of a possible protest, but rather, for his own reasons, to help the Jews of Rome as best he could while preventing a confrontation between the Holy See and Nazi Germany. In his telegram, Weizsäcker made it perfectly clear that the Pope was close to making a public protest. He made the protest seem more probable by evoking the responses of some French bishops[20] to the deportations of Jews from France in August 1942, and by stressing a comparison, though not necessarily accurate, with a supposedly more decisive Pius XI.

18 This telegram from the archives of the German Ministry of Foreign Affairs is printed in full in Friedländer, *Pius XII and the Third Reich*, pp. 206-207.

19 Graham, "La strana condotta di E. von Weizsäcker," pp. 455-471.

20 Serge Klarsfeld, *Vichy-Auschwitz*, two volumes (Paris: Fayard, 1983-1985), pp. 353-355, 369, 405, 412-413.

Despite the greater or lesser efforts of the Pope, Maglione, Weizsäcker, Stahel, Gumpert, and others, 1,023 Roman Jewish men, women and children were deported to Auschwitz in the early morning of Monday, October 18.[21] Within a week, all but 149 men and 47 women had been gassed. Sixteen men and one woman survived to return to Italy after the war.[22] And despite all the talk of a possible papal protest "if things continued," the Pope did not protest. The closest he came to a protest occurred on October 25-26, with an article in *L'Osservatore Romano*, after most of the Jews had been killed. There were in fact two short articles, side by side, on the front page that day. The first article lamented in broad and general terms the sufferings of all innocents in the war. The second spoke of the Pope's reaction to that suffering in a manner that made it clear that he was referring to the recent roundup in Rome. It said:

> As is well known, the August Pontiff, after having tried in vain to prevent the outbreak of the war [...] has not for one moment ceased employing all the means in His power to alleviate the sufferings that are, in whatever form, the consequence of this cruel conflagration. With the growth of so much evil, the universally paternal charity of the Supreme Pontiff has become, one could say, even more active; it does not pause before boundaries of nationality, religion or descent [stirpe]. This manifold and incessant activity of Pius XII has been greatly intensified recently by the increased sufferings of so many unfortunate people.[23]

This was the first of only two times during the war that the Pope, or individuals speaking in his name, mentioned those who were suffering because of their *religion*.

In an assessment for his superiors in Berlin two days later, Weizsäcker wrote:

21 The number of deportees has sometimes been given as 1,007, but according to Liliana Picciotto Fargion, *Il libro della memoria: Gli ebrei deportati dall'Italia (1943-1945)* (Milan: Mursia, 2002; first published in 1991), p. 882, it is now recognized to be at least 1,023.

22 Ibid., p. 44.

23 "La carità del Santo Padre," *L'Osservatore Romano*, October 25-26, 1943, p. 1.

> By all accounts, the Pope, although harassed from various quarters, has not allowed himself to be stampeded into making any demonstrative pronouncement against the removal of the Jews from Rome [...] he has done everything he can, even in this delicate matter, not to injure the relationship between the Vatican and the German government or the German authorities in Rome. As there will presumably be no further German action taken with regard to the Jews here in Rome, this question, with its unpleasant possibilities for German-Vatican relations, may be considered as liquidated.[24]

According to Weizsäcker, then, the Pope had made no protest.

The question at hand today is whether European historians agree with American historians on this interpretation, i.e., that there was no real protest from the Vatican to the Rome roundup. This question, however, is misleading, because American historians themselves are not in total agreement any more than their European counterparts. I have tried to demonstrate this in my remarks.

I would like to conclude by asking one more question: Was anything achieved by Pius XII's *threats* to protest, and do historians agree on this issue? We have seen that some historians claim that the roundup ended abruptly because of the Hudal letter, and I have shown that this is impossible. Another source of disagreement involves the release of some 250 people arrested on October 16. The confusion on this point seems to stem from a report that Sir D'Arcy Osborne, the British ambassador to the Holy See, sent to his government on October 31, 1943. According to Osborne, Cardinal Maglione told him of his meeting with Weizsäcker on October 16. Further, according to Osborne, Maglione said that Weizsäcker had relayed Maglione's threat of a protest to Berlin, and as a result, "a good number of persons were released." Osborne concluded: "It seems, therefore, that the Vatican intervention has been

24 Weizsäcker to Berlin, October 28, 1943, from the archives of the German Ministry of Foreign Affairs, printed in full in Friedländer, *Pius XII and the Third Reich*, pp. 207-208. Without knowing of Weizsäcker's letter, the editors of *L'Osservatore Romano* published just one other short article related to the roundup on October 29, 1943. In similar terms, it referred to the Pope's charity and compassion for those suffering because of their nationality, religion or race. This was the second of only two papal references during the war to those suffering because of their religion.

effective in saving a great number of these unhappy people."[25] In the confusion of the time, Osborne certainly believed this, and Maglione may have believed it, too.

Many historians have accepted this statement at face value. But a look at the chronology makes it clear that Maglione's claims were incorrect. According to Arminio Wachsberger, a survivor of the Rome roundup and deportation to Auschwitz, the arrested Jews underwent a selection on the afternoon of October 16. Of the 1,259 arrested, 252 non-Jews, half-Jews and Jews in mixed marriages were declared exempt from deportation. They were released either that evening or at dawn the following day.[26] They were thus selected for release *before* the Hudal letter, about a possible papal protest, had been forwarded to Berlin. Weizsäcker's report about a possible papal protest, which Maglione credited with the releases, was not sent until the following day. The 252 prisoners were therefore released not because of Vatican pressure, but because the German SS was not deporting individuals in their categories. On October 17 and the days that followed, Vatican representatives did try to secure the release of other individuals—usually, by their own admission, Jews who had converted. They had no success.[27]

Second, some historians, including Robert Graham, Pierre Blet, and Owen Chadwick, have claimed that because of the Pope's threat of a protest, in Graham's words, "Rome was excluded from the mass deportations of Jews."[28] Nothing could be further from the truth. After October 16, Jews in Rome went into hiding, so dramatic mass roundups were no longer possible, but hundreds were arrested on an individual basis. Due to the numbers of unregistered Jewish refugees in the city, the exact number of Jews arrested and deported after the October 16

25 Document in the archives of the British Foreign Office, printed in ADSS, vol. IX, doc. 3, p. 506; and Riccardi, *L'Inverno più lungo*, p. 134.

26 Arminio Wachsberger, "Testimonianza di un deportato da Roma," and Kappler report, both in Picciotto Fargion, *L'occupazione tedesca*, pp. 19, 177-178.

27 Vatican efforts in the days following October 16 are documented in the ADSS, vol. IX. Relevant documents include nos. 307, 375, 376, 377, 381, 385, 397, 404, 407, 416, 426 and 449.

28 Graham, "La strana condotta di E. von Weizsäcker," p. 470. For some others who make a similar assertion, see Blet, *Pius XII and the Second World War*, p. 217; and Chadwick, "Weizsäcker, the Vatican, and the Jews of Rome," p. 199.

roundup is not clear, but it was at least 670, and perhaps many more.[29] That number, not including those arrested in the roundup of October 16, exceeded the total number of Jews deported from any other Italian city, including Trieste. And the Pope never again threatened to protest.

One final point: According to a captured German document now in the National Archives in Washington, Eberhard von Thadden, an official in Ribbentrop's Ministry of Foreign Affairs, sent a memorandum to Adolf Eichmann, chief of the Gestapo section dealing with Jews, on October 23, describing Hudal's letter and Weizsäcker's confirmation of a possible papal protest.[30] Eichmann testified at his trial in Israel in 1961 that he immediately consulted with his superior, Heinrich Mueller, asking him "to indicate to me what was to be done."[31] Obviously it was too late by October 23 to do anything to save the Jews arrested in Rome on October 16. Over 800 of them had been gassed and cremated at Auschwitz that very day. But equally obvious, the SS were concerned about the impact of a papal protest. A strong threat of a protest once the roundup had actually begun was probably too late to be effective in that particular case. But why could the Pope not have issued that threat a week or two earlier or later? What effect might it have had then?

Presenter II: Sergio Minerbi

I will present a series of facts that were precedent to the October 16 meeting of Maglione with Weizsäcker, and at the end I will also suggest possible ideas for which I have only circumstantial evidence.

Rome was on the way to being occupied by the Nazis over two days: September 8-10, 1943. I personally remember this event. With the exception of armed resistance near Porta San Paolo, there was practically no impediment to the German occupation of Rome. On September 9, when the fate of Rome was not yet clear to anybody, Maglione already knew what to do. He summoned Weizsäcker, the German ambassador, and told him immediately that the purpose of the meeting was to avoid a

29 Picciotto Fargion, *Il libro della memoria*, p. 30.

30 Thadden's memorandum, in the National Archives in Washington, D.C., is cited in Katz, *The Battle for Rome*, p. 114.

31 Ibid., for the quotation from Eichmann's trial testimony.

German invasion of the Vatican and to obtain German protection in case of a Communist insurgence.[32] These were the two main preoccupations of the Vatican throughout the German occupation: One, to safeguard the neutrality of the Vatican, i.e., "don't invade us"; and two, to avoid a Communist insurgence.

On September 11, Weizsäcker sent a telegram to Berlin, and Goebbels wrote in his diary: "The Vatican requested our ambassador to safeguard its rights. The Führer gave an affirmative answer."[33] There are several testimonies to the contrary, that instead of accepting to respect the Vatican's neutrality, Hitler was planning to invade the Vatican and probably kidnap the Pope.[34] It's not clear how true this was, but at least at that time that was the general belief.

On September 15, the Dean of the Diplomatic Corps to the Holy See, the Brazilian Ambassador, said to the diplomatic corps: "If the Pope is kidnapped, we will demand the right to go with him; we will go with him."[35]

On September 17, the Secretariat of State of the Holy See expressed for the first time the fear that perhaps measures would be taken against the Jews in Italy.[36] On September 18, Monsignor Giuseppe Di Meglio said that a Jewish lawyer came to the Vatican requesting they take in Jewish refugees.[37] Roman Jews were apparently not so happy to extend aid to Jewish refugees, except for the few Zionists, who wanted to help as much as possible.

On September 25, General Rainer Stahel, the military commander of Rome, got wind of an order sent by Himmler to Herbert Kappler, chief of the SS in Rome. Although they were not addressed to him, Stahel read the incoming and outgoing messages, and therefore knew that the orders had arrived. This was a top-secret order dated September 25, regarding

32 Owen Chadwick, *Britain and the Vatican during the Second World War* (Cambridge: Cambridge University Press, 1988), p. 272.

33 Quoted in Michaelis, *Mussolini and the Jews*, p. 347.

34 Dan Kurzman, *A Special Mission: Hitler's Secret Plot to Seize the Vatican and Kidnap Pope Pius XII* (Cambridge, MA: Da Capo Press, 2007) p. 285.

35 Chadwick, *Britain and the Vatican*, p. 273.

36 ADSS, vol. IX, doc. 336, p. 480; Note by the Secretariat of State.

37 Ibid., doc. 338, p. 482; Note by Di Meglio, of the Secretariat of State.

the deportation of the Roman Jews to Germany "for liquidation."[38] It's very important to remember that at this early stage, certain news about the deportation of the Jews in Rome had already arrived. Kappler, for reasons unclear until now, ordered the immediate confiscation of 50 kilograms of gold from the Jews. What happened to my family—excuse me for being personal—is typical, and I will explain why. My father, an engineer who had spent one year in Heidelberg learning German, said immediately: "I know German culture, they are men of honor; if they say they will take the gold and nothing else, that is what will happen." My mother—from Warsaw—said: "I also know the Germans. I was in Warsaw in March-April 1940 [she went with an Italian passport to Warsaw and took her parents to Rome, which was quite an extraordinary exploit at that time].[39] They will take the gold, and the people immediately after. Therefore, we leave our house tomorrow morning." And as the Italian saying goes, "*A casa mia il padrone sono io, ma chi comanda è mia moglie*" (In my house I am the master, but the one who gives the orders is my wife.) So at least they acknowledged the reality, and the next morning, we were out.

It took several more days, until October 4, for Foreign Minister Ribbentrop to answer what Maglione had asked on September 9, when it was not yet clear that the Germans would occupy Rome. Ribbentrop replied: "We will respect the sovereignty and integrity of the Vatican State, but we would welcome the Curia publishing an unambiguous account of the situation."[40]

Kappler took the 50 kilos of gold in 36 hours. The Vatican was alerted; according to its own documents, it said that if needed, it would loan 15 kilograms. Contrary to what is commonly believed, nothing was in fact given by the Vatican. It was not necessary, because within 36 hours more gold than needed was collected.

So on October 4, Ribbentrop cabled Weizsäcker: "We will respect the Vatican's sovereignty, and in exchange we ask for an official declaration

38 E.F. Möllhausen, *La carta perdente: Memorie diplomatiche, 26 Luglio 1943 - 2 Maggio 1945* (Rome: Sestante, 1948), p. 112. The author was *chargé d'affaires* at the German Embassy to Italy in Rome.

39 Sergio Minerbi, "La diplomazia italiana e il salvataggio di ebrei e polacchi," *Nuova Storia Contemporanea*, anno XII, no. 2, March-April 2008, pp. 13-32.

40 Friedländer, *Pius XII and the Third Reich*, p. 201.

of 'good behavior.'" Two days later, Kappler alerted Karl Wolff, Higher SS and Police Leader of Italy, of the arrival of Eichmann's representative Theodor Dannecker. At the time, Consul Eitel Möllhausen was the last German diplomat remaining in Rome. His ambassador had gone to the North; he and Gerhard Gumpert were the only ones who had stayed in Rome.

Möllhausen wanted to save Jews! This is amazing! He decided to repeat what he claimed he and his ambassador Rahm had done in Tunisia, i.e., instead of deporting them, send the Jews to work; transform the Jews into forced laborers. Moreover, Möllhausen did something that was absolutely extraordinary: On October 6, he sent an urgent cable to Hitler saying that 8,000 Jews would be sent to Northern Italy to be liquidated. Now, the fact that he sent a cable to Hitler is very significant, but in addition, nobody in the diplomatic service of Germany had the right to use the word "liquidate." Moreover, since the cable was sent to Hitler, the OSS agent immediately thought it must be a very important cable[41] and had it translated and brought to Roosevelt the same day. Roosevelt did nothing.[42]

The next day, October 7, Weizsäcker read Ribbentrop's cable reassuring him that the Vatican's rights would be respected. Immediately, Weizsäcker went to Secretary of State Maglione, who explained to him that they had to save Rome and avoid turning it into a battleground. This was one of the main preoccupations of the Vatican: To have Rome declared an open city in order to save it from being bombed. The city was of cardinal importance to civilization. And from that very moment, I have the feeling that Weizsäcker had the time and the opportunity to alert the Jews. Weizsäcker wrote in his memoirs that in fact, he did so. It may be true, and Maglione said he recommended that the German commanders avoid taking harsh measures in Rome.[43] What did "harsh measures" mean? Deportations?

Two days later, on October 9, Weizsäcker was received by the Pope himself in a private audience, a very important audience, about which Cardinal Maglione wrote in his notes of the same day. Weizsäcker said

41 Ibid., p. 204.

42 Katz, *The Battle for Rome*, p. 81.

43 Alberto Giovannetti, *Roma cittá aperta* (Milan: Ancora, 1962), p. 174.

that Germany was determined to respect the sovereign rights and integrity of the Vatican.[44]

During the roundup of October 16, the Germans came to deport the family of Advocate Foligno at 171 Via Flaminia. A neighbor, a simple Italian lady, came out of her apartment, shouting at a German officer: "What are you doing? You should not take him!" The German officer answered: "Lady, your own Pope said a few days ago, when he met our ambassador, that if you have to organize the deportation of the Jews, do it quickly."[45] This document was printed by the Vatican in its collection. Whether the Pope was rightly quoted by the German officer or not, does not really matter. The four editors of the Vatican documents thought it necessary to include this document in their official selection.

There is a series of very interesting footnotes to this document. One says this fact was immediately denied; the story was not true.[46] But footnote no. 2 says that the last meeting between Weizsäcker and the Pope took place on October 9. So we know on which day the Pope "did not say" what the officer claimed. We know also from Maglione's note that the meeting took place on October 9. Perhaps the Pope said something of this kind, which is, in a certain way, supported by Eichmann. In his diary he wrote: "Considering the influence of the Catholic Church, especially in Italy, it was necessary to carry out a 'surprise' action."[47]

When raising the question of his arrest by the Germans, the Pope laughed and said something like: "You know what I would do? I would remain in Rome." The Pope did not react publicly to the roundup of Roman Jews. Perhaps he thought a public condemnation might provoke immediate Nazi retaliation. The Pope kept his silence and obtained the non-execution of his own deportation, German protection against a

44 ADSS, vol. VII, doc. 428, p. 664.

45 As noted in the introduction, quotations represent the essence and not always the precise formulation of what can be found in the original document. For the exact quote see: Ibid., doc. 383, p. 519.

46 Andrea Riccardi also refers to this document and to the comment of Father Pfeiffer, who didn't consider this fact as true, due to the fact that he believed only the SS were involved in the roundup. Riccardi wrote: "This is not true since, as it appears in the war diary, three police groups—and other units—under the German commander, were available for the operation." Andrea Riccardi, *L'inverno più lungo*, p. 146.

47 Eichmann's journal (in German), par. 376/AE 56.

Communist uprising, and the retention of his postwar role as mediator. Just like his predecessor Benedict XV, he, too, dreamed of finishing the war as a mediator.

On October 11, a special message from the Italian Secret Service warned that 3,000 SS men would search homes in Rome. It was not difficult to imagine that the action was intended to look for Jews.[48] On October 14, Maglione received Weizsäcker again, but they did not speak about the Jews. Maglione wanted to be reassured that there were "sufficient [German] police forces to maintain public order."[49] At the end of the conversation by the door—this is a general diplomatic rule, you say important things in a confidential way—Maglione said something like: You know, if I were you, I would be really very, very cautious not to do things that could upset the situation. Two days later, the Jews were seized.

We must remember that after October 16 there were some additional arrests of Jews from Rome. Susan Zuccotti claims that around 700 were arrested, but in fact more than 1,000 Jews were taken after October 16. The difference may perhaps lie in the fact that the German SS carried out the *aktion* of October 16, but the arrests after October 16 were carried out by the Fascist Italian Police. The result, however, was the same: Auschwitz.

This is the evidence so far. We have only circumstantial evidence that there may have been some kind of a deal to the following effect: I, Pius XII, will keep silent. You, Germans, finish quickly what you have to do and safeguard the neutrality of the Vatican.

Respondent I: Andrea Tornielli

To hypothesize [Professor Minerbi] that the Pope had given the go-ahead to the deportation of Jews in order to save the Vatican, as long as it was done quickly—excuse me, but this really is too much. If he gave the green light to do so in the first place, why did he then summon the ambassador to protest? (We agree that it was not a formal diplomatic

48 October 11, 1943, ADSS, vol. IX, doc. 363, p. 501.

49 ADSS, vol. VII, doc. 435, p. 670.

protest. But this is not the issue.) We have a document—the testimony of the unknown German officer, although not all that was said by German officers is necessarily accurate—that among others is found in the ADSS, which claims that the Pope allegedly gave a quick go-ahead. But that does not necessarily mean that it is true. Moreover, the Pope was advised by Princess Pignatelli Aragona, who arrived in the Vatican in the early morning when the Pope was still praying. Surprised, the Pope told Maglione to summon Weizsäcker. This is the same Pope who allegedly said a few days earlier: "If you have to do it, do it quickly and take them away." To believe such an exaggeration, which has no historical basis, seems to me too much.

A short remark on a comment made by Professor Zuccotti concerning the doubt surrounding Monsignor Hudal being contacted by Carlo Pacelli: In his letter, Hudal said that a prominent Vatican dignitary who was very close to the Holy Father had told him that the same morning. This is Hudal, who in his letter cites another Vatican dignitary very close to the Holy Father. It is certified and documented that Carlo Pacelli, one of Pius XII's nephews, used to convey these kinds of informal messages (they had obtained a special permit for him from the German command to walk around freely); he was even awarded a silver medal by the Partisan Liberation Committee for this activity. There is therefore no doubt that Carlo Pacelli contacted Hudal.

As to the gold issue, Professor Minerbi claims that according to the Vatican documents, they were possibly involved in this. In this case as well, there is written documentation and there is also the testimony of a person whose name you mentioned, who went to the Vatican.

Sergio Minerbi: Israel Zolli, Chief Rabbi of Rome.

Andrea Tornielli: A written note by Bernardino Nogara, head of the Institute of Religious Activities (*Istituto per le Opere di Religione*—IOR), reads: "This morning Zolli was here. He asked, and we offered, a loan of 15 kilograms [of gold]." Thereafter, there is another note saying that it was unnecessary, because the missing 15 kilograms had been collected from Catholic families. So, as you said, not even one gram of gold came from the Vatican, but you presented it as if doubting that there was the will or the interest…

Sergio Minerbi: No, I didn't doubt that.

Andrea Tornielli: Regarding additional interventions—Hudal's letter, the involvement of Father Pancrazio Pfeiffer, and the testimony of Nikolaus Kunkel, who witnessed the delivery of a letter addressed to Ambassador von Weizsäcker before the beginning of the roundup by General Stahel (who wanted to intervene in order to stop the roundup)—Kunkel talks about a phone call made by Stahel to Himmler. My question to Professor Zuccotti is: Was there no communication between Berlin and Rome on October 16? Was there no order by Himmler to put the roundup of the ghetto on hold?

Remarks from the audience.[50]

Andrea Tornielli: So there was no such order by Himmler. Yet, I don't think we can exclude a communication by phone.

As to the important question made by Professor Zuccotti as to why there wasn't a public protest, which is a fundamental point, I think it is a little demeaning to present this issue only as the Pope's fear of a German invasion of the Vatican. The October 25 article in *L'Osservatore Romano* entitled "The Charity of the Holy Father" (*La Carità del Santo Padre*) states: "The August Pontiff [...] has not for one moment ceased employing all the means in His power to alleviate the sufferings [...] the universally paternal charity of the Supreme Pontiff [...] does not pause before boundaries of nationality, religion or descent [*stirpe*]."[51] The word *stirpe* is important since the Pope wanted to let people know that he was helping Jews.

In addition, we must bear in mind that here they were not talking about the buildings of the Vatican, of their fear that the *Wehrmacht* or the SS would march into St. Peter; they were talking about hundreds of religious institutes and houses that had obtained Stahel's permit by having somehow declared "extraterritoriality" (that, in fact, could not be applied because often they were institutes that did not have extraterritoriality), and after the ghetto roundup (but not only after, we have the testimony of that Jew who turned to Montini; his request is even

50 The remarks from the audience were impossible to transcribe.

51 "La carità del Santo Padre," *L'Osservatore Romano*, October 25-26, 1943.

documented in the ADSS), these institutes began to take in refugees. Now, did the Pope know? Was he afraid? Was he not afraid also that a public protest would spur the SS (as in fact happened in the two cases mentioned earlier) to go into all the religious institutes and houses where these placards were hung?

So when the request was made that if the Germans guaranteed the extraterritoriality of the Vatican, the Vatican would say that the behavior of the German soldiers had been proper (this was said repeatedly, in diplomatic meetings as well), we must bear in mind that the convents, the religious institutes, were packed with refugees, including Jews. Were the doors opened? Was the cloistering called off due to some spontaneous initiative? Let's leave this question for the moment. It was known that it was a very delicate situation, one that could have been reversed very easily, because these institutions could have been subjected to raids and deportations.

Respondent II: Thomas Brechenmacher

First, a question: When was the Holy See and, in particular, the Pope, informed about the planned raid? Specifically, was it already on October 9-10? And how did they interpret the situation before they were certain?

Second, I would like to add some remarks with regard to the role of Bishop Hudal.

Concerning the first point, the state of information: There is a lack of sufficient sources. There is a short memo by the Secretary of State from October 11. It reports that Field Marshal Kesselring requested from Erwin Rommel 3,000 SS men to carry out house searches (the original text speaks of *Perquisizioni domiciliari*) in Rome in cooperation with Italian-Fascist units. The memo also reports that this action was supposed to begin on October 18, and that it would be finished within three days.[52] The memo reports a planned action directed against the whole Roman population. It does not refer to specific actions against the Jews.

52 ADSS, vol. XI, p.501.

Second: The statement of the German officer, documented in a memo by Maglione on October 23, which has been cited several times here.[53] This memo reports a statement on October 16 by a German officer with an unknown function during the arrest of a Jewish family living in Via Flaminia. Answering a Roman woman protesting against the arrest, the German soldier stated that the Pope had told the German Ambassador that if the deportation of the Jews had to be carried out, it should be done as soon as possible. The value of these two sources is obviously limited. In one source, an unspecific action against the whole Roman population is mentioned. The other, as already stated by Andrea Tornielli, is a third-hand report, moreover from a German who had to justify the arrest to a Roman woman. Here, the German uses an alleged papal quote.

Then there is the statement of the embassy employee Möllhausen, mentioned by Robert Katz, that he had handed over a telegram to Weizsäcker on October 9, in which Weizsäcker was ordered not to interfere with the upcoming deportation. He (Möllhausen) also asked Weizsäcker to pass that information on to the Vatican. Möllhausen gave this statement orally, in an interview after the war. I don't believe there is any document from 1943 that substantiates this account.

On the basis of these sources, we can only guess as to whether or not the Vatican knew of the upcoming roundup. The question is what we know about the specific actions of the Holy See. On that specific question, the documentation is far better. Apart from whether or not the Holy See was informed on October 9 that an action against the Jews of Rome was imminent, we know that the Vatican anticipated excesses against the Jews from the beginning of the German occupation in mid-September and that the question as to what could be done to help the Jews had been raised.[54]

A decision was made to take diplomatic steps directed at the German ambassador, Weizsäcker. Monsignor Tardini noted on September 17 that the Cardinal Secretary of State had already spoken with Weizsäcker twice about the situation of the Jews—on September 10 and 13.[55] There

53 Ibid., p. 519.

54 Ibid., vol. IX, p. 480.

55 Ibid., pp. 480-481; vol. VII, pp. 616, 622-623.

are corresponding remarks by the counselor of the embassy Albrecht von Kessel, which have received too little attention in this context. In his memoirs, drafted immediately following the end of war, von Kessel wrote about the week of September 10-17. Stating that he had consulted with Weizsäcker on the 10th regarding possible measures to help the Jews of Rome, von Kessel wrote: "Parallel to my efforts [following September 11], Weizsäcker visited the Pope and warned him not to protest publicly. For such a protest would not save a single Jew. Also, it would drive Hitler to extreme fury, that would not stop even at his—the Pope's—person."[56] This part of von Kessel's memoirs was published in the context of *The Deputy* controversy. But a few years ago, Harald Vocke, who wrote an extensive book about Albrecht von Kessel, included these reminiscences taken from his estate.[57]

Von Kessel's memoirs match the testimony of embassy employee Gumpert. Weizsäcker told him: "Back then, I had a confidential conversation with Montini and informed him that a statement by the Pope would lead to the transports being carried out all the more." Once again, Weizsäcker: "I know the reactions of these people on our side. Montini, by the way, understood my argument." This is cited in the Weizsäcker documents, kept by the Institute for Contemporary History in Munich.[58]

We can conclude, therefore, that the memoirs of von Kessel, the statement of Gumpert, and the note of the Secretary of State from September 17, together form a coherent picture. Evidently, the Holy See took the words of Weizsäcker to heart, and decided to abstain from protesting openly against the anti-Jewish actions. Instead, the protest was voiced utilizing the diplomatic channels.

At that time there were grave concerns that the German occupiers might disrespect the neutrality of the Vatican's territory. For that reason, on September 18, a representative of the Roman Jewish community was urgently advised that a group of some 150 French and Polish Jews

56 Harald Vocke, *Albrecht von Kessel: Als Diplomat für Versöhnung mit Osteuropa* (Freiburg: Herder, 2001), pp. 274-275.

57 Ibid.

58 Quoted in Dieter Albrecht, *Notenwechsel*, vol. 2, S. XVIII, note 11.

should leave the city and move to the Abruzzi, i.e., escape from the German police.[59]

In the following days, with the assurance that the neutral territory of the Vatican would be respected, another possibility arose—to open the enclave of the monasteries and convents to hide Jews.

I would like to point to a precedent already mentioned by Sister Loparco—the document of October 10, 1943. This document shows that with papal approval, a convent of sisters on Gianicolo Hill in western Rome opened its gates for an elderly Jewish couple.[60] That means that by the end of September there was a change in strategy. The more it became apparent that the German occupiers respected the inviolability of the Vatican and its religious institutions, the more the Vatican opened the convents.

A few words concerning Hudal: As far as I know, the only source for the thesis that Carlo Pacelli asked Hudal to compose a letter is the letter itself. As you may know, we have opened Hudal's archive in Santa Maria dell'Anima, and by now we have reviewed nearly all of its contents. We have been able to find, amongst other files, Hudal's original letters in duplicate scripts. They contain the passage Andrea Tornielli was citing earlier regarding his being asked by a high representative, close to the Pope. Hudal did not only include this phrase in his memoirs, it was actually part of the original letter. Unfortunately, the archives of Hudal don't hold any other documents that could shed light on this question.

The question is: What are the arguments against a possible request to Hudal? Certainly that he was *persona non grata* at the Holy See by no later than 1938. His book *The Foundations of National Socialism* was clearly disapproved of by the Pope. And in 1938 tensions arose again when Hudal planned to celebrate a thanksgiving service in the Anima for the *Anschluss* (annexation) of Austria. It was forbidden by the Secretary of State. Hudal was *persona non grata* in 1943, so why should anyone come to the conclusion that it would be a good idea to ask Hudal? Which facts hint towards a request to Hudal? One reason might be that Hudal had good contacts in Germany, at the highest levels of the military establishment. Concerning the question Professor

59 ADSS, vol. IX, pp. 482-483.

60 Ibid., p. 496.

Zuccotti brought up: Was anything achieved? It seems that the raid was halted at about 2 p.m., and the letters of Hudal and Weizsäcker arrived no earlier than late in the evening or the next day. Whatever caused the raid to stop, the Holy See must have gotten the impression that its initiative had contributed to its end. They may have come to the conclusion that their strategy of diplomatic intervention in combination with remonstrative letters (maybe even the letter of Hudal) had proven to be an effective approach.

Since Sergio Minerbi put forward a strong thesis, allow me to voice a strong antithesis, although I cannot prove this with any document.

I have the impression that on October 16 the Holy See quite possibly followed a two fold strategy. First, they utilized Weizsäcker in a diplomatic approach. But although he pledged to look into it, and in spite of a promise made to Maglione, he was not to be trusted. So they chose an additional approach, and that was the request to Hudal.

The second part of my thesis is, as Sister Loparco explained, that the strategy of the Holy See following October 16 was to open the convents in cooperation with the embassy and, partly, with General Stahel. Reference to that can be found in the memoirs of Albrecht von Kessel. The embassy provided posters—certificates—that announced: "Extraterritorial Vatican Area." So in this case, the strategy was not to protest openly, but to act. The intention was to use the convents to save as many Jews as possible.

Discussion

Paul O'Shea: One of the things that strikes me about the whole Roman affair—that just adds to what I believe, at the risk of compounding the provocations, was a potentially unavoidable tragedy—is that the Vatican was sitting down with the Devil and attempting to strike a deal with him, and was doing it as Thomas Brechenmacher expressed, on two tracks: trying to find a way out of an impossible situation without imperiling the Vatican's neutrality or at least the façade of neutrality (I don't think anyone took it particularly seriously). Whether or not the Vatican curia believed that the Germans would invade, there is some evidence to suggest that they did. Certainly the Pope was prepared to die as a martyr.

The primary question I have with regard to the whole tragedy is: Given that the Vatican, and certainly the Pope, knew that something was going to happen to the Jews of Rome, whatever that would be, and given that Pius knew his enemy all too well—by this stage of the war he knew what was happening in the East, people knew that deported Jews did not come back, Italian soldiers and the general public knew what was happening—why then was there not some effort made to inform the Jewish community in Rome that something was up? Something was going to happen?

Now, I have not found any documentation, I haven't seen anything in the ADSS, but surely from a purely humanitarian point of view, if ordinary Italians spontaneously opened their doors to take in people who were being hunted down, why didn't the Vatican, or the Vatican officials—Maglione, Montini, Tardini, Tisserant or the Pope—at least pass on the information they were receiving to the leadership of the Roman community, either the rabbinical leadership, Delasem[61] in Rome or the communal leadership? This question remains unanswered.

Jean-Dominique Durand: I would like to go back to Weizsäcker's document—a rather ambiguous channel, of which we are more or less being held prisoners. We must look at it methodologically: What is the nature of this document? Who wrote it? To whom is it addressed? These are basic questions that we teach our students when evaluating a document.

Here we have a German ambassador who was definitely not a Nazi, at least not a member of the Nazi party. But what did he want? What was his plan? I do not wish to disparage the value of diplomatic dispatches (in particular in the presence of such an esteemed ambassador as Ambassador Minerbi), but we know well that, like prefects, diplomats often write what the addressee expects to hear. So can we totally trust this document? I think it must be handled with caution.

I would like to refer to another example, this time a French one, which opens the way to a comparison. We have a letter from the ambassador of Vichy, Leon Bérard, from the period during which the Vichy govern-

61 Delasem (Delegazione Assistenza Emigranti Ebrei) was a Jewish organization which helped Jewish refugees in Italy from 1939. After September 1943 it operated, with the assistance of many clerics, to save Jews.

ment was preparing its anti-Jewish legislation. He wrote that the Pope would have nothing to say against an anti-Jewish law. This document has caused much controversy, many discussions, and many disputes.

On the other hand, in the archives of the Spanish Ministry of Foreign Affairs, I found a letter from the Spanish Ambassador to Vichy, José Félix de Lequerica, a truly hardcore Fascist. He wrote to his minister that he was tremendously angry with the Nuncio to France Valerio Valeri, since the latter had apparently said in a conversation that Bérard was not telling the truth: The Pope did not agree with the law for the Jews.

Therefore, I would like to emphasize again the need to be very careful, from a methodological point of view. As far as prudence in the interpretation of documents is concerned, it is vital that we take all the various aspects into consideration. As historians, we know that documents should not always be taken *au pied de la lettre*—literally.

Matteo Napolitano: I do not wish to add anything to what Thomas Brechenmacher has already said, but I have the impression that the Vatican's argument was self-defeating. In other words, the Vatican masochistically published a series of documents that clearly demonstrate that the Pope was, in fact, indifferent with regard to the Jews.

I would like to discuss the famous minutes mentioned earlier. My first point is that the report of the Maglione-Weizsäcker conversation dated October 16 is the only direct source available. As already mentioned, Weizsäcker asked that this conversation not be reported to Berlin. In the report, as far as I remember (and I will cite a small segment from it), Maglione leaves to Weizsäcker the liberty to report the conversation to Berlin or not. As far as the Vatican is concerned, it is not very important. So what was important? Maglione explained this subsequently: It is important that this thing be stopped immediately, because it's happening "under the very windows of the Pope" (in Susan Zuccotti's words).

Still, is it disapproval or a protest? I would like to cite something that so far, due to lack of time, has remained implicit. Maglione concludes his report as follows: "However, I also had to tell him that the Holy See should not be put in a position where he would be compelled to protest: Should he be constrained to do so, the Holy See would have to rely on the Divine Providence for the consequences."[62] I don't know if this phrase is sufficiently clear, but it seems to me that "protest" could be the equivalent of disapproval, or that disapproval might be a preamble to protest. However, "protest" was the word Maglione used in his report.

Another element I wish to discuss concerns Osborne's telegram. Professor Zuccotti has explained the timeframe very well. However, from the final paragraph of the telegram, I wonder whether Osborne was wrong with respect to the Pope's general intention, because he says (I quote from memory): "I asked whether I could report to my government the interest of the Holy See in the Jews, and I was told not to, because any publication of information would lead to new persecutions." This is Osborne's report.

The whole case of Weizsäcker is also revealed by Jacques Nobécourt, an author who possibly has nothing to do with Pius XII and who has not always been favorable toward the Pope. He said that Weizsäcker, in fact, concealed the truth from his government.

Michael Phayer: If we agree, and I do, with Sergio Minerbi that the two main preoccupations of the Vatican immediately prior to October 16 was the possibility of a Communist uprising in Rome and Vatican neutrality, then we are saying that the Jews were a lesser priority than these two matters.

I believe Sergio Minerbi is right in that respect. Before the Jews had even reached Auschwitz, Pius XII asked the Germans to beef up their manpower policing the streets of Rome in order to reduce the possibility of a Communist uprising.

Furthermore, I found a document in the National Archives in Washington, according to which the Vatican put in an order to a Swiss company for machine guns and ammunition with which they were going to defend the Vatican, not against the Germans, but against the Communists in Rome.

Immediately after the Americans occupied Rome, Pius made the same request: that they increase their policing of the streets of Rome in order to quell a possible Communist uprising.

62 Notes of Cardinal Maglione, October 16, 1943, ADSS, vol. 9, p. 506.

I do not agree, however, with Sergio Minerbi's hypothesis that if you have to do something, do it quick. I believe that von Kessel's memory is correct, that he and Gumpert and Stahel dictated the so-called "Hudal letter" and then told him to sign it. That indicates that there was a considerable amount of cooperation among the German diplomatic staff in Rome. My question to Thomas Brechenmacher is: Do you agree with von Kessel's recollection that this is indeed the origin of the Hudal letter?

If this is the case, then it seems that the German diplomatic staff, quite possibly with the cooperation (or at least with the knowledge) of the Vatican, was working together to do what it could to safeguard the Jews, or at least reduce any further danger to them. This is important, because it comes back to Sergio Minerbi's first two points. If things could have been accomplished through the Germans, then the Vatican was not putting itself at risk in the eyes of Berlin, including any potential invasion of the Vatican by German groups or the possible kidnapping of the Pope, which probably in retrospect is a little bit ridiculous but everybody believed it at the time. Everybody in the Vatican as well as the German diplomats took this threat literally. As Sergio Minerbi pointed out, all of the diplomats at the Vatican said that if they took the Pope, they would go also.

Dan Michman: A short remark. What I think we are trying to decipher is whether certain directives regarding the Jews came from the Pope to the lower echelons. Analyzing the situation at that time: Italy and Rome had been conquered by the Germans and, as was mentioned, there was danger to the Vatican, to its independence, which was at the heart of the Church. Therefore, the Church set its political preferences on what to do with the Germans.

Regarding the lower echelons: What were they expecting to happen if the Vatican really fell apart? If there was no central government, would they act on their own instead of waiting for orders, as would normally happen in a regular state? We had this experience with other states in 1939 and 1940, when the government fell apart and the others, the lower echelons, had to run the country. Here we're speaking about the convents and the bishops, etc., who would now have to think for themselves. A new way of thinking was born, one in which they could not expect the Pope would give a clear order in that situation. I believe he made his preferences known, and it was not a central matter on his mind, but they also became much more independent. This is just a suggestion, but I'm trying to look at the situation that existed in September-October 1943.

Iael Nidam-Orvieto: Several very important things have been discussed, for example the question raised earlier: Why didn't they let the Jews, the Jewish leadership, know? This question is fascinating when placed in the context of the Jewish community in Rome. Here the case of the Chief Rabbi Israel Zolli is extremely important. I have no doubt that he went to the Vatican, that he was at least one of the liaisons with the Vatican in this case, and he received promises of aid. But Rabbi Zolli was not popular with the Jewish community. He was probably the only leader—again, as an Eastern European—who knew what violent antisemitism was; he was afraid of the invasion and he was quite aware of the danger to the Roman and Italian Jews, and in fact he tried to convince the rest of the Jewish leadership in Rome about the danger. But the Jewish leadership was fearful that his attitude would spread panic. Dante Almansi, President of the Union of Jewish Communities, was very afraid and wanted to avoid panic and, as he didn't admire Zolli, he was unable to accept Zolli's scenario and advice.

We also know that Zolli tried, in September 1943, to warn the Jews of the community, and some of those who were convinced went into hiding. It is from them that we know the story.

Therefore, this question is even more vexing because of the context. A historian cannot really ask himself what would have happened *if*, because there really is no "if," and yet, in this case, the question really tickles me: How would Almansi, who couldn't believe the worst scenario, or Ugo Foa, who a few weeks after the *razzia* wrote a memoir and still didn't admit that Zolli was right and he was wrong, have reacted if the Vatican had passed them some information? This "ahistorical" question bothers me greatly.

We have been discussing the question of an order, or an initiative. I don't believe that there was such an order. We will never find it. But perhaps we should phrase the question differently: Was this an initiative of the local institutions, of the people in the field, or was it an initiative from the top?

Grazia Loparco mentioned that we have some documentation of a few superiors in institutions who were quite hesitant. But when they heard that the Holy See suggested, agreed or asked them to hide Jews, they opened their gates. In other cases, we have a clear initiative from the field, and retroactively, maybe, they received the encouragement, the agreement, from the Pope. So what was the rule here?

We have here an assortment of issues. We are far away from a clear picture. I very much hope that one day, when the Vatican's archives are opened, we will have a clearer picture, although I don't think we will ever have "the picture." We will never have the whole answer, but we will have much more clarity about many of these aspects.

Another final comment on something that has come up in each session: Many of the participants often mention the fact that after the war, a number of Jews thanked the Vatican and the Pope. This is true. Many Jews thanked them. Many Jews were saved by Catholic institutions. It is natural that they would go to the Pope to thank him. We must also remember, and if you look at their diaries you will see, many of them expected the Pope to help. Jews believed that the Pope would protect them.

Lately, I've been working on rumors—it's fascinating which rumors circulated about the Pope and his intention to help. For example, one day after the story of the gold ransom, Lorelei Weiss—who was in Norcia in September 1943—wrote in her diary about a rumor that the Pope donated a large amount of gold to save the Jews. It is intriguing how fast the rumor spread and how incorrect it was. So, at the end of the war, expectations engendered their natural will to thank the Pope; this should not surprise any of us. It does not prove anything; it only proves the very special relationship between the Jews and the Pope, which research has yet to explain sufficiently.

I would also like to say that it is natural not to agree on many of the topics we are dealing with. For example, the issue of the importance of oral testimonies, as well as the question of converted Jews—whether we consider those cases as a rescue of Jews or not—it's clear we disagree on that. We have different perceptions and this is part of our efforts to find a way of understanding how things were perceived at the time.

Sergio Minerbi: Professor Napolitano, even if it is self-defeating, it's okay with me. But the interest of the Pope in the Jews is not only documented by what I have already said, it is also documented by two diplomatic meetings he had after the roundup. On October 18, two days after the roundup, he received the British representative, Osborne. Not a word about the Jews! Not a word! He had nothing more to lose, but not a word was uttered. The only problem was Rome and the police, etc.

On October 19, American Ambassador Harold Titman was received by the Pope (his report is in documents in the *Foreign Relations of the United States*) and again, not a word about the Jews! Three days later! So he couldn't have cared less. Later, when the people in the field started saving Jews, he did not oppose their actions. Maybe he even gave his blessing after the event.

It is very important to note that while the Pope refrains from making any public statement on the Jews because he doesn't want to hurt relations with Germany, he does not refrain from public speech when he has to praise German behavior. On October 28, after the roundup, after the Jews had been sent to and killed in Auschwitz, he had the gall to publish in *L'Osservatore Romano* what Ribbentrop asked for back on October 4, i.e., the certificate of good behavior.

As to the Maglione-Weizsäcker meeting: Was it a protest or not? It's not so difficult to understand. In 1904 or 1905, Sergei Sasonov was the Russian Ambassador to the Holy See. Rafael Merry Del Val, then Secretary of State, presented him with a note of protest by the Vatican to the Tsar. Sasonov responded by asking Merry Del Val's permission not to give this document to the Tsar, because he believed that the relations between their two states would be disturbed. What did Merry Del Val answer? Did he say what Maglione said? No! He said that he guessed that the Holy Father would convoke him to say goodbye. Very nice, very politely—go home! Sasonov eventually transmitted the note to the Tsar. So when you want to do something, you do it.

Matteo Napolitano: It's not the same situation. In this case, Weizsäcker did not receive a verbal note from the Vatican.

Sergio Minerbi: That is true. And that proves that from the very beginning it was not meant to be a protest.

Matteo Napolitano: But he did not exclude it.

Sergio Minerbi: If you continuously say, "Don't provoke me because I may react" and you do nothing, your threat becomes void. This is what the threats of the Vatican to the Germans were meant to be.

My last point concerns Almansi. It is true, at the very beginning he had very little understanding of Jewish refugees, of German authorities and activities. They learned the hard way. Almansi did not have a clue what to do at first. Zolli, because of his Polish origin, was the opposite.

Almansi had one more task. If, on September 9, he had listened to what Zolli rightly advised, he would have spread panic in a community, the majority of whom were poor people who had no means to leave. You tell them: "You have to get out immediately." Where to? Nothing had been prepared. What Almansi should have said was: "Zolli, you are right. Let's sit here, together, and prepare a relief plan so that within seven days everybody will be out of their house." This is what he should have done. But it's not what happened.

Susan Zuccotti: I have a few small points.

The question that Andrea Tornielli asked about Himmler and the calling off of the roundup: Gumpert said that Hudal's letter was sent to the Foreign Office. Father Blet said that it was sent to Himmler, and apparently this information came from Hudal, who reported that Stahel had told him on October 17 that Himmler had stopped the raid because of the special character of Rome, not the published Vatican document. So the information saying that Himmler was involved in calling off the raid came from Stahel to Hudal, and both of them had reason to indicate that they were doing something, that their work had had some effect. However, October 17 was far too late. We know that the roundup came to an end at 2 p.m. on the 16th. So again, the chronology speaks for itself.

On another point, I would say that convents and monasteries certainly were not full of Jews on October 16. So any reason for the Pope to be reticent about protesting in order to protect Jews in convents was a later factor perhaps, but not on October 16. They did go in, but not that day. Most did not enter until after the 16th.

As to the question of the placards and the protection offered by them to institutions of the Church—the whole issue is very confusing. I am sure it was a joint effort. But I believe the major purpose of this effort was not to protect Jews, but rather the institutions; the placards were sent before many Jews were in the institutions. You certainly wouldn't put a placard on an institution saying—don't invade because there are Jews here. It's much more complicated than that. We all know the placards existed, but we don't know too much about the background.

Thomas Brechenmacher: Only a short remark regarding what Paul O'Shea said: I believe the question of neutrality is a key point. If you do not recognize this idea of Pacelli, you won't be able to understand the policy of the Holy See during that time. "We must remain neutral to be able to promote peace." This question is crucial for understanding the whole approach.

Concerning the letter by Hudal: I do not know if it was dictated by von Kessel. As far as I remember, von Kessel only noted that a revised version of the Hudal letter was made and sent to the Ministry of Foreign Affairs. I can merely say that after our review of the Hudal archive, this matter remained unclear.

Andrea Tornielli: I don't believe that the fact that the Pope did not mention the ghetto roundup in his audiences with Titman and Osborne leaves one to deduce that he didn't care about the Jews. This would mean not putting together all the elements. If he couldn't care less, why was the ambassador summoned? True, he did not issue a written protest like Merry Del Val did to the Tsar in a completely different situation, but in the drawers of the Third Reich's Ministry of Foreign Affairs there were 70 formal protest notes by the Vatican, left there without even being honored with an answer. We must bear in mind that they knew who their counterpart was. They were dealing with Hitler. Therefore, I don't think that this conclusion can be deduced.

Concerning the Zolli case that was so eloquently explained, Zolli said they should give an order to close the offices. They should inform the Jews about the danger to the thousands of persons who were living in the ghetto. The only fear was panic. I think Zolli was right, but at that moment the leaders of the Jewish community preferred to ignore his suggestion, both in order to avoid panic, and due to skepticism and a lack of action (I'm quoting from an article by Minerbi).

Finally, Michael Tagliacozzo wrote about how, when he searched for hospitality in a convent, they shut the door in his face. Afterwards, the superiors of the convent themselves contacted him, offering him hospitality.

The fact is that more than 200 institutes and religious houses in Rome opened their doors (Iael Nidam-Orvieto is correct, some of them did and some of them did not). It therefore seems unimaginable that there was no encouragement or oral indication, when in the city of the Pope there was a connection between Rome and the religious institutes. They were one element, a whole. Of course, different answers were given. We must remember that there was an internal debate even inside the Vatican. There is documentation of the sudden death in the Vatican of a Monsignor who had hosted a Jewish family. Cardinal Nicola Canali, the vicar of Vatican City, immediately ordered the Jewish family to be thrown out of his house. The Pope was advised, and he told Montini to talk to Canali and tell him to revoke his order. So such communication channels did exist.

Therefore, there was an internal debate, and different standpoints were confronted. We have documents demonstrating that within the Vatican itself there were those who said, "Why do we have to put ourselves at risk on account of the Jews?" We are clearly not talking about unanimity. However, the fact that more than 200 institutes and convents in Rome hosted refugees indicates, from a merely statistical point of view, that there must have been some indication and encouragement from above.

Session Six: Pius XII – Post-war Assistance to Fleeing Nazis and Policies on Hidden Jewish Children

What was Pius XII's involvement in the assistance extended by the Vatican to Nazi war criminals after the war? What was the Vatican policy toward Jewish children (baptized and unbaptized) hidden in religious houses?

Presenter: Michael Phayer

Before I begin, let me suggest that what happened after the war throws a very interesting light on Pius XII with regard to what happened during the war.

In the postwar years—1946 and 1947—within about one year, three distinguished Jewish men visited Pius XII separately to ask him for his help in finding Jewish children who had been hidden by Catholics during the war. The three visitors were Gerhart Riegner, who ran the Switzerland desk in the World Jewish Congress and was very important for getting the word out about the Holocaust—as most of you probably know—in a very timely fashion.[1] The second visitor was Leon Kubowitzki, Secretary General of the World Jewish Congress.[2] The third was Chief Rabbi Isaac Herzog from Jerusalem. They all came to Pius XII asking the same thing: We need help finding our children. Riegner was the first to come. Later, he described the meeting with Monsignor Montini as one of the most bitter experiences of his life. He told Montini that somewhere between

1 For more details see Walter Laqueur, *The Terrible Secret: Suppression of the Truth about Hitler's "Final Solution"* (Boston: Little Brown Press, 1980); Christopher Browning, *The Origins of the Final Solution: The Evolution of Nazi Jewish Policy, September 1939-March 1942* (Lincoln: University of Nebraska Press, 2004).

2 His name was changed to Aryeh Kubovi. He later became Chairman of the Directorate of Yad Vashem.

a million and a million-and-a-half Jewish children had perished during the Holocaust, and Montini said that that was impossible and couldn't be true. The two men sat there and argued about it for 30 minutes before Montini finally gave in. This shows to what little extent the Vatican had internalized what had happened to the Jews during the Holocaust. Pius XII welcomed each of these three men warmly, and gave them the impression that he was interested in the plight of the hidden children, each of whom, as Riegner had pointed out, represented a thousand children and they had to recover each one of them. But Pius did nothing to help them. On the contrary, at the very time he was receiving these men, he was abetting the escape of the murderers of these children and other Jews. Think about the hypocrisy of Pius at that moment. I will now address the topic of the "ratlines," the escape routes of the Nazis. Three books have been written about this topic, discounting John Loftus and Mark Aaron's book, which was written a long time ago, and which was rather sensational and didn't get much academic attention.[3] The first book, by Uki Goñi, an Argentinian author, is called *The Real Odessa*; the second, which I wrote, was published in 2008; and the third, recently published by a German, Gerald Steinacher, is called *Nazis auf der Flucht* (Nazis on the Run).[4] The public reaction to these books was incredulity. No! That couldn't have happened! The Vatican wouldn't have helped these criminals escape. I understand that that would be the reaction of many people. If, however, you look—and I'm just going to touch upon this briefly—at the origin of these ratlines, you see the evolution of the process and how the Vatican got to the point of using these escape routes for Nazis. As I've said before, in 1942 Pope Pius XII is on record as having said that he did not believe the Allies could win the war. He envisaged a Nazified Europe. And he knew, because he knew the Nazis, that in a Nazified Europe, Catholics were going to suffer. The leadership of the Catholic Church was going to suffer. He knew that on June 30, 1934, in the so-called "Night of Long Knives," Erich Klausner, the most well-known lay German Catholic, was murdered. So in 1942, Pius XII

3 John Loftus and Mark Aaron, *Unholy Trinity: How the Vatican's Nazi Networks Betrayed Western Intelligence to the Soviets* (New York: St. Martin's Press, 1992).

4 Uki Goñi, *The Real Odessa: Smuggling the Nazis to Perón's Argentina* (London, New York: Granta Books, 2002); Michael Phayer, *Pius XII, the Holocaust, and the Cold War* (Bloomington: Indiana University Press, 2008); Gerald Steinacher, *Nazis auf der Flucht: Wie Kriegsverbrecher über Italien nach Übersee entkamen* (Innsbruck: Studienverlag, 2008).

cooperated with an initiative of Argentina, Germany, and the Vatican to allow for the emigration of Catholics after the war. When the Argentinian diplomat Juan Carlos Goyeneche went to the Germans and talked to them about this, they latched on to the idea of a cooperation of Vichy-type European countries, including Spain and other Vichy friends, in setting up a new bloc of worldwide influence. Ribbentrop and Himmler listened to Goyeneche's ideas. Goyeneche went to Rome and later came back to talk to Himmler and Ribbentrop again, but when he mentioned religion, saying that Argentina was a Catholic country so religion had to be part of this new setup, Himmler's eyes glazed over. This was in 1942.

In 1943, when things no longer looked as promising for the Nazis, the situation changed and Goyeneche returned to Germany for talks about the same process once again. This time, Himmler told Goyeneche to notify the Pope that he was quite open to negotiations with regard to religion in this scheme. To my mind this was a ridiculous scheme because Himmler, who was guilty of the murder of tens of thousands of Catholic Poles, was telling Goyeneche to advise the Pope that he was open to negotiations on religion.

So in 1943, the emigration scheme was already set up, to be used by Catholics who would be under the heel of Communist countries in Eastern Europe—after the war, presumably—as well as Nazis who would have to get out of Europe because it would be common knowledge that they were guilty of having perpetrated atrocities.

Thus, the origin of the ratlines was actually to help Catholics, but because the situation changed in 1943, it ended up being an escape route not only for persecuted Catholics from Eastern Europe, but also for Nazis.[5]

How the ratlines worked was as follows: First, the Pontifical Committee of Assistance—better known as the Vatican Emigration Bureau—was set up. Every nationality that wanted to get papers to leave Europe needed an intercessor in the commission—one for the Germans, one for the Croatians, one for the Hungarians, and so on.

The three people who have written about this—Steinacher, Goñi, and I—all agree on how this worked. There were tens of thousands,

5 Signed statement of Walter Schellenberg, head of Sicherheitsdienst (or SD – the intelligence and surveillance branch of the SS), February 7, 1946, U.S. National Archives and Records Administration (NARA), Entry 1088, Box 25, RG 226, location 250/48/30/07.

if not hundreds of thousands, of people in Rome using this system, because they had to find some place to go. Most likely, 95 percent of all the people who went through this process would actually have been persecuted in Eastern Europe. But a few criminals were also making use of it.

So a suspected criminal "on the run" would get to Rome, to a designated person, and get a voucher. This was nothing but a signed piece of paper stating that "so and so" (they changed the name of the suspected criminal to some other name) is well known to us and is in good standing. That was it. He then took this piece of paper to the Red Cross and on the evidence of this flimsy little piece of paper, the Red Cross gave him a visa to leave the country.

The criminal then hung out in Rome until he got enough money to pay for passage to another country. Where did the money come from? Mostly, the United States. Although American Catholics didn't know they were contributing to a ratline, that is actually what was taking place. Cardinal Francis Spellman in New York sent Hudal 150,000 dollars a month, a princely sum in the postwar years in Italy.

One of the main players was Bishop Hudal,[6] the most notorious pro-Nazi in Rome during the war, who was in charge of the German-speaking ratline. Everybody knows who Hudal was, although somehow Father Robert Graham got the idea that the Vatican didn't know, didn't remember who Hudal was, and almost made the man a cardinal in the 1930s!

Kronislaw Draganovic was in charge of the Croat-Ustashe ratline and if you were an Ustashe criminal, you went to this Croatian priest. If you were a Hungarian member of the Arrow Cross, you went to Father Gallov, who furnished you with the piece of paper, and so on. That was how the operation worked.

I discovered one more ratline: in Spain. It ran in a different way. It actually came into existence before the Italian ratline, and was run by two Catholic priests—Father José La Boos and the German Jesuit, Father Karl Sauer.

6 The Austrian Bishop Alois Hudal was the rector of the ecclesiastical college at the Church of Santa Maria dell'Anima in Rome. He was a very controversial person, known for being pro-Nazi. For his activity in the war period see session 5B.

Now, the question is: Did the Pope know what was happening? Was he running it? Under whose authority was it operating? It's like asking the question: Did Hitler know about the Holocaust? There's no written record from Hitler that says: "Kill the Jews." However, there is a written record that can be traced back to Pius XII with regard to these ratlines, which I'll get to momentarily.

The man put in charge of the Vatican Emigration Bureau was Monsignor Montini, who went to Pius XII every day for a long interview about what was going on. Is it possible that Montini, who ran the whole network of ratlines from Europe to South America, kept it a secret from Pius XII? Pius XII, the micro-manager? No, that is impossible. It is simply not possible that a worldwide operation of the Catholic Church could be run without the knowledge of the Pope. As I said before, Hudal and Draganovic were well-known Fascists. The Vatican appointed them to head their national groups. It was like putting the proverbial fox in charge of the hen house. It's obvious what would have happened if a Nazi perpetrator, a criminal, had come to Hudal. He would make sure that this person escaped. When Uki Goñi's book was published, it was reviewed in *The London Tablet*. It was a very good book, but it did not prove that Pope Pius XII knew what was going on. So Goñi went back to the Foreign Office files in the Public Record Archives in Britain and found the documents tracing back to Pius XII, and with the correct citations, I used those documents in my book, too. Why did Pius XII do this? He wanted to fight Communism. The Vatican had been fighting Communism for more than half a century by that time, and it wanted to use these able-bodied war criminals for a good cause. So he tried to get them directed to South America, where they could finally do some good, fighting international Marxism. The American secret service knew exactly what was going on. They wrote reports to America, saying that although it gave the appearance of an escape route for people who were going to be persecuted by the Soviets, it was actually not that at all; it was set up to send anti-communist activists to South America.[7] There are numerous reports by intelligence agents detailing

7 Report of Captain Henry R. Nigrelli, June 5, 1946, NARA, Entry 212, Box 5, RG 226, location 250/64/33/5.

this. They all gave the same opinion. The reason for the ratline was to fight Communism in South America.

Respondent: Matteo Napolitano

I'll start with Michael Phayer's last remarks. I would be more cautious, as far as Pius XII is concerned, in judging Goñi's book as reliable. Furthermore, there are in fact two editions of Goñi's book. The first edition contains accusations against the Vatican that were not documented. When Goñi was made aware of his poor methodology, in the afterword of the second edition he apologized, saying: "As far as Papal complicity was concerned, the charge that the English hardback edition of *The Real Odessa* walked on thin documentary ground was not without merit. This was admittedly one of the very few instances in which the book dared to elevate an assumption to the level of certainty. Fortunately, however, such evidence does now exist, [thanks to] the Public Record Office in London."[8]

Goñi's book—I have not yet had the chance to read the other two books, since they were published only recently—is an example of how not to write history. It's a paradigm of "serial quotations," where one takes whatever one needs from a document while eliminating the rest, because the unquoted parts may not support the thesis one is trying to sustain. This is a very dangerous tactic, one to which all historians must pay attention. I can demonstrate here and now the things Goñi "chiseled" to adapt to his thesis. Furthermore, when I read his book, I was overwhelmed by a sense of discomfort. The book has many troublesome citations; an honest historian must acknowledge this inconvenient truth. There were cases in which many members of the clergy, with a propensity towards one war criminal or another, acted on their own initiative.

I took the same documents Goñi used, footnote by footnote, and examined them. After reassessing them as a whole, I was presented with a completely different picture. Allow me to highlight just two points.

8 Uki Goñi, *The Real Odessa*, pp. 327-328.

One: Goñi does not demonstrate in any way whatsoever Pius XII's involvement in the ratlines. Even if we use the "La Vista" dossier[9] to demonstrate the involvement of Pius XII, we are going too far afield. But since the documents are available to us, we can certainly discuss this matter.[10]

The British Foreign Office documents demonstrate (and Goñi conveniently leaves this out) that the Vatican had no intention of saving war criminals from an international court of justice; it wanted to save them from Tito's court of justice. Who would have put any ordinary criminal in the hands of Tito? Inspected as a whole, the Foreign Office documents used by Goñi demonstrate that for Tito, the concept of war criminal was quite wide. It even included the "enemy of the people," if I may briefly synthesize.[11] So where can proof of the involvement of the Vatican be found? As already mentioned, there is the Pontifical Committee for Assistance, but inside the Holy See there are discussions on the Committee's activity and its initiatives by various individuals. I believe that even Tardini, while talking to a British representative in Italy, said: "The Pontifical Committee for Assistance is not the Vatican." I can't subscribe to such a comment for reasons of honesty, naturally, but I just wanted to point out that the questions are very complex.

I would like to dwell on another point raised in Michael Phayer's presentation: That the Vatican issued the passports. Recent research in the archives of the International Red Cross revealed that the passports were, in fact, issued by the International Committee of the Red Cross.[12] I would like to add that ascertaining the identity of people in a period in which the registry office was not functioning—when Italy was occupied—was probably near impossible; no one knew who was who and what he had done. Even the Red Cross issued passports based

9 Vincent La Vista was sent by the U.S. State Department to investigate the organization of the emigration of war criminals from Italy. La Vista filed a report in May 1947 detailing the Vatican's involvement.

10 La Vista to Cummings, May 15, 1947, National Archives, College Park MD, FW 800.0128/5-1547.

11 See, for example, PRO, Kew, FO 371, R17586/58/92; and, most important, Williams' dispatch to Osborne, May 14, 1947, National Archives, College Park MD, RG 58/97/92; retrievable even in PRO, FO 371/67376.

12 Stefano Picciaredda, *Diplomazia umanitaria: la Croce Rossa nella seconda guerra mondiale* (Bologna: Il Mulino, 2003).

merely on the testimony of two persons accompanying the applicant, saying, "This is so-and-so, and he is a refugee from Germany for such-and-such reasons."

Another observation: Pius XII's "prosecutors" say he was informed of the ratlines, yet they deny he was informed of the assistance extended to the Jews. It seems to me that these two aspects must be interpreted using the same criteria. Moreover, Pius XII's anti-communism was not Perón's anti-communism, which challenged the anti-communism of the United States. There are entire volumes written about the relationship between Argentina and the United States, between Perón and U.S. presidents Harry Truman and Dwight Eisenhower. They did not like each other at all! Here, too, the issue of anti-communism, which must be considered in its entirety, does not seem to be the criterion by which to evaluate Pius XII's actions.

One more point: Was the Holy See really so masochistic as to save Germans who, for so many years, had denied religious freedom in Germany; who had assassinated, deported, and killed priests? Did they really want to hurt themselves? This idea must be reconsidered.

However, from a methodological point of view—and this is the last point I would like to emphasize—using the documents in their entirety, unlike Goñi, Goñi's thesis cannot be proved. We could, of course, wait for the opening of the Vatican archives, and hope they allow us to investigate this period further. But to me, Goñi's conclusions seem to be hasty (I do not intend to dwell on Loftus and Aaron's book), and irrelevant.

It is clear, however, that there were individual initiatives—there is no use pretending they did not exist because they did—and these are backed up by documents, reports made by the American secret service in Rome.

I would like to move on to the second issue: The Jewish children. I'll start with a small provocation: The whole question arose within the Catholic Church as an internal Catholic matter. It's the same old story of the good Pope vs. the bad Pope. We know how the events came about—Michael Phayer referred earlier to Riegner and I believe Ambassador Minerbi dealt with it as well and even interviewed Riegner. Riegner himself tells the whole story in his memoirs. Professor Phayer appropriately mentioned Riegner's conversation with Montini, which was indeed a very painful dialogue, though I must correct him: It lasted 20 minutes, not half an hour. Anyway, Montini did not believe the story and to quote Riegner: "Montini replied, 'That is not possible. They probably emigrated.'" They continued to argue, however, Montini's final words according to Riegner were: "Point out to me where these children are and I will assist you in recovering them." This was not cited earlier by Michael Phayer. Riegner replied, "If I knew that, I wouldn't need you."[13] To look for the children in the convents was obviously very difficult.

The matter was continued when Chief Rabbi Isaac Herzog addressed Pius XII, as was mentioned earlier, and made the same request, saying that these children didn't have their parents anymore; they were therefore very important to them. Herzog added that the Jewish people would never ever forget what the Church did for the Jews.

In the time I have left I'll just mention briefly that in a document found in the archive of the Secretariat of State, Angelo Roncalli, the future John XXIII (an important figure in this story) was informed by the Chief Rabbi of France and by the French bishops in August 1946 of a very painful fact: In certain religious houses the small children had been baptized, contradicting the instructions of the French bishops. The situation was distressing indeed, and so on October 23, 1946, Roncalli issued the famous instructions (either his own instructions or attributable to him) that *Il Corriere della Sera* attributed to Pius XII. It is important to understand, these were not the instructions of Pius XII. First of all, they were written in French, and the Secretariat of State did not communicate with its nuncio in French. Second, the instructions were included in a dossier that contained that same French document—an elaboration of the real instructions. I will quote the instructions word for word, since they are very important: "[The Eminent Fathers]... have decided that, as far as possible, the request of the Chief Rabbi of Jerusalem should not be answered." And further, regarding responses: "In any case, should it be necessary to say anything in this regard, it must be done orally, due to the [anti-Catholic] abuse that could result from any written document coming from the Holy See on

13 Gerhart M. Riegner, *Never Despair: Sixty Years in the Service of the Jewish People and the Cause of Human Rights* (Chicago: Ivan R. Dee in association with the United States Holocaust Memorial Museum, 2006), p. 122.

this matter." And these words should be considered in the context of the time: "Eventually…the Church must further investigate and ascertain the various cases, in order to discern one case from another. Evidently, those children who have possibly been baptized cannot be entrusted to institutions that cannot guarantee their Christian education."[14] Here we are not talking about parents asking for their children, since unfortunately they perished in the Shoah. Furthermore, as long as they were not able to take care of themselves—namely until they came of age—those children who had not been baptized and who had no relatives, once they were entrusted to the Church could not be abandoned by the Church, or consigned illegally to anyone else. Under the Natural Law, the Church did not consider a Jewish organization—even of the highest prestige—a father, mother, uncle, or grandfather.

Things would have been different had the children been requested by their relatives. The situation would have changed. But these are the only instructions relevant to us, because they were found in the archive of the Secretariat of State. The situation is, therefore, extremely complex.

I would like to focus now on what happened in Italy. The only Italian case dates back to 1947. It concerns a mother who survived the Shoah and arrived at a convent in Via Balduina to reclaim her children, whom she herself had asked to be baptized. As Sister Grazia Loparco and also Professor Durand mentioned, the issue was passed across the institutional channels, namely to the Vicariate of Rome and then on to the Secretariat of State. There is a note by the Secretariat of State—which I'm not authorized at the moment to show to you—that the Holy Father ordered that these children be returned to their mother. Then he added a reprimand for her behavior—for asking that they be baptized first and then…—and reminded her that they were indeed baptized. Nevertheless, the Papal order was to give them back. This was done within 24 hours, between November 5 and 6, 1947. I repeat: This is a very complex situation that has been simplified by saying Pius XII kidnapped Jewish children. The circumstances were much more complicated, and must be judged in the historical context.

14 The source of the document from which this quotation was taken is still inaccessible to the public.

Discussion

Paul O'Shea: Thank you both for very stimulating and provocative presentations. I have two questions. The first is directed specifically to Michael Phayer: How on earth was Bishop Hudal, the *Brown Bishop*, whom the OSS described as one of the most revolting people they'd ever come across—"the worst of the clerical kind" is, I believe, how they described him in one of their reports—allowed to keep working? How was someone who had such a reputation—and this reputation was seemingly very well known around Rome, and certainly in Allied circles—allowed to keep his job?

Secondly: Do we have any idea how many Jewish children who were baptized—hidden children, who were not reunited with Jewish families for whatever reason and who grew up as Christians—discovered or rediscovered their Jewish ancestors or Jewish origin?

Jean-Dominique Durand: One quick remark with regard to the anti-communism of Pius XII: We have said this already, but I believe we must insist that we are careful not to incorporate his anti-communism into everything, because it was not so strong that it would have led him to organize the escape of war criminals personally.

I would also like to say something with regard to Michel Phayer's comment, that the Pope had a hierarchy of priorities: first to fight Communism, and second to defend the Jews.

We must bear in mind that in September-October 1943, Communism was not a threat in Italy. The Church could have considered Communism as a threat later on, when numerous young people were recruited to the Communist squads of the resistance. But when Rome was liberated there was no real fear of a Communist danger. I believe, therefore, that Pacelli's anti-communism should be regarded as a reality, while paying attention to chronology and the nature of this anti-communism.

Sergio Minerbi: Regarding the question of the escape of war criminals: I became interested in Monsignor Hudal in 1948, because it was on record that many war criminals, both Ustashe and Nazis, were helped by him. This proves nothing, but it was a well-known fact in Rome. I would be grateful to Michael Phayer if he could tell us his opinion of

Goñi's book. Concerning the children, the situation is complex, but it is far from the given description.

First, when it suited the Church, even after 60 years, cases were revealed in which children were returned; when it was inconvenient, no such cases were disclosed. One example of this comes from those who praise John Paul II, who sustained (I don't know how, since it came up 50 years later) that when he was still in Krakow, around 1946, a Polish Catholic couple came to him with a child aged five or six and said: "We received this child from his Jewish parents, and we raised him as a Catholic. We would like to know now, after the liberation, what to do." This priest, who was conveniently identified, who knows how, by the name of Wojtyła, supposedly said: "If he is of Jewish origin, you should hand him over to a Jewish organization." This is undoubtedly true, but it is slightly different to what we believe to have been the practice.

Second, immediately after the liberation, I and some Jewish soldiers from the Land of Israel went around Rome from one convent to another asking whether there were any Jewish children left there without their parents. I obtained nothing, but I was very young, so this fact may have also played a role in our lack of success.

In France, contrary to what Matteo Napolitano told us, two brothers, the Finali brothers, were detained for eight years during an endless legal dispute, because their close relatives wanted them to be sent to Israel. (Since they still live in Israel, they can be contacted, if required.) The Church managed to smuggle them to Spain and make them do whatever they wished, but they did not hand them over to their relatives, except when compelled to do so by a court of justice. I think that on the issue of the children, the conduct of the Church could have been more generous.

Jean-Dominique Durand: By a court of justice, but also by Cardinal Gerlier, Archbishop of Lyon.

Thomas Brechenmacher: Some remarks concerning Hudal and the ratlines. First, I would like to add a very valuable book to the references. Unfortunately, it has only been published in German: Heinz Schneppen,

Odessa und das Vierte Reich (Odessa and the Fourth Reich).[15] It was published about three years ago. This book is very important, especially due to its references to the Hudal archive. Heinz Schneppen offers a much more differentiated view than Goñi. Matteo Napolitano and I agree that Goñi's book is problematic, especially regarding the references and the line of argument. Hudal was never appointed Cardinal. That is misinformation. On the contrary, Hudal was *persona non grata* from 1937/1938 because of his book *Die Grundlagen des Nationalsozialismus* (The Foundations of National Socialism).[16] It immediately received the disapproval of the Pope and Pacelli (at that time still Secretary of State).

The *Osservatore Romano* published a Vatican statement clearly distancing itself from the contentions of the book. Until the 1940s, Hudal was excluded from all functions in the Curia. He did not hold any office of relevance. We have already discussed how the events of 1943 fit into this context.

As to why he was not divested of his office: The college Maria dell' Anima is under authority of the Austrian bishops. The principal is appointed by the Austrian bishops, and for a long time they refused to dismiss him. It was not a matter of the Pope, but of the bishops. Probably they were frightened that Hudal might have caused even more damage if he would have been dismissed from his position in the college. In the end he was dismissed in 1952, tellingly due to pressure imposed by Montini on the Austrian bishops. The order of dismissal came directly from the Vatican.

Concerning Hudal's participation in the ratlines: The documents in Hudal's archive show that Hudal had helped some 1,500 refugees to flee. We have to assume that the vast majority of these refugees were not war criminals. But on the other hand, we know that among them were Franz Stangl, commander of Treblinka; Otto Gustav Wächter, Governor of the District of Galicia; and the former "Kreisleiter" of Braunschweig, Bernhard Heilig. These war criminals were identified without any doubt.

15 Heinz Schneppen, *Odessa und das vierte Reich:Mythen der Zeitgeschichte* (Berlin: Metropol Verlag, 2007).

16 Alois Hudal, *Die Grundlagen des Nationalsozialismus: Eine ideengeschichtliche Untersuchung* (Leipzig: Johannes Günther Verlag, 1937).

The question is: What did Hudal know about the actual identities of these people? Michael Phayer and Matteo Napolitano have referred to this topic. They arrived with Red Cross identification cards and in all cases had changed their identity. On the other hand, it has to be noted that no one made any effort to verify these identities. Generally, the assurance that these people were officers persecuted by the Communists was usually sufficient. It touched Hudal's sense of honor. Due to that, these "refugees" were given aid without checking their true identity. Hudal was not involved in the flight of Adolf Eichmann, who chose to follow another path. He escaped through Genoa.

Dan Michman: I also wish to comment on Professor Napolitano's presentation. The issue of the children was of critical importance in the Jewish world immediately after liberation. This had to do with local realities, with legislation that differed in each country, but it was also connected to the Church in general, because many children were hidden in monasteries, etc., making it not only a question of local churches.

There are issues that must be taken into consideration. Rabbi Herzog was mentioned and there is a lot of documentation on him. Shulamit Eliash wrote about his activities in her Ph.D. thesis.[17] There is also hearsay that, after he left the Pope, Rabbi Herzog asked for a ritual bath to purify himself. This is a very strong expression. He asked to go for a ritual bath in order to purify himself because he was so disappointed with what he had heard.

We know that except for the Finali affair, mentioned by Professor Minerbi, there was also the Anneke Beekman affair, an issue definitely connected to the Church, not the local authorities. The girl was smuggled out of Holland to Belgium. Cardinal van Roey was involved, and he reacted in a very disappointing way. I know this through personal stories from home, because at the time the police were after Anneke Beekman,

17 See, for example, Shulamit Eliash, "The Political Role of the Chief Rabbinate of Palestine during the Mandate: Its Character and Nature," *Jewish Social Studies* 47/1 (Winter, 1985), pp. 33-50; Idem, "The 'Rescue' Policy of the Chief Rabbinate of Palestine before and during World War II," *Modern Judaism* 3/3 (October, 1983), pp. 291-308; Idem, "'He Who Is Negligent in Fulfilling the Commandment of Saving Human Life Is As Though He Has Shed Blood of Israel': Rabbi Herzog and the Holocaust," in Dina Porat, ed., *When Disaster Comes from Afar: Leading Personalities in the Land of Israel Confront Nazism and the Holocaust, 1933-1948* (Hebrew) (Jerusalem: Yad Ben-Zvi, 2009), pp. 103-136, esp. pp. 120-121.

my father was editor of the Dutch Jewish weekly *Nieuw Israëlietisch Weekblad*. The police entered the house where she was living but didn't find her. Her bed, however, was still warm, so she must have been taken away just minutes before. Today, she lives in southern France. That story deeply concerned the entire Dutch Jewish community—and many other people.

Belgium also had many problematic cases regarding events during the occupation and the hiding of children. There is a very important article by a former priest, Professor Luc Dequeker of the University of Leuven, in a book that I edited on Belgium and the Holocaust, regarding the baptizing of children hidden in monasteries.[18] Dequeker clearly shows that both children under age seven and adolescents were baptized in violation of the Church and canon law. Children older than seven (which is considered the age of reason) cannot be baptized against their own free will and without the consent of the bishop, but this was nevertheless done. The Church never really came to terms with this internal principle.

So there is a whole range of issues from the postwar period that the Jewish community was very sensitive to, regarding which Church authorities in several countries reacted in a dubious way (I won't go into details of Poland here, which is a very complicated issue, but a student of mine wrote a Ph.D. thesis on that, including the quarreling among the Jewish organizations[19]).

Moreover, this is an issue to which central directives or even an indication from Rome would have made an enormous difference. The cases in which children were not returned to their parents often involved very religious Catholics, albeit with very basic theological knowledge, such as in the case of Anneke Beekman. In these cases, an intervention from the Vatican would have made an enormous difference.

Andrea Tornielli: With regard to the story that Herzog purified himself after having met Pius XII, I would like to remind you that when Pius

18 Luc Dequeker, "Baptism and Conversion of Jews in Belgium, 1939-1945," in Dan Michman, ed., *Belgium and the Holocaust: Jews, Belgians, Germans* (Jerusalem: Yad Vashem, 1998), pp. 235-273.

19 Emunah Nachmany Gafny, *Dividing Hearts: The Removal of Jewish Children from Gentile Families in Poland in the Immediate Post-Holocaust Years* (Jerusalem: Yad Vashem, 2009).

XII died, Herzog said that his death was a great loss for the entire free world. That the Catholics were not the only ones to mourn his death.

In order to demonstrate the complexity of the situation, it should also be mentioned that in 1945 the Secretary of the World Jewish Congress, Leon Kubowitzki (later Kubovi), gave Monsignor Montini a check for 20,000 dollars. I don't think he would have given that money to an institution that had harmed the Jews.

Concerning the issue of the baptized children: I would like to mention an oral testimony I collected from someone who is still alive, Dan Vittorio Segre, a colleague at my newspaper. During the disputes concerning the Melloni document,[20] he told me what had happened to him. (I'm telling you this in order to demonstrate how multifaceted the situation was.) As part of the Jewish Brigade from Palestine, he went to get a child in Piedmont. He gave only the name of the child's parents, because he did not have any documentation for the child himself. The religious people with whom the child was staying gave him up just like that, based on trust, given that Segre belonged to the Jewish Brigade.

With respect to the Finali case: We must not forget that eventually not only Gerlier intervened (in order to return the children) but also the Secretariat of State, and that it all began when the headmistress of the institute that had housed the baptized children refused to give them back. Therefore, here as well, the situation was very complex.

I would like to conclude with a general comment. I've heard repeatedly here that the Vatican and Pius XII knew everything about the Final Solution; they knew in advance of the roundup in the ghetto of Rome; and the Pope knew, and virtually commanded, the operation for the escape of Nazi criminals. The only thing he was totally unaware of was the rescue of Jews in the convents. This seems to me incredible. When it concerned rescuing Jews, the Pope was absolutely unaware of anything; he knew nothing, no orders were given, no indications whatsoever. However, concerning the ratlines, where there is not even one document that supports the claim that he was aware of them, here, it

20 On December 28, 2004, Alberto Melloni of Bologna University published in *Corriere della Sera* a document written by the Vatican in 1946, instructing that Jewish children who were baptized during the German occupation of France should not be allowed to return to their families.

was said, he must have known. I believe this approach doesn't provide us with a complete picture of the situation.

Michael Phayer: We should not forget the 1943 Moscow Declaration, an agreement between the United States, England, and the Soviet Union that all war criminals should be returned to the country where they committed their crimes and put on trial there.

So the endeavors of the Vatican to provide war criminals with safe passage out of the country were an effort to allow them to escape from the bar of justice at Nuremberg, as well as the so-called postwar "army trials" in the four areas of Germany. Time-wise (and maybe this helps us understand a little more), in 1945 the Vatican began with a position that they were going to allow any criminal to escape. Naturally, they didn't know the names of all the criminals and they didn't know all that the criminals had perpetrated. But Hudal frequently knew the names of the criminals; while still in Germany they knew to seek him out. The same is true for the Ustashe criminals. So in a sense, because the Vatican appointed these people, in 1945 they were flying in the face of postwar justice.

Professor Napolitano mentioned the Tito tribunals. After 1945, moving closer to the beginning of the Cold War in mid-1947, it became increasingly obvious that under Tito, justice was absent in Yugoslavia's tribunals. So at that point, the Allies, especially the United States and England, no longer knew whether they should comply with the Moscow Declaration. They decided that they would continue to comply as long as there was *prima facie* evidence against the person in question, in which case the person would be returned to the country in which the crimes were committed. In cases where it was doubtful, the Allies decided not to return them. As they got closer and closer to the summer of 1947, the Allies got closer and closer to the Vatican's position, so by mid-1947 or shortly thereafter, months perhaps, the Vatican ratline became the ratline also used by the United States in its secret operations to smuggle Nazis out of Europe.

Why was this allowed to continue? My answer is, why not? They knew what Hudal was doing in Rome, it had been reported to Montini, and he was doing the exact same thing the Vatican was doing in Spain.

Further evidence that the Vatican knew what was going on was a May 1947 meeting that took place in Madrid. Attending the meeting were the Papal Nuncio to Spain, the Cardinal Primate of Toledo, the Spanish Minister for Foreign Affairs Serrano Suñer, Father Boos, and Father Sauer. The purpose of this meeting was to continue the operation of the Spanish ratline. Could a meeting of people of that stature have taken place without the Pope's knowledge? I doubt it.

What Thomas Brechenmacher said about Hudal is basically correct. He was fired and he was *persona non grata* in the Vatican after about 1938; however, he was eager to get back into the good graces of the Vatican, and he maneuvered his way into the position of head of the German-speaking ratline. He got the ball rolling immediately after the war and, as was mentioned, at one point the Secret Service thought he was harmless. They considered him and his associates a small band of idiots. But that small band of idiots would then be appointed to do the work of the ratline. Of course, they did a lot of good work as well. Many perfectly legitimate people escaped through that ratline. This is how Hudal finally regained his standing in Rome, until he was discharged in 1952.

There is too much to say about the children, but I will make a brief comment. Dan Michman mentioned the story that Rabbi Herzog requested a ritual purification after he met with Pius XII; after his audience with him he described Pius XII as a political animal. Leon Kubowitzki also got the indication, according to the papers Michael Marrus employed, that Pius was not being very forthright in seeming to offer his help. He'd say things like: "Get me some information, so that I can follow up on this." That was precisely the problem: There was no information regarding where these children were and how many of them were there.

I wish to conclude with one observation. We must understand that if a six- or eight-year-old Jewish child arrived at a convent, it was to that child's benefit to be baptized and to learn the prayers, so that he or she could pass as a gentile. But there were many convents (how many, I don't know) where children were taken in and were not baptized.

One prime example is the conduct of Sister Matylda Getter in Poland. She refused to baptize these children, unless the parents told her to do so. After the war she returned the children to their nearest relatives, even though they frequently didn't want to go. Today there is a tree in memory of Matylda Getter on Yad Vashem's Avenue of the Righteous Among the Nations. I'm not saying that this was typical, but there was a great variety of conduct among the people who hid the children. Of course this caused difficulties in the identity of these children, but when they grew up they tried to make sense of it all.

David Bankier: I would like to ask a question regarding the postwar escape. Professor Phayer referred to the Latin-American connection and the Spanish connection. My question concerns the French connection, the Vatican, and the "Pius X" sect, or organization, which recently earned great notoriety. What do we know about the hiding of Paul Touvier or others in the convents after the war? Can you also say in this case that it must have somehow gotten to the ears of the Vatican that in southern France people who had been involved in the persecution of Jews were being provided safe haven by Church institutions?

Matteo Napolitano: Two quick comments. The ratlines began in 1945. I would be even more careful in this regard, because the documents (I'm referring to Osborne's telegrams to the British Foreign Office) tell us that in 1945 no Croatian officials were considered war prisoners. So if the document in question is the one dated August 27, 1945, it is not conclusive in this regard.

Moreover, what did the Apostolic Nuncio of Italy write to the Secretariat of State? After the war the Vatican was informed about these interned people, many of whom were Croatians, and a note dispatched by the Apostolic Nuncio of Italy in May 1946 said that the Secretariat of State could assure the families of the internees that the presumed criminals would not be handed over to Tito, but to international tribunals.

Moreover, the British claimed that in a list provided by the Vatican, that except for a few names, there were "no monsters." This is very difficult to comment on briefly; a whole new discussion should be opened on this topic.

Bernard Griffin, the Archbishop of Westminster, said to Ernest Bevin, the British Foreign Secretary, that in no case should a released Croatian be handed over to the Yugoslav government, unless it had been established undeniably that he was a war criminal, and that his case had been carefully examined by the American and British authorities. Goñi caused great dispute by omitting to cite this.

With regard to the baptized Jewish children: I agree that this is a complex issue and that what the Jews believed from their point of view was true. Many people had died in the Shoah, and these children were a resource for Judaism. But the viewpoint of the Church must also be understood. When faced with the fact that those who came and knocked at the convents' doors were not the parents of these children but representatives of Jewish institutions, it made no sense whatsoever to hand over to them those children who had stayed with them for years. It had nothing to do with the children's natural rights. We can discuss this further, we can agree or disagree, but in 1945-1946 that was the situation.

Finally, I would like to repeat that the only decision made by the Pope in person that we know about—and I repeat that I am not authorized to show you this document, although I really don't think that it would jeopardize anything to show it to you—was to return baptized Jewish children requested by their mothers within 24 hours. Beyond this, the situation was very complex and cannot be discussed in brief.

Jean-Dominique Durand: Professor Bankier asked a question about the Touvier case in France, which I cannot elaborate on here, but which I have been largely working on since I was a member of the commission that studied the case of Cardinal Albert Florent Augustin Decourtray, Archbishop of Lyon—a commission chaired by Professor René Rémond, who worked for two years on this case almost incessantly. I cannot go into all the details of the Touvier case, but our published report was very well accepted, by the French press in particular. We held a press conference with some 100-150 journalists, a big event. It was well received because they understood that as historians, we had carried out in-depth, important, systematic work in all the ecclesiastic archives in France to the extent that a rather anti-clerical French journal, *Le Canard Enchaîné*, wrote an article claiming that the Church was making this an example, because the state had denied access to its archives.

The conclusion is actually quite simple and complex at the same time. Touvier was a war criminal who operated in Lyon during the war and was later sentenced for war crimes. Immediately after the war, he converted to Catholicism (though how profoundly is up for debate). As such, he then found help within a whole network of ecclesiastic institutions, including convents and priests. Our conclusion was that these were personal initiatives, because Touvier was quite convincing, presenting himself as a victim. He got married and had children, but he lived a more-or-less clandestine life. At a certain point, however, he lived in the open; everyone knew him in his birth town of Chambéry, and he enjoyed a certain protection from the police, because at that time he had already been sentenced to death. And from the sect of Pius X he got nothing. He received help from a secretary of Archbishop Cardinal Gerlier, a very kind, simple person, well known in Lyon for helping the poor and the wretched. He took Touvier into his care. The problem was that later he became secretary to Gerlier's successor Cardinal Jean-Marie Villot, which complicated the situation greatly. When Villot was summoned to Rome to be Secretary of State to Paul VI, Touvier followed him to Rome and, behind the back of the Archbishop, he continued to help Touvier, including through official steps, mainly with the President of the French Republic, Georges Pompidou, by means of documents addressed to the Archbishop of Lyon and afterwards also to the Secretary of State.

Conclusion

Dan Michman: To talk about a "conclusion" is obviously an exaggeration. While we all agree that we have not yet reached any conclusion, we have initiated a very important process: the effort to bring together diverse positions, different ways of interpreting what we have encountered. Until now, much of the historical controversy has stemmed from statements or books written by certain individuals, but there have been no meetings such as this one to analyze in depth the documentation and the problems that have arisen. On several occasions here, for example, we have encountered the complexities of interpreting a document: On the one hand paying the utmost attention to the broader context, and on the other, taking into account the apparently minor details, such as the date heading a particular paragraph.

We have discussed here a very important issue, which could be further investigated. It might even form the basis of a much larger project, because it is very clear after this debate—especially to those who have written Ph.D.s and books on this subject—that it is a vast subject, encompassing many countries and many institutions. Even the number of languages involved is such that one scholar cannot cope with it all.

It is also clear that many topics remain unexplored. There are certain issues that everybody jumps on, but during our discussions we discovered many more that were apparently on the sidelines and entirely unexplored, but in reality are of great importance. There also remain, in many places, many sources to be analyzed. Not only is all the documentation in the Vatican archives not yet accessible—and we look forward to their opening for research—there are other archives and collections that still need to be examined. Don't forget, five decades ago we couldn't have foreseen Holocaust research expanding to such magnitude. Many basic questions have not yet been asked. The moment you ask a new question you go into another, unexplored direction that demands the investigation of more material and the scrutiny of additional archives.

On the analytical level, if we want to get some overall answers on the question of the Catholic Church and the Holocaust, we'll have to deal with a broad variety of protagonists: not only the personality of Pius XII, on whom much of the research interest is focused today, but also the many Church institutions and the faithful. Sometimes, in current debates, the interaction between the different protagonists is not clear. For example, regarding the acts of the lower echelons. While some scholars argue that we have no proof that what was done by the faithful was encouraged or ordered or directed by the higher Church hierarchy, others say that it could not have been done *without* directions from above.

I also wish to add this observation: As pointed out earlier, we have here "two parties"—those who come from Catholic ecclesiastical institutions and tackle the entire topic from that standpoint, and those who look at the topic from other perspectives.

Another basic issue is politics and theology; politics and morality. The Church is a worldwide institution with moral-religious dimensions, but the Vatican is also a state with political dimensions, and in many studies the balance between these aspects is sometimes forgotten. Even at this workshop, the theological aspect was hardly touched upon. I believe that this is an aspect of major importance.

Relating to the chronology of the Holocaust, I would like to emphasize a period we did not deal with here, from the end of 1942 to the beginning of 1943. These months were a watershed within the Holocaust history, because it was then that events leading to profound changes in the course of World War II took place: El Alamein, the declaration of the Allies of December 17, 1942, the Pope's Christmas speech, and finally Stalingrad. In this period, too, official statements about what was happening to the Jews were released by authoritative figures. These events are the foundations of a new awareness, and the knowledge of both (the turning point in the war and the official statements on the murder of the Jews) had a major impact on what people were planning for the future. From this point onwards, certain rescue activities were initiated, and leaders began to ponder the proper ways to react; it was also during 1943 that the Soviet Union planned the postwar period—a special commission was established for that purpose. The Allies started to think about the war crimes trials. Therefore, within this context we also have to ask about the Church and the Pope. What did he foresee for the future?

In September 1943 there was the German occupation of Italy and the consequent arrest and deportation of the Jews, as well as the assistance provided to them. The challenge for the Vatican was how to react to the German occupation while it was also being threatened by them. What has not been touched upon, either by us or in most of the studies, is the general development of the war and the knowledge of what the Germans were doing to the Jews. A certain broader context of what was happening is being forgotten while we zoom in on the small details (which are very important, but are not the only framework that can help us understand the behavior of the different parties involved).

Another issue is that we have taken Italy and Rome as a case study, but we have only briefly touched upon the topic of the Church in the free world—in South American states, in North America, and in the free world in general. One country that is important for a fuller assessment of the Vatican's approach is Ireland, and its policy vis-à-vis the fate of the Jews under the Nazi yoke. A recent book by Shulamit Eliash about Ireland, Zionism, and the Jews also relates to World War II.[1] In this book, Eliash demonstrates how the Holy See influenced Irish politics during that period; Ireland actually distanced itself from any rescue activity. This aspect should also be included in our overview.

As a university professor I'm thinking about our future students; this workshop raised many excellent topics for Ph.D. theses. But it is also clear that we need future encounters and perhaps the publication of more documentation with references that point to the different interpretations found in the scholarly literature.

I would say, in conclusion, that this has been a very fruitful encounter. I'm glad we embarked on this venture and I'm sure it will also bring more documents to public knowledge.

Roberto Spataro: The core of my address comprises three points: What have we accomplished? What did we not accomplish? And what should we accomplish?

1 Shulamit Eliash, *The Harp and the Shield of David: Ireland, Zionism and the State of Israel* (New York: Routledge, 2007).

What have we accomplished? First of all, we met in an atmosphere of confidence, trust, and mutual respect. This was the hope that His Excellency, the Apostolic Nuncio expressed yesterday, at the beginning of our meeting. If this was one of the objectives, we have reached it and we are satisfied. Around this table scholars and historians have come together who work with great seriousness, and they have proved it.

Second, we have shared the documentation gathered by each of us and this was one of the objectives Director Shalev indicated. So we have successfully reached this objective, too. Naturally, there were divergences in the interpretation of the documents and in the adopted methodology, but I believe they were complementary.

What did we not accomplish? First of all, as Professor Michman extensively underlined, we have not discussed in depth all the topics we have touched upon. But we were aware of this from the beginning. We have also not reached an agreement on contentious topics, the most controversial of which is the role of Pius XII.

I do hope, however, that the proposition expressed by Professor Loparco has earned the accord and support of all of us. Almost at the end of her address, Professor Loparco said: "There was no written direction by Pius XII; the movement (at least in Rome, in Italy) to host persecuted Jews was born, in part, spontaneously, despite being a phenomenon of a very complex nature. However, I believe that there existed some form of encouragement [Ambassador Minerbi used another expression—a blessing] of the Pope." I hope that on this proposition, at least to a minimal extent, there is agreement.

What should we accomplish? Three things come to mind. First, we must continue studying with the same scientific seriousness I have mentioned. Second (and this is obviously addressed to those who promoted this initiative), we must collect the material that has been produced, enhance it, and distribute it. Third, we must assess what has been proposed—both by Yad Vashem and the other bodies present. We have invested serious work and effort in order to be able to progress in this research, as well as in the evaluation of the data that the research offers.

Appendix: Accompanying Documents to the Presentations

- Extract of letter from Eugenio Pacelli to his brother Francesco, April 28, 1924
- Extract from the diary of meetings—Father Giacomo Martegani, Jesuit Director of *La Civiltà Cattolica*, November 1, 1943
- Letter of Cardinal Eugenio Pacelli to Cardinal Eugenio Tisserant (Secretary of the Saint Congregation for the Oriental Church), May 21, 1938
- Extract of a radio speech given by Pope Pius XII, December 24, 1940
- The plan of Pope Pius XII—Report on the visit of Charles De Gaulle, June 30, 1944
- Document referring to the conversation between Marshal Pétain and the Apostolic Nuncio about the Bérard Report
- Dossier on a meeting held by the International Red Cross on the Jewish topic, February 12, 1943
- Memorandum of Moshe Waldmann about his talk with Chief Rabbi Dr. Prato, May 26, 1938
- Correspondence between Orsenigo and the Holy See
- Extract of letter from the Mother General of the Franciscan Missionaries of Mary, March 1944
- Extract of "The Charity of Pius XII," October 25-26, 1943
- Extract of letter from Monsignor Hudal to General Stahel
- Notes of Cardinal Maglione
- Mgr. Anichini to Pope Pius XII
- Notes of the Secretariat of State
- Documents Pertaining to the Holocaust
- The Origin of the Vatican's Emigration Policy

Extract of letter from Eugenio Pacelli to his brother Francesco, April 28, 1924

[…] The Bavarian Concordat was solemnly signed here in Munich, last March 29. We are still awaiting approval of the Landtag or Parliament, which, following the new elections and in the face of the recent awful anti-Catholic storm from the nationalist parties that involved violent attacks against the Holy See, the Cardinal Archbishop, etc., creates much serious concern. In general, the whole situation is very hard now and extremely preoccupying in Germany, precisely because of the progress of the nationalist parties, which are fanatically anti-Catholic. I can tell you that I am beginning to grow tired, physically too, and I believe that after seven years of nunciature in Germany, in the midst of the worst of misfortunes, they could release me.

Monaco 28.4.24

Carissimo Francesco

Perdonami se rispondo con tanto ritardo alla carissima tua del 29 Marzo. La pubblicazione fatta sui giornali della ricorrenza del mio giubileo sacerdotale, che non so proprio come si è risaputo, (pubblicazione, che ho in tutti i modi, ma invano, cercato di evitare) è stata per un vero disastro. Mi si è riversata addosso una valanga di telegrammi, di lettere, anche di alti personaggi, e me ne continuano a giungere tuttora non poche, sebbene sia passato quasi un mese. Carico come sono di lavoro, si è aggiunta così una ulteriore fatica, tanto più sgradevole, in quanto che, nonostante tutti gli sforzi, una grande quantità di quelle lettere, è rimasta ancora e rimarrà forse per sempre senza risposta. Mi è stato così anche impossibile di inviare gli auguri a Giulio ed a Marcantonio per le loro feste; li mando ora affettuosissimi per tuo mezzo, pregando di scusare l'involontario ritardo.

Ti ringrazio dell'affettuoso pensiero delle Lire cinquecento, ma mi sembra che non sia proprio il caso. Tu hai già abbastanza spese per la famiglia. Ho pensato, del resto, anche io e pregato in modo anche più speciale in quel giorno per Elisa.....

L'istanza per il "Fuersorge Verein" di Muenster mi è stata rimessa qui da Roma soltanto l'altro ieri. Siccome la distribuzione dei sussidi si fa non da me direttamente, ma dal Caritasverband, ho raccomandato a questo che, se nulla osta, quella domanda sia presa in speciale considerazione, inviando Lire 5000 di sussidio. Sarà bene però di dare all'interessato una risposta più generale, almeno fino a cose fatte, dicendo che la istanza è giunta ora e sarà presa in speciale considerazione. Non sono infatti del tutto sicuro se, visto l'enorme numero delle domande, il Caritasverband potrà dare una (relativamente) somma così elevata.

Ho letto su qualche giornale italiano di un nuovo decreto e di un nuovo elenco dei titoli di nobiltà. Nè tu nè io abbiamo mai dato peso a tali cose. Siccome tuttavia è un privilegio, che appartiene non a noi personalmente, ma alla famiglia, alla quale (chi può saperlo?) un giorno potrebbe essere utile, credo che sarebbe necessario di vedere se vi sono delle pratiche da fare per la conservazione di quel diritto.

Il Concordato bavarese fu solennemente firmato qui in Roma, il 29 Marzo scorso. Rimane però l'approvazione del Landtag o Parlamento, la quale,-dopo le nuove elezioni, e visto il furioso vento anticattolico, che spira in questo momento da parte dei partiti nazionalisti, con violenti attacchi contro la S. Sede, contro il Cardinale Arcivescovo, ecc.,-dà le più gravi preoccupazioni. - Tutta la situazione è in generale ora difficilissima ed assai preoccupante in Germania, a causa appunto dei progressi dei partiti nazionalisti fanaticamente anticattolici. Ti assicuro che comincio a sentirmi stanco, anche fisicamente, e penso che, dopo ormai sette anni compiuti di Nunziatura in Germania in mezzo alle più ardue traversie, mi si potrebbe lasciare libero. Il corrispondente della Koelnische Volkszeitung da Parigi dice di aver appreso in quella Nunziatura che Mons. Cerretti sarà fra breve nominato Cardinale. Essendo egli stato mio successore nella Segreteria degli Affari Eccles. Straordinari, credo che, qualora quella notizia (come sembrebebbe, data la fonte) fosse vera, avrei ben diritto, non di divenire Cardinale anche io (quod absit), ma di ritirarmi ad una vita più confacente alle mie inclinazioni.

In fretta con saluti e ringraziamenti affettuosissimi a tutti

† Eugenio

P.S. Anche Giuseppe mi ha scritto una cara letterina. Dio sa però quando potrà rispondere. Ti pregherei, qualora avessi occasione di vederlo o di scrivergli, di ringraziarlo intanto da mia parte.

Extract from the diary of meetings—Father Giacomo Martegani, Jesuit Director of La Civiltà Cattolica, *November 1, 1943*[*]

[…] Concerning Rome, the Holy Father told me about the negotiations he is having with both fighting sides for its safety: keeping it as an "open city" and allowing supplies into the city. He also took an interest on behalf of the Jews. Concerning the relations with the Germans, as of now there is nothing to complain about, and the given assurances will also be valid in the future.

* *La Civiltà Cattolica* archives.

non si esaurisce nei fatti contingenti per non disinteressarsene mai. Finalmente si è interessato e ha benedetto in pratiche per l'acquisto di una nostra tipografia, fatto avvenuto con segni di protezione divina veramente straordinaria. Quanto al modo con cui si è svolto l'armistizio, disse di disapprovare la "lunga diplomazia"; e dichiarò di non conoscere alcun personale mandatario.
Si ammettono articoli e notizie pronte

1 Novembre 1943

Assenti i PP. Messineo e Marii

A proposito della città di Roma, il S. Padre ha parlato delle trattative che sta svolgendo con entrambi i belligeranti per la sua incolumità: pel suo rispetto quale città aperta, e pel suo approvvigionamento. S'è anche interessato a bene degli ebrei. Quanto alle relazioni coi tedeschi, finora non c'è nulla da lamentare, e le assicurazioni date varrebbero anche per l'avvenire. Conoscendo la carestia che incombe minacciosa nei paesi ove passa la guerra, il S. Padre si è interessato presso i paesi neutrali più ricchi di derrate per ottenerne tempestivi aiuti. Finalmente ha benedetto di cuore la nostra tipografia.
Si ammettono articoli e notizie pronte

5 novembre 1943

Circa il recente bombardamento avvenuto nella Città del Vaticano, mancano prove apodittiche per stabilirne i responsabili. Il S. Padre ha ripetuto la sua preoccupazione e i suoi interventi per soccorrere le popolazioni più colpite dalla guerra.
Si ammettono articoli e notizie pronte. Si insiste perché i Padri collaborino al lavoro delle recensioni, che langue.

20 novembre '43

Assenti i PP. Zeiller e Marii – Presente il P. Cavalli, nuovo "adiutor scriptorum". –
Il S. Padre ha avuto occasione di nominare Hitler, e si è trattenuto dicendo che nei suoi scritti ci sono degli errori, e che

Letter of Cardinal Eugenio Pacelli to Cardinal Eugenio Tisserant (Secretary of the Saint Congregation for the Oriental Church), May 21, 1938[*]

SECRETARY OF STATE
OF HIS HOLINESS

ASS. AMIS CARD. TISSERANT
543019
FROM THE VATICAN, 21 MAY 1938

No. 1892/38
TO QUOTE IN ANSWER

With the venerable letter of last April 6,

Your Reverend Eminence kindly informed me about the article in a newspaper, according to which the Polish government introduced a law that intends to forbid the slaughtering of animals as imposed on the Israelites by their religious laws. This would constitute a real persecution against the Jews. You therefore suggested the possible intervention of the Apostolic Nuncio in order to stop such a measure.

I have engaged His Excellency Monsignor Cortesi in this matter, and I am now glad to send Your Eminence, hereby attached, his report No. 89 from last May 7, which includes precise information on the subject.

I am glad to take this opportunity to express to Your Eminence my most profound veneration, and I profess myself humbly, kissing your hand.

The most humble true
servant of His Eminence
E. Card. Pacelli

To His Reverent Eminence
CARDINAL EUGENIO TISSERANT
Secretary of the S. Congregation for the
Oriental Church

with attachment

* Courtesy of the Tisserant family private collection.

GIUNIA

Ass. Amis Card. TISSERANT

543019

DAL VATICANO, 21 Maggio 1938

SEGRETERIA DI STATO

DI SVA SANTITA'

N° 1892/38

DA CITARSI NELLA RISPOSTA

E.mo e Rev.mo Signor Mio Oss.mo,

Con la venerata Lettera in data 6 aprile scorso l'Eminenza Vostra Reverendissima si compiaceva segnalarmi la notizia di un giornale, secondo la quale il Governo di Polonia avrebbe introdotto una legge che tenderebbe a proibire la macellazione per giugulamento, imposta agli israeliti dai loro precetti religiosi, e che costituirebbe perciò per gli ebrei una vera persecuzione. Ella insinuava, pertanto, la convenienza di un passo di Monsignor Nunzio Apostolico per impedire un tale provvedimento.

Non ho mancato d'interessare al riguardo l'Ecc.mo Monsignor Cortesi, e sono lieto ora di poter rimettere all'Eminenza Vostra, qui accluso in copia, il suo Rapporto N. 89 del 7 maggio corrente, il quale contiene precise notizie sul problema in questione.

Profitto volentieri dell'incontro per esprimere a Vostra Eminenza i sensi della più profonda venerazione con cui baciandoLe umilissimamente le mani mi professo

di Vostra Eminenza Rev.ma

Umil.mo Dev.mo Servitor vero

E. Card. Pacelli

A Sua Eminenza Rev.ma
IL SIGNOR CARDINALE EUGENIO TISSERANT
Segretario della S.Congregazione per la Chiesa Orientale

con allegato

Extract of a radio speech given by Pope Pius XII, December 24, 1940[*]

[…] Not less of a comfort is it for us that we were able to support, with both the moral and spiritual assistance from our representatives and with the support of our donations, a high number of refugees, exiles and emigrants, even among the "non-Aryans."

* *Acta Apostolicae Sedis*, 1941 (Annus XXXIII, series II, vol. VIII), p. 10.

giunti, altra opera di non piccola mole abbiamo iniziato ed andiamo attivamente svolgendo e sviluppando, per chiedere e trasmettere notizie, ove appena sia possibile e lecito il farlo, non solo di moltissimi prigionieri, ma altresì di profughi e di quanti le presenti calamità tristamente separano dalla loro patria e dal loro focolare. Abbiamo in questo modo potuto sentir palpitare vicino al Nostro migliaia di cuori con il commosso tumulto dei loro più intimi affetti o nell'anelante tensione e nell'incubo grave della incertezza, nell'esultante gioia della ricuperata sicurezza, nella profonda pena e pacata rassegnazione sulla sorte dei loro cari.

Nè minore conforto è per Noi l'essere stati in grado di consolare, con l'assistenza morale e spirituale dei Nostri Rappresentanti o con l'obolo dei Nostri sussidi, ingente numero di profughi, di espatriati, di emigranti, anche fra i «non ariani»: ai polacchi ha potuto essere particolarmente largo il Nostro soccorso, come a quelli per i quali il contributo della carità dei Nostri figli degli Stati Uniti d'America Ci rendeva più facile il Nostro paterno interessamento.

***

Or è un anno, Venerabili Fratelli e diletti figli, Noi facemmo da questo luogo alcune dichiarazioni di massima su presupposti essenziali di una pace conforme ai principî di giustizia, di equità e di onore, tale quindi da essere duratura. E se il successivo svolgersi degli avvenimenti ne ha rimandato a tempo più lontano l'attuazione, i pensieri allora esposti nulla hanno perduto della loro intrinseca verità e aderenza alla realtà, nè del loro valore di morale obbligazione.

Oggi Ci troviamo in presenza di un fatto che ha una notevole importanza sintomatica. Dalle polemiche appassionate delle parti in lotta sugli scopi della guerra e sul regolamento della pace, emerge sempre più chiara una quasi *communis opinio*, la quale asserisce che così l'Europa anteriore alla guerra, come i suoi pubblici ordinamenti, si trovano in un processo di trasformazione tale da contrasse-

JEAN-DOMINIQUE DURAND

The plan of Pope Pius XII— Report on the visit of Charles De Gaulle, June 30, 1944[*]

The Holy Father receives me. Behind the kind welcome and the simplicity of his words, I am captured by the sensibility and the strength of his ideas. Pius XII assesses everything from a point of view that rises above people—their endeavors and their quarrels. And yet he knows what these cost them and he suffers with all of them at the same time. You can feel the supernatural burden—with which he is the only one invested in the entire world—laying heavy on his soul, but still he carries it and lets nothing wear him down, certain of the goal, sure of the way. His reflections and knowledge will not allow him to ignore any of the events that are dramatically changing the world. His clear thoughts are focused on the consequence: the outburst of the confused ideologies of Communism and Nationalism in large parts of the world. His inspiration reveals to him that only faith, hope and Christian charity may prevail over them, although they will exist everywhere, submerged for a long period of time. So for him, everything depends upon the politics, the actions and the language of the Church, and the way it is conducted. This is why the Pontiff keeps this domain entirely to himself, and this is where he implements all the gifts of authority, radiance and eloquence that God bestowed upon him. Pious, pitiful and political, in the utmost

* Charles De Gaulle, *Mémoires de Guerre, L'Unité: 1942-1944* (Paris: Plon, 1956), pp. 286-287.

meaning that these terms can assume, is how he seemed to me, through the respect that he, this Pontiff and sovereign, inspires.

We are talking about Catholic people, whose destiny is insecure. Regarding France, he thinks it will be threatened, mainly by no one else but itself. He foresees that despite the ordeals, it will find an occasion to play an important role in a world in which many human values have been reduced to despair, but he also sees the danger it incurs by falling back into divisions that paralyze its intellect. Regarding Germany, a people that in many respects is particularly dear to him, he expresses his main concerns: "Poor people!" he repeats to me. "How they will suffer!" In Italy he foresees a lengthy period of confusion, though he does not display excessive anxiety about it. Maybe he thinks that after the fall of Fascism and the end of the monarchy, the Church—a very powerful institution in this country—will remain the only authority enforcing order and unity; a perspective that he seems quite willing to envision. While he allows me to understand, I reflect on what the evidence has just shown me. As soon as the battle was over yesterday, an enormous crowd of one movement came to Saint Peter's Square to acclaim the Pope, as if he were the sovereign of Rome and Italy's remedy. But it's the Soviets' actions—today on Polish land and tomorrow all over the entire territory of Central Europe—that fills the Holy Father with anguish. In our conversation he evokes the events taking place in Galicia where, behind the Red Army, persecutions of the faithful and the priests have already begun. Thus, he thinks that Christianity will be subjected to very cruel trials, and that only a tight union between the European countries inspired by Catholicism—namely Germany, France, Italy, Spain, Belgium and Portugal—will be able to contain the danger. I presume this is Pope Pius XII's great plan. He blesses me. I leave.

**Le dessein du pape Pie XII,
Compte rendu de la visite du général de Gaulle,
30 juin 1944**

Le Saint-Père me reçoit. Sous la bienveillance de l'accueil et la simplicité du propos, je suis saisi par ce que sa pensée a de sensible et de puissant. Pie XII juge chaque chose d'un point de vue qui dépasse les hommes, leurs entreprises et leurs querelles. Mais il sait ce que celles-ci leur coûtent et souffre avec tous à la fois. La charge surnaturelle, dont seul au monde il est investi, on sent qu'elle est lourde à son âme, mais qu'il la porte sans que rien ne le lasse, certain du but, assuré du chemin. Du drame qui bouleverse l'univers, ses réflexions et son information ne lui laissent rien ignorer. Sa lucide pensée est fixée sur la conséquence : déchaînement des idéologies confondues du communisme et du nationalisme sur une grande partie de la terre. Son inspiration lui révèle que, seules, pourront les surmonter la foi, l'espérance, la charité chrétiennes, lors même que celles-ci seraient partout et longtemps submergées. Pour lui, tout dépend donc de la politique de l'Église, de son action, de son langage, de la manière dont elle est conduite. C'est pourquoi le Pasteur en fait un domaine qu'il réserve personnellement et où il déploie les dons d'autorité, de rayonnement, d'éloquence, que Dieu lui a impartis. Pieux, pitoyable, politique, au sens le plus élevé que puissent revêtir ces termes, tel m'apparaît, à travers le respect qu'il m'inspire, ce pontife et ce souverain.

Nous parlons des peuples catholiques dont le sort est en balance. De la France, il croit qu'elle ne sera, d'abord, menacée que par elle-même. Il aperçoit l'occasion qu'elle va trouver, malgré ses épreuves, de jouer un grand rôle dans un monde où tant de valeurs humaines sont réduites aux abois, mais aussi le danger qu'elle court de retomber dans les divisions qui, trop souvent, paralysent son génie. Vers l'Allemagne, qui par beaucoup de côtés lui est particulièrement chère, se porte en ce moment sa principale sollicitude. « Pauvre peuple ! me répète-t-il. Comme il va souffrir ! » Il prévoit une longue confusion en Italie, sans en éprouver, toutefois, une inquiétude excessive. Peut-être pense-t-il qu'après l'effondrement du fascisme et la chute de la monarchie, l'Église, moralement très puissante dans ce pays, y demeurera la seule force d'ordre et d'unité; perspective qu'il semble envisager assez volontiers. Tandis qu'il me le laisse entendre, je songe à ce que, tout à l'heure, des témoins m'ont rapporté. À peine finie la bataille d'hier, une foule énorme, d'un seul mouvement, s'est portée sur la place Saint-Pierre pour acclamer le Pape, tout comme s'il était le souverain délivré de Rome et le recours de l'Italie. Mais c'est l'action des Soviets, aujourd'hui sur les terres polonaises, demain dans toute l'Europe centrale, qui remplit d'angoisse le Saint-Père. Dans notre conversation, il évoque ce qui se passe déjà en Galicie où, derrière l'armée Rouge, commence la persécution contre les fidèles et les prêtres. Il croit que, de ce fait, la Chrétienté va subir de très cruelles épreuves et que, seule, l'union étroite des États européens inspirés par le catholicisme : Allemagne, France, Italie, Espagne, Belgique, Portugal, pourra endiguer le péril. Je discerne que tel est le grand dessein du pape Pie XII. Il me bénit. Je me retire.

Ch. de Gaulle,
Mémoires de guerre. L'Unité 1942-1944,
Paris, Plon, 1956, p. 286-287.

*Document referring to the conversation between Marshal Pétain and the Apostolic Nuncio about the Bérard Report**

Vichy, September 15, 1941

E-6 Re: The Marshal, the Nuncio and the Jews
No. 550
Politics / Europe
Confidential

Your Excellency:
I had the opportunity to hear an odd dialogue between the French Head of State and the Nuncio of Your Holiness on returning to Vichy after a month-and-a-half's holiday. It was following the dinner given by the Marshall to the Diplomatic Corps, last Saturday, the 13th. A meal, by the way, that was extremely pleasant, in which the Marshall was surprisingly youthful. He stood for more than one hour during the coffee hour, mingling with one group and the other, with a witty word for everybody. Earlier he ate, displaying an exceptional appetite (when talking about such an historical figure, no detail is superfluous). An entire half-truffled partridge was the second course of meat, to which he did the honors without any reservation.

After joking with the Nuncio who, being more austere, did not taste the main course—a detail well observed by the Marshall—he said, "I received a letter from our Ambassador in the Vatican, M. Leon Bérard, that gave an account of a conversation with the Pope in which he introduced the measures adopted by France regarding the Jewish Problem.

The Pope found them in order and expressed his approval." "That's impossible, that's impossible!" replied the representative of the Holy See, jumping up, extremely nervous. "The Holy Father would not have approved such measures."

"I will show you the letter," replied the Marshall. "Come and see me and I will read it to you, since Bérard tells me that the Pope gave his consent."

* MEAE R2295/7, Ministry of Foreign Affairs, Spain.

"That's impossible, that's impossible," insisted the Nuncio, a fervent Christian Democrat and, I believe, a not so cautious supporter of the Anglo-Saxon democracies.

Then I said, "I am not at all surprised by this approval, Mr. Marshall. When the Catholic Kings adopted much more radical measures against the Jews in Spain, not only did they get his consent, but they even got the congratulations of the Holy Father."

The Nuncio, with a purple face, as if he had already been given the hat, which, it seems, was offered to him during his last trip to Rome, answered, "The Pope of that time, the Pope of that time!"

"As real as the current one," I had to respond.

I recall this dialogue since it reveals the mood, at least in part, of the ecclesiastic elements in the Vatican concerning such a delicate issue as the regulations against the Jews.

Visible, mainly, is the effort not to displease North America, where the representatives of the chosen race are so powerful.

In contrast to the moderate but cautious policy of the Church over many centuries, inspired by the wish not to impede countries from defending themselves against internal enemies, as in the case of the Catholic Kings in Spain, we can now see a purpose entirely different among the influential prelates. Maybe because they are as keen on the United States as they are hostile towards Germany, a country considered to be the contemporary promoter of the response against the Semite threat.

The almost violent attitude of such a placid man as the Apostolic Nuncio in Vichy, in the presence of three or four persons and in front of the Head of State, is a good example of the aforementioned theory.

Being that Valerio Valeri did not much like my recalling of the Catholic Kings, and being a very admirable and kind-hearted person with whom I have very good relations, I later took him home in my car and invited him for lunch tomorrow, Tuesday.

God save Your Excellency for many years.
The Spanish Ambassador

(Jose F. de Lequerica)

AMAE R 2295/7
Ministerio Español de Asuntos Exteriores [Exteriones]

Vichy, 16 de Septiembre 1941.

R-6

Nº. 55c

POLITICA-EUROPA.

RESERVADO

ASUNTO : El Mariscal, el Nuncio y los judíos.

Excmo. Sr.:

Pude escuchar un diálogo curioso entre el Jefe del Estado francés y el Nuncio de Su Santidad recién vuelto a Vichy después de mes y medio de vacaciones. Era a continuación de la comida con que el Mariscal obsequió al Cuerpo Diplomático el sábado pasado día trece. Comida, entre paréntesis, agradabilísima y en la cual el Mariscal estuvo sorprendente de juventud. Más de una hora permaneció de pie yendo de grupo en grupo a la hora del café con una palabra ingeniosa para todo el mundo. Antes -tratándose de un personaje tan incorporado a la historia no hay detalle inútil- había comido con un apetito excepcional. Media perdiz trufada entera fué el segundo plato de carne al cual hizo honor sin limitación ninguna.

Después de bromear precisamente con el Nuncio, que mucho más sobrio no había probado el plato fuerte, detalle muy observado por el Mariscal, éste le dijo:

-"He tenido una carta de nuestro Embajador en el Vaticano, M. Léon Bérard, dándome cuenta de una conversación con el Papa en la cual le ha expuesto las medidas adoptadas por Francia en el problema de los judíos. El Papa las ha encontrado bien y mostrado su aprobación".

-"No es posible, no es posible ,-saltó, nerviosísimo, el representante de la Santa Sede-. El Santo Padre no ha podido aprobar semejantes medidas".

-"Le enseñaré a usted la carta -replicó el Mariscal-. Venga a verme y se la leeré, pues me dice Bérard

Ce document relate la conversation entre le maréchal Pétain et le nonce apostolique sur le rapport Bérard.

- 3 -

que el Papa ha dado su conformidad".

-"No es posible, no es posible", insistía el Nuncio ferveroso demócrata cristiano y creo yo partidario escasamente cauto de las democracias anglosajonas.

Entonces dije yo:

-No me sorprende nada esta aprobación, Sr. Mariscal. Cuando los Reyes Católicos tomaron medidas mucho más radicales contra los judíos de España, no sólo tuvieron el asentimiento sino hasta la felicitación del Santo Padre.

El Nuncio, con el rostro de púrpura, como si ya le hubieran dado el capelo, que según parece le ofrecieron en su último viaje a Roma, me replicó:

-"El Papa de la época, el Papa de la época".

-"Tan auténtico como el actual", hube de responderle.

Recojo este diálogo por revelar el estado de espíritu, de una parte al menos, de los elementos eclesiásticos del Vaticano con relación a cuestión tan delicada como las de las precisas regulaciones contra los judíos.

Es visible, sobre todo, el empeño de no desagradar a Norteamérica donde tan poderosos son los representantes de la raza elegida.

En contraste con la moderada pero cauta política de la Iglesia durante tantos siglos, inspirada en el deseo de no impedir a los Estados defenderse contra sus enemigos interiores, como fué el caso de los Reyes Católicos en España, ahora se observa en influyentes prelados un propósito enteramente contrario. Tanto quizás como por la simpatía hacia los Estados Unidos, entra en ello la hostilidad a Alemania, país considerado como el iniciador en la época contemporánea de las reac-

- 3 -

ciones frente al peligro semita.

La ~~reacción~~ actitud, casi violenta, de hombre tan apacible como el Nuncio apostólico en Vichy, delante de tres o cuatro personas y frente al Jefe del Estado, es buen síntoma de ello. ~~[illegible]~~.

Como le gustó muy poco a Mgr. Valerio Valeri mi recuerdo de los Reyes Católicos, y es persona estimable y bondadosa con la cual mantengo muy buenas relaciones, le conduje luego a casa en automóvil y le tengo invitado a almorzar mañana martes.

Dios guarde a V. E. muchos años.

EL EMBAJADOR DE ESPAÑA:

(José F. de LEQUERICA)

*Dossier on a meeting held by the International Red Cross on the Jewish topic, February 12, 1943**

JES/HL

G.59
February 18, 1943
Copy as original

CICR ARCHIVES

NOTE
on the meeting convoked for February 12, 1943
by Melle Ferrière, in the Metropole
("round table")

Following a decision of the Coordination Committee, Melle Ferrière invited by phone the following people in order to have them deliver a short report on the Jewish question:

Monsignor Rast, representative of the Nunciature,
Mr. Lawrie, of the YMCA,
Pastor Freudenberg, of the Ecumenical Council,
Mr. MacLeland, of the International Union of Aid for Children,
Melle Hohermuth, of Aid for Emigrants.

Melle Ferrière explained the project that had been presented to the coordinating members.

Following this presentation, a discussion began relating to the question of whether the committee should increase its dealings with the Jewish questions without, however, harming its other activities. The general opinion was that the committee could not shirk this task and that it was the only one capable of deploying useful activity in this matter. Mr. Lawrie added that he regretted that in America they ignored this part of the committee's activity and asked if it was possible to more widely inform the public in the United States. All the invitees understood

* Archives du Comité international de la Croix-Rouge, B G 59, Israélites.

well the need to proceed with discretion. Above all, they approved the Committee's decision not to make any major public declarations aimed at general denunciations of the Jewish persecutions. This would not have any value.

The participants warmly thanked Melle Ferrière for having given them this information that interests them greatly and they hoped that in the future they would be equally informed by the committee on this matter.

A collaboration and contribution from the represented organizations cannot, it seems, be taken for granted. The representative of the nunciature was reserved. He took many notes, since he obviously wanted to keep informed the authorities from which he depends. In private, he expressed to me several times the great satisfaction of the nunciature for the contact that is about to be established with the committee, contact he hopes will be fruitful.

J. Schwarzenberg

JES/HL

G.59

18 février 1943.

Copie conforme

ARCHIVES DU CICR

G 85 / V...

NOTE

sur la séance convoquée pour le 12 février 1943

par Melle Ferrière, à la Métropole.

("round table").

Comme suite à une décision de la Commission de Coordination, Melle Ferrière a fait inviter par téléphone les personnes suivantes en vue de leur faire un petit exposé sur la question israélite:

Msgr. RAST, représentant la Nonciature,

Mr. LAWRIE, du YMCA,

le pasteur FREUDENBERG, du Conseil oecuménique,

Mr. MacLeland, de l'Union internationale de secours aux enfants,

Melle HOHERMUTH, de l'Aide aux Emigrés.

Melle Ferrière a fait un exposé selon le projet qui avait été porté à la connaissance des membres de la Coordination.

A la suite de cet exposé, une discussion s'est engagée sur la question de savoir si le Comité devait s'occuper d'une façon accrue des questions israélites, sans toutefois que cela nuise à ses autres activités. L'opinion générale a été que le Comité ne pouvait pas se dérober à cette tâche et qu'il était seul en mesure de déployer une activité utile dans ce domaine. M. Lawrie a ajouté qu'il regrettait qu'on ignorât en Amérique ce côté de l'activité du Comité. Il a demandé si une information plus ample du public des Etats-Unis ne serait pas possible. Tous les invités ont bien compris la nécessité de procéder avec discrétion. Ils ont surtout approuvé la décision du Comité de ne pas faire de grande déclaration publique dénonçant les persécutions juives d'une façon générale. Ceci n'aurait aucune valeur.

Les invités ont remercié chaleureusement Melle Ferrière de leur avoir donné ces informations qui les ont vivement intéressés et ils espèrent qu'à l'avenir également on leur fera part de temps à autre des efforts faits par le Comité dans ce domaine.

Une collaboration et une contribution quelconques de la part des organisations représentées par les invités ne peut, semble-t-il, pas être escomptée. Le représentant de la Nonciature s'est tenu sur la réserve. Il a cependant pris de nombreuses notes, voulant évidemment tenir au courant les autorités dont il dépend. Seul à seul, il m'a exprimé à plusieurs reprises la grande satisfaction de la Nonciature en ce qui concerne le contact qui vient d'être établi avec le Comité, contact dont il espère qu'il sera fructueux.

J. Schwarzenberg

*Memorandum of Moshe Waldmann about his talk with Chief Rabbi Dr. Prato, May 26, 1938**

Confidential Haifa, 26.5.1938

Talk with Chief Rabbi Dr. Prato (Rome)

During my stay in Rome I discussed with Dr. Dante Lattes, among other matters, the question of our relationship with the Vatican. Dr. Lattes informed me that, in recent months, Chief Rabbi Prato had created a better than bearable relationship with Cardinal Secretary Pacelli. Lattes advised me to talk to Prato.

Following my conversation with Lattes, I called upon Dr. Prato and he told me, among other things, the following:

The hostility of the Vatican against the new paganism of National Socialism is fundamental. Due to this fact, a peculiar psychological state had developed, i.e., a greater open-mindedness regarding Jewish demands. In fact, a few weeks ago, at a reception of Polish Cardinals and Archbishops, the Pope urgently indicated that he would not appreciate seeing the Polish Church act with any antisemitic tendencies in union with Polish-Fascist elements. Due to an earlier intervention by Pacelli regarding the matter of *Shechita* [kosher slaughtering—T.B.], the Pope brought up this question in his talk with the Polish Church high dignitaries, saying that the Catholic Church had to beware of

* Courtesy of the Central Zionist Archives, S25/3759.

helping to impose moral constraints on the Jews in this important matter. Further, Prato spoke comprehensively with Pacelli about the Jewish law in Hungary. The final Prato-Pacelli conversation on this question took place in the afternoon of Sunday, May 15, shortly before the departure of Pacelli to the Eucharistic Congress in Budapest. In this conversation Pacelli promised Prato that he would work on the Hungarian Catholics in order that the Jewish law would meet with a refusal at the Upper House in Budapest, or at least would be changed substantially. The question of how much these efforts are accompanied by success is still unclear. However, the willingness of Pacelli, i.e., the Curia, to support the Jews in this matter is significant.

In view of this psychological favorable situation that Prato described to me in detail, it seemed obvious to turn the conversation to our relationship with the Catholic Church on matters of Jewish Palestine. Prato told me that, until now, he had anxiously avoided touching on this subject in his many meetings with high Vatican dignitaries. This was for two reasons. First, he is striving to strengthen his bond of trust with the Curia; and second, he is in no way authorized to bring up this matter, even with the utterance of only one syllable, without the knowledge of the *Sochnut* [the Jewish Agency—T.B.]. But, in his opinion, the time will soon come when feelers can be put out in order to reach, after decades of ongoing efforts, a *modus vivendi* with the Curia in matters of Zionism. This could happen at first in a non-obligatory way, meaning that Prato would be informed in detail of the existing material on this question and then at upcoming opportunities, based on this knowledge, he could direct the conversation towards this matter.

It is to be considered that the Vatican will say or do nothing against its man of confidence, i.e., without the knowledge of the patriarch Monsignor Barlassina in Jerusalem. However, you also have to know what to offer the Church. Our declarations of absolute neutrality and highest respect to the Holy Places of Christianity are matters of course and are not substantial arguments during negotiations with the Roman Curia. More important is the emphasis that today we are already a decisive factor in Palestine and our importance in the country is expected to increase. Also, in the case that a Jewish nation is founded, even excluding Jerusalem [by creating] a British corridor, our influence on Jerusalem and everything within it cannot be underestimated. This means that for both sides it can only be to our advantage if we, the Church and the Jews in Palestine have peaceful relations with one another. Furthermore, emphasis is to be put on the determination of Article 14 of the Palestine Mandate regarding the constitution of an inter-Christian committee for the administration of the Holy Places. The point of controversy lies in the question of the presidency that will probably have to fall, *rebus stantibus* (sic), considering the mandatory power, to a high Protestant cleric. But due to reasons of prestige, the Roman Church cannot agree to such a regulation. The commission has not been constituted, because Rome has the opinion that without the biggest Greek-Orthodox power (Russia) no Orthodox representative can be called into this inter-Christian committee. This is a lame excuse, as in fact the patriarch of Byzantium is regarded in Greek-Orthodox circles, *primus inter pares* [sic], as a high-church dignitary. We do not have any influence on the constitution of this inter-Christian committee and should withstand this, because even if we had any influence in that direction, we would not have any interest in putting ourselves in a position of opposition with the American, English or Swedish Protestants. But as far as the Jews can judge this question, the presidency of this inter-Christian committee is entitled to Rome, as Rome takes its origins from Peter and Paul and holds the fiction of being the oldest Church, which we, despite knowing that Byzantine is the oldest, can accept. In my opinion, it would do no harm if this question was raised in an extraordinarily careful, legal-scientific manner in respected European papers and treated in the sense of a Roman candidacy recommendation on the presidency of the inter-Christian committee. Pacelli would be informed only afterwards that these statements were made with help from the Jewish circles.

Prato considers having this kind of procedure, to establish close contact with the Curia regarding matters of Zionism, as essential. However, Prato has requested not to be contacted by personal letters regarding these matters. The reasons for this are detailed in my special report about the situation of the Jews in Italy. Instead, it would be preferable to correspond with Dante Lattes, who would then inform Prato and act as the intermediary to relay Prato's messages back to us.

It would be worth convoking a comprehensive meeting on this complex issue.

Moshe Waldmann

Herr Shertok

VERTRAULICH. Haifa, 26.5.1938.

Gespraech mit Oberrabbiner Dr. Prato (Rom).

Waehrend meiner Anwesenheit in Rom habe ich mit Dr. Dante Lattes unter anderem die Frage unserer Beziehungen zum Vatikan eroertert. Dr. Lattes teilte mir mit, dass Oberrabbiner Prato in den letzten Monaten ein mehr als ertraegliches Verhaeltnis zu Kardinalsekretaer Pacelli hergestellt habe. Lattes riet mir, ich moege mich mit Prato unterhalten.

Auf Grund dieses Gespraeches mit Lattes suchte ich Dr. Prato auf und dieser erzaehlte mir u.a. nachstehendes:

Die Gegnerschaft des Vatikans gegen das Neuheidentum des Nationalsozialismus ist fundamental. Durch diese Tatsache hat sich ein psychologisch eigentuemlicher Zustand entwickelt, naemlich, eine groessere Aufgeschlossenheit in Beziehung auf juedische Forderungen. Tatsaechlich hat der Papst vor einigen Wochen bei einem Empfang polnischer Kardinaele und Erzbischoefe diesen eindringlich vor Augen gefuehrt, dass er es ungerne sehe, wenn sich die polnische Kirche in ein antisemitisches Fahrwasser im Bunde mit polnisch-faszistischen Elementen begebe. Auf Grund einer frueher erfolgten Intervention Pratos bei Pacelli in Sachen der Schechita hatte der Papst in seiner Unterredung mit den polnischen Kirchenfuersten auch diese Frage angeschnitten und gesagt, dass die katholische Kirche sich davor hueten muesse, in dieser fuer die Juden wichtigen Angelegenheit, Hilfe zu leisten, dass auf die Juden ein Gewissenszwang ausgeuebt werde. Ferner hat Prato mit Pacelli ausfuehrlich ueber das Judengesetz in Ungarn gesprochen. Die letzte Unterredung Prato - Pacelli in dieser Frage erfolgte am Sonntag, den 15. Mai nachmittags, kurz vor der Abreise Pacellis nach Budapest zum Eucharistischen Kongress. Pacelli hat in dieser Unterredung Prato versprochen, er werde auf die ungarischen Katholiken in dem Sinne einwirken, dass das Judengesetz im Oberhause in Budapest Ablehnung oder zumindest wesentliche Aenderungen erfahre. Wie weit diese Bemuehungen von Erfolg begleitet ~~sein werde~~ steht dahin. Kenntzeichnend ist die Bereitwilligkeit Pacellis, d.h. der Kurie, in dieser Sache fuer die Juden einzutreten.

Angesichts dieser psychologisch guenstigen Situation, die mir Prato eingehend schilderte, war es naheliegend, dass ich das Gespraech auf unsere Beziehungen zur katholischen Kirche in Sachen des Juedischen Palaestina lenkte. Prato sagte mir: Er habe sich bis jetzt aengstlich davor gehuetet, in seinen vielfachen Zusammenkuenften mit hohen vatikanischen Dignitaren diese Frage anzuschneiden. U.zw. aus zwei Gruenden. Erstens bemuehe er sich, sein Vertrauensverhaeltnis zur Kurie noch staerker auszubauen, zweitens sei er in keiner Weise autorisiert, ohne Wissen der Sochnuth auch nur mit einer Silbe diese Angelegenheit anzuschneiden. Seine Meinung aber ist, dass bald der Zeitpunkt gekommen sein wird, an dem man Fuehler ausstrecken kann, um die seit Jahrzehnten andauernden Anstrengungen mit der Kurie zu einem modus vivendi in Sachen des Zionismus zu gelangen, (auszustrecken). Dies koenne am besten zunaechst in unverbindlicher Weise geschehen. D.h. dermassen, dass Prato ueber das vorliegende Material in dieser Frage genauestens informiert sei und dann auf Grund dieser Kenntnisse bei sich darbietenden Gelegenheiten das Gespraech auf diese Fragen lenke. Hierbei ist zu beruecksichtigen, dass der Vatikan nichts gegen seinen Vertrauensmann, d.h. ohne Wissen dieses Vertrauensmannes, naemlich des Patriarchen Barlassina in Jerusalem, sagen oder tun werde. Allerdings muss man auch wissen, was man der Kirche zu bieten habe.

- 2 -

Unsere Deklarationen der absoluten Neutralitaet und des hoechsten Respektes gegenueber den Heiligen Staetten der Christenheit sind Selbstverstandlichkeiten und kein gewichtiges Argument in Verhandlungen mit der roemischen Kurie. Schwerer wiegend ist die Betonung der Tatsache, dass wir schon heute [redacted] in Palaestina, ein ausschlaggebender Faktor sind und dass unsere Bedeutung im Lande aller Voraussicht nach sich steigern wird. Auch im Falle der Gruendung eines Judenstaates, selbst bei Eximierung Jerusalems in einem englischen Korridor, wird unser Einfluss auf Jerusalem und alles, was sich darin befindet, von nicht zu unterschaetzender Bedeutung sein. D.h. fuer beide Teile kann es sich nur vorteilhaft auswirken, wenn wir, Kirche und Judenheit in Palaestina, ein friedliches Verhaeltnis zu einander haben. Ferner ist Gewicht zu legen auf die Bestimmung des Artikels 14/ des Palaestinamandates betreffend die Konstituierung eines interchristlichen Komitess zur Verwaltung der Heiligen Staetten. Streitpunkt hierbei ist die Frage der Praesidentschaft, die, rebus stantibus, wahrscheinlich mit Ruecksicht auf die protestantische Mandatarmacht einem hohen protestantischen Kleriker zufallen muesste. Die roemische Kirche kann aber aus Prestigegruenden einer derartigen Regelung nicht zustimmen. Zur Konstituierung dieser Kommission ist es nicht gekommen, weil Rom der Ansicht ist, ohne die groesste griechisch-rtakxxxxMacht orthodoxe Macht (Russland) koenne kein orthodoxer Vertreter in dieses interchristliche Komitee berufen werden. Das ist eine faule Ausrede. Denn tatsaechlich ist der Patriarch von Byzanz, der in griechisch-orthodoxen Kreisen als Primus inter pares betrachtete xx orthodoxe Kirchenfuerst. Wir haben auf das Zustandekommen xxxxx dieses interchristlichen Komitees keinen Einfluss und sollten uns auch hueten, einen Einfluss darauf zu nehmen, denn wir haben ja auch kein Interesse, uns, auch wenn wir irgend welchen Einfluss nach der Richtung ausueben koennten, in einen Gegensatz zu den amerikanischen, englischen, und schwedischen Protestanten zu setzen. Soweit die Juden diese Frage jedoch zu beurteilen vermoegen, so gebuehrt der Vorsitz in diesem interchristlichen Komitee doch Rom. Denn Rom leitet seine Herkunft vom Petrus und Paul ab und haelt an der Fiktion aufrecht, die aelteste Kirche zu sein, was wir, wenn auch wissend, dass die Byzantinische die aeltere ist, gelten lassen koennen. Meiner Meinung nach koennte es nicht schaden, wenn in ausserordentlich vorsichtiger, juristisch-wissenschaftlich verbraemter Form in angesehenen europaeischen Zeitschriften diese Frage angeschnitten und im Sinne einer Empfehlung der roemischen Anwartschaft auf die Praesidentschaft im interchristlichen Komitee behandelt wuerde. Pacelli muesste nur hinterher erfahren, dass diese Aeusserungen nicht ohne Zutun juedischer [redacted] erfolgt seien.

Prato haelt eine derartige Prozedur fuer nicht unwesentlich, Tuchfuehlung mit der Kurie in Sachen des Zionismus zu bekommen. Allerdings bittet Prato in diesen Dingen brieflich mit ihm persoenlich nicht in Verbindung zu treten. Die Gruende hierfuer sind ausfuehrlich in meinem Sonderbericht ueber die Lage der Juden in Italien angegeben. Es waere der Weg eines privaten Briefwechsels mit Dante Lattes vorzuziehen. Lattes wuerde alsdann Prato informieren und auch der Vermittler der Mitteilungen Pratos an uns sein.

Es wuerde sich verlohnen, ueber diesen ganzen Komplex eine ausfuehrliche Besprechung anzuberaumen.

Moshe Waldmann.

Correspondence between Orsenigo and the Holy See

1. Orsenigo to Pacelli, Berlin, March 26, 1933, regarding the withdrawal of the statement by the German bishops of the incongruity of Catholicism and National Socialism:

   [...] In my opinion, one [of the bishops] should perhaps have demanded precisely worded concessions [of the German government] regarding the freedom of the Catholic organizations, but the Episcopacy preferred—hoped—to formulate its statement without establishing any contact, not even secretly, with the government. Therefore, since no negotiations took place, no concessions by the counterpart could be expected.

   [Prot. No. 6781], Archivio della Congregazione degli Affari Ecclesiastici Straordinari (AES) Germany, pos. 621, file 139, fol. 77r-78r.[1]

2. Orsenigo to Pacelli, Berlin, April 11, 1933, regarding the beginning of the persecution of the Jews by the National Socialists:

   [...] Regretfully, the antisemitic doctrine of the [German] government as a whole was accepted and approved, and, regretfully, this fact shall stick like a badge of disgraceful malice on the first pages of the history of German National Socialism!

   [Prot. No. 6954], AES Germany, pos. 643, file 158, fol. 6rv.

3. Orsenigo to Pacelli, Berlin, September 14, 1935, regarding National Socialist ideology and the Reich Party Day of 1935.

a) Regarding anti-Bolshevism, which merely provided the National Socialists with a pretext to persecute the Jews:

   [...] this congress, which seemed to pursue the purpose of instigating a boundless war of all nations against Bolshevism, for which only the Jews are deemed responsible. This speech, delivered on Party Day, full of numbers, names and facts, made a deep impression and

1 All these documents can be found at: http://www.dhi-roma.it/orsenigo.html

terribly inflamed the minds of the German people. It appealed to the German mentality, despite its specific inclination to examination, calculation and statistics. One should therefore not be surprised that after this Party Day, antisemitic persecution resumed even more fervently. Moreover, since [the Jews] were blamed for Bolshevism, it is conveniently justified in the eyes of the people, so that it is difficult to find a non-Jewish German who dares to reject it outright, while the more moderate people confine themselves to raising some objections to the methods by which this war is conducted. [...]

I don't know if Russian Bolshevism as a whole is the work of the Jews alone; but here a way was found to make this allegation believable and, as a consequence, one should take action against the Jews. If the National Socialist government remains in power for a long time, and it seems that this will be the case, the Jews will be condemned to vanish from this nation.

[Prot. No. 14482], AES Germany, Scatola 9a, fol. 32r–33r.

b) Orsenigo to Pacelli, Berlin, September 17, 1935 regarding Hitler's non-Christian worldview.

[...] Hitler's speech of Monday evening was a display of a strange, if not arrogant, philosophy of the history of the German people, also in view of his relationship with Christianity. Regretfully, it revealed the absence of any belief, whether the Christian faith or any other. Any meaningful contribution of religion to the greatness of Germany was contested; it was attributed to National Socialism alone, and is expected exclusively from the party and the army.

[Prot. Nr. 14518], AES Germany, Scatola 9a, fol. 60rv.

4. Orsenigo to Pacelli, Berlin, Novemer 15, 1938 regarding the night of the pogrom:

Subject: Antisemitic Vandalism [...]

I must add some more observations to the information already published in the newspapers of 9 and 10 November regarding the antisemitic excesses:

1) *The destruction started, as if upon orders, on the night immediately following the announcement of the death of a young diplomat in Paris [the assassination of the embassy secretary Ernst vom Rath by Herschel Grynszpan]. The latter was killed by the shots of a young Jew, whose parents had been deported from Germany to Poland some days earlier. The blind revenge of the people evolved everywhere according to the same pattern: In the night, people smashed all the display windows [of Jewish businesses] and set synagogues on fire; the next day the businesses—now unprotected—were plundered, and the goods, even the most valuable ones, were destroyed in the wildest manner.*

2) *Only on the afternoon of November 10, after a day in which the mob had satisfied its barbaric urges—without being hindered by any police officer—did Minister Göbbels give the command to stop, and called the incidents an expression of the "anger of the German people." This single term was enough to restore the peace.*

By this, one could easily suppose that the order, or the permission, to commit these excesses came from the very highest echelons.

By his statement that the so-called "antisemitic reaction" [to the assassination of embassy secretary Ernst vom Rath by Herschel Grynszpan in Paris—T.B.] was "an act of the German people," Göbbels did great injustice to the real, sound German people, to which certainly the majority of Germans belong: An eighty-year-old retired Protestant Superintendent entered the Nunciature in order to protest specifically against these words of Göbbels. [...]

[Prot. Nr. 25341], AES Germany, pos. 742, file 356, fol. 40r–41r.

*Extract of letter from the Mother General of the Franciscan Missionaries of Mary, March 1944**

[…] Before anything else I wish to talk to you about the Holy Father and to convey manifold blessings especially for you: Blessings that support you in your hard work well before you are aware of them.

First is the Christmas letter, bearing the revered signature: A letter without which—one scarcely dares admit—has become an annual tradition. What a blessing, my beloved daughters! I submit it to your highly respectful filial piety, at the same time underscoring the dual *watchword*, an echo of the word of the Holy Father, and—not without emotion—the *constant benevolence* that inspires the final blessing:

The Christmas holidays have given you the opportunity to once again express to Us, in delicate terms, the filial adherence of the Franciscan Missionaries of Mary to all the directives of the Holy Church and its head, to whom at the same time you proffer, with a gracious image of the Virgin, your vows and the assurance of your fervent prayers. We are very responsive to all these signs of faithful commitment, no less than to the resolution that drives, you tell us, all your religious to radiate, more than ever, in the midst of the present calamities, the rich contents of the two "watchwords": prayer and charity.

We wholeheartedly hope that in the course of the New Year God will continue to accompany with his graces each and every one of your

* "Lettre générale de Mère," *Chronique Intime*, No. 5, June 1947, pp. 175-177.

works and your persons, and We are most pleased to reiterate to you the entreated Apostolic blessing, as a pledge of these divine favors and a token of Our unwavering goodwill toward your Institution.

From the Vatican, December 31, 1943.

PIUS P. P. XII

The much valued image thus came to continue its own tradition also … and this year, it is as beautiful as a missal page. On the back it bore the following autograph:

Jesus gives himself to us unreservedly in the poverty of Bethlehem, in the suffering on the cross, in the silence of the Tabernacle: Would we have the courage to refuse Him anything He asks of us for his poor, suffering and abandoned brethren?
Christmas 1943

PIUS P. P. XII

May this moving call—I would go so far as to say a "lamentation"—which penetrates our hearts coming from the heavenly Master, awaken the ingenuity of a love which *can* and *must* go to the souls and the anguish, be they what they may, at least through prayer, sacrifice, the gift of the self. This is both apostalate and almsgiving, always available to our generosity, with which is associated our spirit of poverty, that allows the authorities to be more generous in performing effective works of charity.

And I will go further, my dear daughters, conveying to you something about the Audience of the Sovereign Pontiff on January 25. As usual, it was full of blessings for the Institute and lasted […] over half an hour.

The Holy Father's charity spares no effort to relieve the multiple woes abundant among the stricken, the refugees, the starving; it takes all forms and we are often its humble messengers. Thus the faith of the Holy See has again called us to a new administrative office, related specifically to charity. I had to thank His Holiness for this and I did so in your name too, because whether from near or far, everything that relates to the heart of the Institute affects you, just as the revered "watchwords" are for all your counterparts as well.

At one point, as I set out to the Holy Father the most pressing concerns, I concluded by saying, "I place all of this entirely in God's hands." And the Holy Father, repeating these words in an animated fashion and with such an encouraging smile, said, "*Yes, we are in God's hands,* **in his hand**." This was such a clear and sweet call to have faith that I was profoundly comforted by it.

Rome, Juin 1947

No. 5 Vingt-sixième Année

SOMMAIRE

Lettre générale de Mère.

Rome, 27 Mars 1944.

Mes chères Filles,
P. C. C.

Nous avons été tout particulièrement unies dans la prière ces deux derniers jours. D'abord pour redire de toute notre âme *l'Ecce Ancilla Domini* qui caractérise notre voie, puis aussi pour nous réunir en esprit autour de la chère tombe de la chapelle bleue, en ce dimanche de la Passion, et repasser là, les pensées fortes et profondes que nous offrait la méditation du matin.

Comme de plus en plus les événements confirment notre vocation spéciale dans l'Eglise, celle dont Mère Fondatrice a été pour nous l'initiatrice et l'exemple! Sacrifice *pur*, sacrifice *entier*, elle nous le disait hier, c'est nous rapprocher de Jésus, la divine et souveraine Victime. Tant de faiblesses, tant de misères inhérentes à notre pauvre nature reprennent sans cesse, non pas notre parole, mais la fleur d'amour de cet holocauste! Si chaque matin dans l'action de grâces de la Communion nous redisions la chère formule de nos vœux, peut-être s'imprimerait-elle mieux dans notre vie?

176

Quoi qu'il en soit, mes bien chères filles, l'heure presse et Jésus veut des saintes, c'est-à-dire des âmes généreuses, *profondément* fidèles et qui ne se paient pas seulement de mots. La vague du grand châtiment, appelée par la malice et l'indifférence coupable des hommes, pèse sur le monde. On a voulu se passer de Dieu, et Il nous laisse un temps nous débattre contre les œuvres du mal. Châtiment pour les uns, épreuve pour les autres, la justice divine y trouve la réparation obligatoire, mais aussi la miséricorde nous rappelle que le pardon est proche pour tous ceux qui le voudront. Pendant cette quinzaine de douleur, de la plus grande douleur qui fut jamais, celle de la Passion, comme nous pouvons contempler encore l'effroyable tableau de la justice et l'abîme d'amour du pardon! Le Cœur de Jésus nous le dira de la part du "Père" et nous nous tiendrons tout près de Lui d'esprit et de cœur, afin de mieux nous faire les humbles petites coopératrices de la Rédemption pour les âmes de notre temps.

*

Avant toute autre chose, je veux vous parler du Saint Père et vous transmettre des bénédictions successives qui vous sont spécialement destinées, et qui soutiennent votre rude labeur bien avant que vous en ayez connaissance.

D'abord c'est la lettre de Noël, portant la vénérée signature, lettre devenue maintenant — sans qu'on ose presque se l'avouer — une tradition de chaque année. Quelle grâce, mes bien chères filles! Je la livre à votre piété très respectueusement filiale, et vous souligne le double *mot d'ordre,* écho de la parole du Saint Père, et non sans émotion, la *constante bienveillance* qui inspire la bénédiction finale:

Les fêtes de Noël vous ont fourni l'occasion de Nous exprimer une fois de plus, en termes délicats, la filiale adhésion des Franciscaines Missionnaires de Marie à toutes les directives de la Sainte Eglise et de son Chef, auquel vous offrez en même temps, avec une gracieuse image de la Vierge, vos voeux et l'assurance de vos ferventes prières. Nous sommes très sensible à toutes ces marques de fidèle attachement, non moins qu'à la résolution qui anime, Nous dites-vous, toutes vos religieuses, de faire rayonner plus que jamais, au milieu des calamités présentes, le riche contenu des deux "mots d'ordre": prière et charité.

De tout coeur Nous Nous plaisons à souhaiter que Dieu continue à accompagner de ses grâces, au cours de la nouvelle année, toutes et chacune de vos oeuvres et de vos personnes, et bien volontiers Nous vous renouvelons, comme gage de ces divines faveurs et témoignage de Notre constante bienveillance envers votre Institut, la Bénédiction Apostolique implorée.

Du Vatican, le 31 décembre 1943.

Pius P. P. XII

La précieuse image vint aussi continuer *sa* tradition à elle ... et cette année, belle comme une page de missel. Elle portait au verso l'autographe que voici:

Jésus se donne à nous sans réserve dans la pauvreté de Bethléem, dans les souffrances du Calvaire, dans le silence du Tabernacle: aurions-nous le courage de Lui refuser quoi que ce soit qu'Il nous demande pour ses frères pauvres, souffrants et abandonnés?
Noël 1943.

Pius P. P. XII

Que cet appel émouvant, cette "plainte" dirai-je, arrivant à notre cœur de la part du divin Maître, éveille l'ingéniosité d'une charité qui *peut* et qui *doit* aller aux âmes et aux détresses quelles qu'elles soient, tout au moins par la prière, le sacrifice, le don de soi. C'est un apostolat et une aumône toujours à la disposition de notre générosité, à laquelle s'associe notre esprit de pauvreté, qui permet à l'autorité de faire part plus large à la charité effective.

Et je continuerai encore, mes chères filles, en vous disant un mot de l'Audience du Souverain Pontife, le 25 janvier. Elle fut, comme de coutume, bien pénétrée de grâces pour l'Institut et dura ...plus d'une demi-heure.

La charité du Saint Père se prodigue inlassablement pour tant de misères qui abondent parmi les sinistrés, les réfugiés, les affamés; elle prend toutes les formes et souvent nous en sommes les humbles messagères. C'est ainsi que la confiance du Saint Siège nous a encore appelées à un nouveau bureau administratif, justement en rapport avec la charité. J'avais à en remercier Sa Sainteté et je l'ai fait en votre nom aussi, car de près ou de loin, tout ce qui touche le cœur de l'Institut vous atteint, comme les vénérés "mots d'ordre" sont pour toutes aussi.

A un moment, exposant au Saint Père des préoccupations plus vives, j'achevais en disant: "Je remets tout cela entre les mains de Dieu." Reprenant ces mots avec animation et un si encourageant sourire: "*Oui,* dit le Saint Père, *nous sommes entre les mains de Dieu,* **dans sa main.**" C'était une invitation à la confiance, si claire et si douce, que j'en fus profondément réconfortée.

Lorsque les Assistantes Générales m'eurent rejointe, et que le Pape éleva la main pour bénir, il eut une formule plus longue et plus complète que jamais, vous tenant présentes toutes, et même vos familles. Je sentais que cela vous serait une grande consolation, alors que l'éloignement et les barrières vous laissent dans un si pénible et parfois si angoissant silence sur tout ce qui les concerne. Le bon Dieu, par le "Père" unique et commun à tous, a voulu donner là une joie intime que vous n'aurez pas moins en pensant que vous et tous d'ailleurs, nous sommes "*entre les mains de Dieu,*" mieux encore: "**dans** sa main."

Au commencement de mars ce fut l'anniversaire de l'élection du Pape. A notre télégramme de respectueuses félicitations, le Cardinal Maglione répondit par un autre ainsi conçu:

"*Sa Sainteté très touchée filial geste remercie paternellement voeux Renouvelle tout Institut Bénédiction Apostolique.*"

Et quelques jours après, me communiquant l'affectation d'un don très généreux dont le Saint Père faisait bénéficier une de nos missions, le Cardinal ajoutait:

"*Voglia vedere in questo sovrano atto dell'Augusto Pontefice un segno della sua particolare predilezione verso le Missionarie Francescane di Maria e del suo compiacimento per le opere di bene ch'esse con tanto zelo fomentano per la diffusione della fede.*"

"Particolare predilezione", lisez ce mot, mes chères filles, avec une profonde gratitude. On est confondu, n'est-il pas vrai, de ces incessantes bontés paternelles, mais aussi "noblesse oblige" et ce devoir est très doux.

Filiale obéissance, avidité de connaître les directives du Souverain Pontife pour mieux y répondre, dévouement sans limites, voilà bien ce que doit être notre réponse, avec la mise en œuvre de la parole de Mère Fondatrice: "Pour l'Eglise, pour le Pape, vivons sans interruption d'amour, de sacrifice et de prière."

Extract of "The Charity of Pius XII," October 25-26, 1943[*]

[…] *As is well known, the August Pontiff, after having tried in vain to prevent the outbreak of the war* […] *has not for one moment ceased employing all the means in His power to alleviate the sufferings that are, in whatever form, the consequence of this cruel conflagration. With the growth of so much evil, the universally paternal charity of the Supreme Pontiff has become, one could say, even more active for all people; it does not pause before boundaries of nationality, religion or descent* [stirpe]. *This manifold and incessant activity of Pius XII has been greatly intensified recently by the increased sufferings of so many unfortunate people.*

May all of this beneficent activity, especially the prayer of the faithful across the whole world, ceaselessly rise to heaven with renewed fervor, bringing about even greater results and hastening the day when peace may return to the world, when men will put down their arms, set aside all discord and rancor, and finally, as brothers, collaborate for the common good.

* "The Charity of Pius XII," *Osservatore Romano*, October 25-26, 1943. The article was published originally in italics.

SUSAN ZUCCOTTI

Extract of letter from Monsignor Hudal to General Stahel[*]

[...] In addition, I would like to address an urgent matter. I have just received a report from a high-ranking Vatican official close to the Holy Father stating that arrests of Jews with Italian citizenship have begun this morning. On behalf of the good mutual understanding between the Vatican and the German military command, I hereby ask for an order to stop the arrests in Rome and the surrounding areas. The German reputation abroad and the risk of a dismissive public statement by the Pope demand these measures be taken. Given that the German Reich wishes to utilize the services of the Vatican for certain tasks in the not too distant future,—I know that the first enquiries were made in March—continued dissent between the Vatican and the Reich caused by persecutions of Jews will damage the cause of peace [sic—most likely 'understanding,' as before].

* *Actes et Documents du Saint Siège relatifs à la Seconde Guerre Mondiale* (ADSS) (Vatican City: Libreria Editrice Vaticana, 1965-1980), vol. IX, pp. 509-510.

372. Le nonce à Berlin Orsenigo au cardinal Maglione

Tél. nr. 567 (A.S.S. Guerra Ital.-Milit.-Germ. 291)

Berlin, 16 octobre 1943

Assistance aux prisonniers de guerre italiens en Allemagne.

Ricevuto telegramma n. 474.[1]

Circa soldati trasferiti Germania come prigionieri, mi fu promesso assistenza religiosa facilitata presenza loro cappellani; circa aiuto materiale et morale, con visita del Nunzio Apostolico, si darà risposta che spero favorevole; circa servizio Ufficio Informazioni, di cui ho illustrato speciali vantaggi... si promette studiarne la possibilità. Ho insistito per una sollecita risposta.[2]

373. Mgr Hudal[1] au général Stahel

(A.E.S. Germania 742, copie)[2]

Rome, 16 octobre 1943

Démarche pour faire cesser les arrestations de Juifs.

Ich darf hier[a] eine sehr dringende Angelegenheit[b] anschliessen. Eben berichtet mir eine hohe Vatikanische Stelle aus der unmittelbaren

---

[1] Voir nr. 358.

[2] Voir infra nr. 400. — En même temps, on promit au Nonce de lui permettre des visites aux camps de prisonniers de guerre; voir AA (Bonn) St. S. du 5 octobre 1943: « Der Nuntius hatte seinerzeit den Herrn Staatssekretär um die Erlaubnis gebeten, Kriegsgefangenenlager zu besuchen. Das Oberkommando der Wehrmacht teilt auf Anfragen des Ausw. Amts mit, daß gegen Besuche der Nuntius in Kriegsgefangenenlagern keine Bedenken bestehen. Es bittet um Angabe, welche Lager der Nuntius su sehen wünscht und wann dies der Fall sein soll. Dies hat der Herr Staatssekretär heute dem Nuntius mitgeteilt » (sér. 819, p. 278063). Mais, en fait, le Nonce ne put faire aucune visite. — Voir infra nr. 438.

---

[a] *corr.* wohl   [b] *omis* hier

---

[1] Mgr Aloïs Hudal, évêque titulaire d'Ela et recteur du Collège de langue allemande S. Maria dell'Anima, voir nr. 71, note 1.

[2] La lettre fut aussi insérée dans un télégramme de l'ambassade d'Allemagne à l'Auswär-

Umgebung des Heiligen Vaters,[3] dass heute morgen die Verhaftungen von Juden italienischer Staatsangehörigkeit begonnen haben. Im Interesse des friedlichen[c] Einvernehmens zwischen Vatikan und deutschem[d] Militärkommando[e] bitte ich vielmals, eine Order zu geben, dass in Rom und Umgebung diese Verhaftungen sofort eingestellt werden.[f] Das deutsche Ansehen im Ausland fordert eine solche Massnahme und auch die Gefahr, dass der Papst öffentlich dagegen Stellung nehmen wird. Da in nicht zu ferner Zeit das Deutsche Reich den Vatikan für bestimmte Aufträge benützen dürfte — ich weiss, dass bereits im März getastet worden ist[4] — würde ein grosser Schaden für die Sache des Friedens herauskommen, wenn die Judenvorfolgungen zu einem weiteren Dissens zwischen Vatikan und Reich führen würden.[f]

[c] *corr.* guten bisherigen [d] *corr.* dem hohen deutschen [e] *ajouté*, das in erster Linie dem politischen Weitblick und der Großherzigkeit Eurer Exzellenz zu verdanken ist und einmal in die Geschichte Roms eingehen wird, [f-f] *corr.* ich fürchte, daß der Papst sonst öffentlich dagegen Stellung nehmen wird, was der deutsch-feindlichen Propaganda als Waffe gegen uns Deutsche dienen muß.

---

tiges Amt, signé par l'attaché Gumpert. Une première partie de la lettre ne se trouve ni dans le télégramme ni dans la copie de la minute conservée aux A.E.S. Les deux textes ne sont pas identiques. Nous publions le texte de la minute en indiquant les variantes du télégramme.

[3] C'est le neveu du Pape, le prince Carlo Pacelli (note de Mgr Hudal).

[4] Mgr Hudal se réfère à des pourparlers privés qu'un officier des S.S. recomandé par le Duc de Mecklenburg, avait commencés à Rome pour sonder les possibilités d'un accord avec le Vatican. Mais il semble que ces tentatives étaient plutôt chimériques, sans autorisation de Berlin, voir R. A. Graham, *Goebbels e il Vaticano* p. 136 sv. — Mgr Hudal annota la réponse téléphonique du général Stahel du 17 octobre: «Habe die Sache an die hiesige Gestapo und an Himmler unmittelbar sofort weitergeleitet, Himmler gab Order, daß mit Rücksicht auf den besonderen Charakter Roms diese Verhaftungen sofort einzustellen sind»; le même jour il reçut une réponse écrite que Mgr Hudal transmit en extrait: «... Bezüglich Ihrer Bemerkungen, daß in Rom und Umgebung Verhaftungen von Juden stattgefunden haben, kann ich Ihnen mitteilen, daß ich persönlich als Militärkommandant damit nichts zu tun habe. Es handelt sich dabei um eine reine Polizeiaktion, auf die ich keinerlei Einfluß habe, da meine Aufgaben auf rein militärischem Gebiete liegen. Trotzdem habe ich selbstverständlich Ihre Bedenken den zuständigen Stellen umgehend zur Kenntnis gebracht» (A.E.S. Germania 742).

368. Notes of Cardinal Maglione*

(A.E.S. 2606/43, autogr.)

Vatican, October 16, 1943

When he heard about the "razzia" against the Roman Jews, the Cardinal summoned the German Ambassador to protest. The Ambassador promised to intervene, but without mentioning the Cardinal's dissent, so as not to prejudice the desired result.

When I came to know that the Germans had rounded up the Jews this morning, I sent for the German Ambassador[1] and asked him to intervene in favor of those unfortunate people. I spoke the best I could in the name of humanity and Christian charity.

The Ambassador, who already knew of the arrests but doubted that it involved Jews specifically, told me in a sincere and emotional tone: "I always expect to be asked why on earth I keep this office."

I exclaimed: No, Mr. Ambassador! I'm not asking you and would never ask you such a question. I only say: His Excellency, who is so warm and tender hearted, please try to save these many innocent people. It is painful for the Holy Father, painful beyond words, that in Rome of all places, under the eyes of the Common Father, so many people are destined to suffering only because they belong to a certain race...

After a few seconds of contemplation, the Ambassador asked me: "What would the Holy See do if such things were to continue?"

I replied: The Holy See would not like to be put in a position of having to express words of disapproval.

The Ambassador observed: For more than four years I've been following and admiring the Holy See's attitude. He succeeded to guide the boat amongst rocks of all sizes and shapes without collision, and although he had greater faith in the Allies, he knew how to maintain

* ADSS, vol. IX, pp. 505-506.

1 Ernst von Weizsäcker. On the morning of October 16, Princess Enza Pignatelli Aragona Cortes informed the Pope; see R. A. Graham, *La Strana Condotta*, p. 466 sv. According to an undated report of the Comitato Ricerche Deportati Ebrei (Committee for Research on Deported Jews), the *razzia* began around 11 p.m. on October 15. The Jews who were caught were taken to the Collegio Militare. The *aktion* continued until 1 p.m. on October 16.

a perfect balance. I'm asking myself whether now, when the boat is just about to reach port, is it the right moment to put everything in danger. I'm thinking about the consequences that a step by the Holy See would trigger… The instructions come from a very high place… "His Excellency allows me not to mention this official conversation."[2]

I pointed out that I was asking for his intervention, addressing his sentiments of humanity. I left it to his judgment whether or not to mention our conversation, which had been so friendly.

I wanted to remind him that the Holy See has been, as he himself had pointed out, very careful in order not to give the German people the impression that he had done or wanted to do anything, even the smallest thing, against Germany, in the time of such a terrible war.

However, I also had to tell him that the Holy See should not be put in a position where he would be compelled to protest: Should he be constrained to do so, the Holy See would have to rely on Divine Providence for the consequences.

"Meanwhile, I repeat: His Excellency told me that he would try to do something for those unfortunate Jews. I am grateful for it. As to the rest of it, I'm leaving the decision in his hands. Should he think that it is more appropriate not to mention our conversation, so be it."[3]

2 See no. 342, where Weizsäcker spoke in the same way.

3 See Weizsäcker, telegram to the Auswärtiges Amt (the German Foreign Office) no. 147, published in S. Friedländer, *Pius XII*, p. 144. The British Minister reported on this conversation on October 31: "As soon as he heard of the arrests of Jews in Rome, the Cardinal Secretary of State sent for the German Ambassador and formulated some [sort] of protest. The Ambassador took immediate action, with the result that large numbers were released… Vatican intervention thus seems to have been effective in saving a number of these unfortunate people. I inquired whether I might report this, and was told that I might do so, but strictly for your information and on no account for publicity, since any publication of information would probably lead to renewed persecution" (tel. no. 400, Foreign Office 371/37255); see *Actes 7*, p. 62.

368. Notes du cardinal Maglione

(A.E.S. 2606/43, autogr.)

Vatican, 16 octobre 1943

Ayant appris la razzia contre les Juifs romains, le cardinal convoqua l'ambassadeur d'Allemagne pour protester. L'ambassadeur promit son intervention, mais sans mentionner la démarche du cardinal pour ne pas compromettre le résultat désiré.

Avendo saputo che i tedeschi hanno fatto stamane una retata di ebrei, ho pregato l'Ambasciatore di Germania [1] di venire da me e gli ho chiesto di voler intervenire a favore di quei poveretti. Gli ho parlato come meglio ho potuto in nome dell'umanità, della carità cristiana.

L'Ambasciatore, che già sapeva degli arresti, ma dubitava si trattasse specificamente di ebrei, mi ha detto con sincero e commosso accento: « Io mi attendo sempre che mi si domandi: Perché mai Voi rimanete in cotesto vostro ufficio? ».

Ho esclamato: No, signor Ambasciatore, io non Le rivolgo e non Le rivolgerò simile domanda. Le dico semplicemente: Eccellenza, che ha un cuore tenero e buono, veda di salvare tanti innocenti. È doloroso per il Santo Padre, doloroso oltre ogni dire che proprio a Roma, sotto gli occhi del Padre Comune siano fatte soffrire tante persone unicamente perché appartengono ad una stirpe determinata...

L'Ambasciatore, dopo alcuni istanti di riflessione, mi ha domandato: « Che farebbe la Santa Sede se le cose avessero a continuare? ».

Ho risposto: La Santa Sede non vorrebbe essere messa nella necessità di dire la sua parola di disapprovazione.

L'Ambasciatore ha osservato: Sono più di quattro anni che seguo ed ammiro l'attitudine della Santa Sede. Essa è riuscita a guidare la barca in mezzo a scogli d'ogni genere e grandezza senza urti e, se pure ha avuto maggior fiducia negli alleati, ha saputo mantenere un perfetto equilibrio. Mi chiedo se, proprio ora che la barca è per giungere in porto, conviene metter tutto in pericolo. Io penso alle conseguenze, che provocherebbe un passo della Santa Sede... Le note direttive ven-

---

[8] On télégraphia au Nonce à Berne le 4 novembre: « V. E. R. riceverà tramite bancario fr. sv. 25.620 da erogarsi secondo suo prudente giudizio » (tél. nr. 148).

---

[1] Ernst von Weizsäcker. Le Pape fut informé le matin du 16 octobre par la princesse Enza Pignatelli Aragona Cortés; voir R. A. Graham, *La strana condotta* p. 466 sv. Suivant un rapport non daté du « Comitato Ricerche Deportati Ebrei » la razzia avait commencé vers les 23 heures du 15 octobre. Les Juifs pris furent conduits au Collegio Militare. L'action dura jusqu'à 13 heures du 16 octobre.

che provocherebbe un passo della Santa Sede... Le note direttive vengono da altissimo luogo... « Vostra Eminenza mi lascia libero di non " faire état " di questa conversazione ufficiale? ».[2]

Ho osservato che io l'avevo pregato d'intervenire facendo appello ai suoi sentimenti d'umanità. Mi rimettevo al suo giudizio di fare o non fare menzione della nostra conversazione, che era stata tanto amichevole.

Volevo ricordargli che la Santa Sede è stata, come egli stesso ha rilevato, tanto prudente per non dare al popolo germanico l'impressione di aver fatto o voler fare contro la Germania la minima cosa durante una guerra terribile.

Dovevo però pur dirgli che la Santa Sede non deve essere messa nella necessità di protestare: qualora la Santa Sede fosse obbligata a farlo, si affiderebbe, per le conseguenze, alla divina Provvidenza.

« Intanto, ripeto: V. E. mi ha detto che cercherà di fare qualche cosa per i poveri ebrei. Ne La ringrazio. Mi rimetto, quanto al resto, al suo giudizio. Se crede più opportuno di non far menzione di questa nostra conversazione, così sia ».[3]

---

[2] Voir nr. 342 où Weizsäcker parla dans le même sens.

[3] Voir v. Weizsäcker, télégramme à l'Auswärtiges Amt nr. 147, publié dans S. FRIEDLÄNDER, *Pius XII*. p. 144. Le ministre de Grande Bretagne rapporta le 31 octobre à propos de cet entretien: « As soon as he heard of the arrests of Jews in Rome Cardinal Secretary of State sent for the German Ambassador and formulated some [sort?] of protest. The Ambassador took immediate action with the result that large numbers were released... Vatican intervention thus seems to have been effective in saving a number of these unfortunate people. I enquired whether I might report this and was told that I might do so but strictly for your information and on no account for publicity, since any publication of information would probably lead to renewed persecution » (tél. nr. 400, F.O. 371/37255); voir *Actes* 7, p. 62.

53. Mgr. Anichini[1] to Pope Pius XII[*]

Unnumbered (A.E.S. St. Eccl. 761, orig.)

Vatican, February 13, 1944

Information regarding the persons who have found refuge in the canons' building in Saint Peter's Basilica.

The paternal kindness of Your Holiness was manifested once again in such a touching manner that I feel the duty to expound on what happened as a result of the action I and some of my canonical colleagues at Saint Peter's undertook, aimed at helping persecuted people of different backgrounds, by hosting them in the rectory area.[2]

When I was finally able to return to Rome last November 1, thanks to the generosity of some people who sent a car for me to my home in Tuscany, I found already gathered in the rectory—which is considered land subjected to the special jurisdiction of the Cardinal Archpriest[3]—a number of individuals who believed their lives to be in serious danger. I could not refuse to take in these people, who were in a precarious situation and were relatives of the people who had organized my happy return.

Besides, neither I nor my colleagues thought we were transgressing any law, since all of our guests were kept well hidden and did not bear upon the Vatican's food administration (*annona*). Finally, we all hoped that their stay would be very short.

Subsequently, other urgent and serious cases came up, in particular concerning those affected by the racial laws, and so new guests were admitted in various rectories—always in the name of fraternal charity—and are listed as follows:

1. At my place, Mr. A. from Adri (Salerno) and his family, refugees, who despite being Catholic, were not considered Aryan and therefore were actively pursued for deportation to Poland; Mr. B., a member of the Swiss Guard, and his cousin C., aged 16 of French origin, both of them sheltered as a measure of precaution.

* ADSS, vol. X, pp. 127-129.

1 Monsignor Guido Anichini, canon of Saint Peter from 1928.

2 Located to the left of the Basilica.

3 Cardinal Federico Tedeschini (1873-1959).

2. At Monsignor Fioretti's place:[4] the parents of the abovementioned A., also Catholic, dislodged and subjected to ruthless persecution because they were not Aryan. With them are their son-in-law and grandson, as well as Prince D. an officer of the Royal Army.

3. At Monsignor Descuffi's place:[5] his cousin E. with his son, Count F., a former officer in the Navy, both of them in danger of being arrested and executed by firing squad, for political reasons. In addition, Monsignor Descuffi also hosted a former student of his, an officer in the Royal Navy, who refused to enroll in the Republican Army; Dr. G., a former officer of the Ministry of the Interior who rejected the new regime, and two young brothers, H. and I., one of them a draft-dodger of the Royal Army and the other of uncertain nationality, born in France.

4. At His Excellency Monsignor Beretti's place:[6] his sisters, with three nephews and engineer K., all of them wanted for not possessing the required Aryan qualities.

5. At Monsignor Roma's place:[7] an army marshal and his nephew (or grandson) with his wife and daughter, also wanted and in danger of serious sanctions.

6. At Monsignor Gromier's place:[8] the young student L., son of Senator M., in danger of being taken hostage; the young diplomat Dr. N., a former staff member of the Royal Embassy in Paris and now actively wanted by the police for this fact alone.

7. At the late Monsignor Bruni's place:[9] before my lamented colleague died, he hosted in his home Dr. O. with his son, threatened with reprisal by Republican Fascists. After the death of Monsignor Bruni, with the approval of Monsignor Descuffi,[10] the executor of Bruni's will and testament, Engineer P. and Colonel Q. (former

4 Monsignor Cesare Fioretti, canon from 1934.

5 Monsignor Ugo Descuffi, canon from 1934.

6 Monsignor Francesco Beretti (1877-1955), titular bishop of Caesarea Philippi from 1936.

7 Monsignor Gaetano Roma, canon from 1924.

8 Monsignor Léon Gromier, canon from 1926.

9 Monsignor Alfonso Bruni, canon from 1931.

10 See footnote 5.

Chief Commander of S. M. of Marshal Cavallero) were hosted in Bruni's house; the first one actively hunted for racial reasons and the latter for political-military motives.

8. Additionally, in the third floor utility rooms, various officials of the Royal Army were lodged who, after having pledged allegiance to the King of Italy, refused to adhere to the Republic and were therefore sought after for revenge. These were: architect R., Mr. S. and Mr. T., all of them highly recommended young men coming from good families.

9. On the same floor, in the quarters of the Sacristan Don Alessandro Ciccarelli, were already hosted: U., an officer in the Royal Army, wanted; V., idem; W., an ex-musketeer of Il Duce, now sought after as a traitor because he applied to join the Palatine Guard; and X., an ex-Jew baptized a long time ago, actively persecuted. They remained hidden in the quarters of priest Ciccarelli: They paid no amount of money or bargained anything in exchange for the hospitality.

10. On the ground floor, with the doormen and the Sacristans, various people were taken in, mostly Jews baptized years ago. Here are their names: Y., born Catholic, former Commissioner for Spain and Portugal, a condemned fugitive wanted by the Police; Z., a non-Aryan Catholic who had already been arrested but had miraculously escaped; A. aged 64, a Jew as above; B. aged 55, a Jew as above; G. and D. former Jews, wanted; E. from the Royal Air Force, an ex-prisoner, escaped, wanted; F. and wife, displaced from Castel Gandolfo where they were hosted in the papal villa, wanted because they were not Aryans; G., a non-Aryan Catholic who had escaped arrest and is wanted along with his wife; H. I., nephew of the vicar's vice; K., persecuted on racial grounds; L., idem; M., wanted because he belonged to the Royal Army.

In all, there were some *fifty* individuals in very serious danger of being arrested and gunned down or deported. Those in less danger have spontaneously left; those who remain prefer to face any danger in the rectory, protected in the Father's house, whom they desperately plea: *salva nos, perimus!*[11]

11 Cf. *Mt* 8, 25.

Notes of Monsignor Tardini:

This letter was written after Mons. Anichini, Descuffi and Roma[12] were summoned by the Papal Commission for Vatican City State[13] and told by his Eminence Cardinal Rossi[14] that they must make all their guests leave. This led to an uproar… in the Sacred College. On February 10—at the funeral of Pius XI[15]—the cardinals asked Cardinal Rossi and the other members of the Commission… not to insist. Cardinal Rossi replied that he spoke on order from above. The cardinals asked Maglione to speak with the Holy Father. In reality…whoever wanted to, left.[16]

12 See footnotes 1, 5 and 7.

13 Members of the Commission were Cardinals Nicola Canardi (1974-1961), Raffaelo Carlo Rossi (1876-1948) and Giuseppe Pizzardo (1877-1970).

14 Cardinal Rossi, secretary of the Consistorial Congregation and member of the Commission.

15 Pius XI died on February 10, 1939.

16 Monsignor Tardini responded on February 15, 1944 (unnumbered, A.E.S., St. Eccl. 761) by correcting an error of Monsignor Anichini on the legal position of the Canonica.

53. Mgr Anichini[1] au pape Pie XII

Sans nr. (A.E.S. St. Eccl. 761, orig.)

Vatican, 13 février 1944

Renseignements sur les personnes réfugiées dans l'immeuble des chanoines de Saint-Pierre.

La paterna bontà della Santità Vostra, manifestatasi ancora una volta in modo così commovente, mi fa sentire il dovere di esporre figlialmente quanto è avvenuto, dato per fatto mio e di alcuni miei colleghi Canonici di S. Pietro, per venire incontro a perseguitati di vario genere accogliendoli nei locali della Canonica.[2]

Quando io, il primo novembre scorso potei finalmente ritornare a Roma mediante la prestazione generosa di persone che mi inviarono una macchina fino a casa in Toscana, trovai che nella Canonica — che si ritiene terreno a sé, posto sotto la particolare giurisdizione del Cardinale Arciprete[3] — erano già stati accolti non pochi individui, che si ritenevano minacciati gravemente nella vita, per cui anch'io ritenni di non dovermi rifiutare a ricevere in casa persone pericolanti e congiunti di chi era stato autore del mio felice ritorno.

D'altronde né io né i miei colleghi ritenevamo di trasgredire alcuna legge in quanto che tutti i nostri ospiti si mantenevano rigorosamente occulti e non gravavano sulla annona del Vaticano, e in fine si sperava da tutti che la dimora sarebbe stata di brevissima durata.

Successivamente altri casi urgenti e gravi si verificavano, specie di gente colpita dai decreti razziali, e per questo in varie abitazioni Canonicali furono accettati nuovi ospiti — a titolo sempre di fraterna carità — che nell'attuale momento possono essere così elencati:

1. Presso di me il signor A. sfollato da Adri (Salerno) con la famiglia, il quale pur essendo di religione cattolica non ha quanto basta per essere considerato ariano e perciò è attivamente ricercato per essere spedito in Polonia. Il signor B., guardia palatina e il suo cugino C. di anni 16 di nazionalità francese ambedue ricoverati per cautela.

2. Presso Mons. Fioretti:[4] i genitori del medesimo A., anch'essi cattolici, sfollati, fatti segno a spietata persecuzione perché non ariani.

---

[1] Mgr Guido Anichini, chanoine de Saint Pierre depuis 1928.

[2] Située à la gauche de la basilique.

[3] Le cardinal Federico Tedeschini (1873-1959).

[4] Mgr Cesare Fioretti, chanoine depuis 1934.

Sono con essi il genero ed il nipote. Inoltre il principe D., ufficiale del R. esercito.

3. Presso Mons. Descuffi: [5] il suo cugino E., col figlio già ufficiale di marina, entrambi in pericolo di essere arrestati e fucilati per motivi politici. Oltre a questi Mons. Descuffi accolse un suo antico allievo conte F., ufficiale del R. esercito che rifiutò di aderire all'armata repubblicana; il dott. G., già funzionario del Ministero dell'Interno che ha rifiutato il nuovo Regime, e due giovani fratelli H. e I., uno renitente a lasciare l'esercito Regio e l'altro di nazionalità incerta essendo nato in Francia.

4. Presso Sua Eccellenza mons. Beretti: [6] le di lui sorelle con tre nipoti e l'ingegnere K., tutti presi di mira per difetto di requisiti ariani.

5. Presso mons. Roma: [7] un maresciallo del Regio esercito, suo nipote con signora e figlia, anch'egli ricercato e in pericolo di gravi sanzioni.

6. Presso Mons. Gromier: [8] il giovane studente L., figlio del Senatore M., sotto la minaccia di essere preso in ostaggio; il giovane diplomatico dott. N., già facente parte della R. Ambasciata a Parigi, e ora attivamente ricercato, per questo solo fatto, dalla polizia.

7. Presso il fu Mons. Bruni: [9] prima che il compianto collega morisse egli aveva ricevuto in casa il dott. O. col figlio minacciato di rappresaglie da parte dei fascisti repubblicani. Dopo la morte di Mons. Bruni col favore dell'esecutore testamentario mons. Descuffi,[10] vennero accolti in quella casa l'ingegnere P. e il colonnello Q. già capo di S. M. del maresciallo Cavallero; il primo ricercato attivamente per pretesti razziali e il secondo per motivi politico-militari.

8. Inoltre al terzo piano, dove sono alcune stanze di ripostiglio, furono ricoverati vari ufficiali del R. esercito, i quali per aver giurato fedeltà al Re d'Italia non si sentivano di passare alla Repubblica e per questo sono ricercati per le relative vendette. Essi sono: l'architetto R., il signor S., il signor T., giovani tutti di buone famiglie e autorevolmente raccomandati.

9. Nello stesso piano, nell'abitazione del sacrista don Alessandro Ciccarelli furono da tempo accolti: U., ufficiale del R. esercito, ricercato; V. id.; W., già moschettiere del Duce e ora ricercato come

[5] Mgr Ugo Descuffi, chanoine depuis 1934.
[6] Mgr Francesco Beretti (1877-1955), évêque titulaire de Césarée de Philippe depuis 1936.
[7] Mgr Gaetano Roma, chanoine depuis 1924.
[8] Mgr Léon Gromier, chanoine depuis 1926.
[9] Mgr Alfonso Bruni, chanoine depuis 1931.
[10] Voir note 5.

traditore, che ha fatto domanda per essere ammesso nella Guardia Palatina; X., già ebreo, — ma da tempo battezzato — perseguitato attivamente. Costoro sono rimasti occulti nell'abitazione del sacerdote Ciccarelli: non risulta affatto che per essere accolti abbiano sborsato somme o mercanteggiato l'ospitalità.

10. Nel piano terreno presso i portieri e sacristi sono state accolte varie persone, la maggior parte ebrei, da vari anni battezzati. Ecco i nomi: Y., cattolico di nascita, ex Commissario per la Spagna e il Portogallo, ricercato a morte dalla polizia; Z., cattolico non ariano già arrestato e miracolosamente fuggito; A. di anni 64, ebreo come sopra; B., di anni 55, ebreo come sopra, G. e D., già ebrei, ricercati; E., della R. Aeronautica già prigioniero, fuggito, ricercato; F. e signora sfollati da Castel Gandolfo dove erano stati accolti nella villa pontificia, ricercati perché non ariani; G., cattolico non ariano sfuggito alla cattura e ricercato con la moglie, H. I., nipote del vice parroco; K., perseguitato per ragioni razziali; L., id.; M., ricercato perché del R. E.

Sono in tutto circa *cinquanta* individui in grave pericolo di essere arrestati e fucilati o deportati. I meno pericolanti si sono già spontaneamente allontanati; i rimasti preferiscono affrontare ogni pericolo nella Canonica all'ombra della casa del Padre a cui rivolgono l'angosciosa invocazione: *salva nos, perimus*! [11]

Note de Mgr Tardini:

Questa lettera fu scritta dopo che Mons. Anichini, Descuffi e Roma [12] furono chiamati dalla Pontificia Commissione per lo S.C.V.[13] e sentirono dirsi dall'em.mo cardinale Rossi [14] che dovevano far uscire tutti gli ospiti. La cosa fece chiasso... nel Sacro Collegio. Il 10 febbraio — ai funerali di Pio XI [15] — gli em.mi cardinali pregarono il cardinal Rossi e i colleghi della commissione di ... non insistere. Il cardinale Rossi rispose che aveva parlato per ordine superiore. I cardinali fecero parlare al S. P. dal cardinale Maglione. In realtà uscì ... chi volle.[16]

[11] Cf. *Mt* 8, 25.

[12] Voir notes 1, 5 et 7.

[13] Membres de cette Commission étaient les cardinaux Nicola Canali (1874-1961), Raffaello Carlo Rossi (1876-1948) et Giuseppe Pizzardo (1877-1970).

[14] Le cardinal Rossi, secrétaire de la Congrégation Consistoriale, membre de la Commission.

[15] Pie XI était mort le 10 février 1939.

[16] Mgr Tardini répondit le 15 février 1944 (Sans nr., A.E.S. St. Eccl. 761) en corrigeant une erreur de Mgr Anichini sur la position juridique de la Canonica.

93. Notes of the Secretariat of State[*]

(A.S.S. Carte Sostituto, orig.)

Vatican, March 7, 1944

On the acceptance by a religious institute of people under threat.
Father Martinelli S. J. asks if he can agree to the wholehearted prayers of mothers who request hospitality for their children.

Note of Monsignor Montini:
Ex Aud. SS.mi, 8-3-44.[**] He leaves to him the responsibility in this matter.

Note of the Office:
Communication: 8-3-44. Father Martinelli gives thanks.

* ADSS, vol. X, p. 171.

** Ex Audienza Santissimi = an audience with the Pope

93. Notes de la Secrétairerie d'Etat

(A.S.S. Carte Sostituto, orig.)

Vatican, 7 mars 1944

Sur la réception dans un institut religieux de gens menacés.

Padre Martinelli [1] S.J. chiede se possa cedere alle preghiere accoratissime di mamme che domandano ospitalità per loro figlioli.

Note de Mgr Montini:

Ex Aud. SS.mi, 8-3-44. Si rimette alla sua responsabilità.

Note d'office:

Comunicato: 8-3-44. P. Martinelli ringrazia.

MICHAEL PHAYER

Documents Pertaining to the Holocaust

1. Settimio Sorani, head of Rome's Delasem (Delgazione Assistenza Emigranti Ebrei) organization to assist Jews, comments on the Vatican and the Holocaust to Harold Tittmann, Florence, January 22, 1962:

   What was expected—an outspoken and loud outcry of condemnation of what was well known to the Vatican, a condemnation in such a way that it would have put a restraint on the part of the Christian world, on the unheard of crimes which were taking place unpunished [which did not occur]. That is the reason we were disillusioned.

   AR 33/44, file 716, archives of the American Jewish Joint Distribution Committee.

2. A postwar statement of Reuben Resnik, staff member of the American Joint Distribution Committee, who was in Rome during the war:

   While I was received in a private audience and otherwise honored by the Vatican, I must be frank to tell you that I was not a great admirer of top Vatican policy with respect to the Holocaust. During its height there was constant apologizing by the Vatican for its inability to do anything about it when, as a matter of fact, no effort was made to do anything about it.

   Reuben B. Resnik, "Efforts in Relief, Rescue and Resettlement during World War II," A talk before the Detroit Jewish Historical Society, June 12, 1988. Oral Histories Collection, archives of the American Jewish Joint Distribution Committee.

The Origin of the Vatican's Emigration Policy

A. Catholic Emigration

1. Ambassador Llobet to Ruiz Guiñazu, October 6, 1942:

   [Maglione] suggested to me that the pontiff would be interested in knowing the willingness of the government of the Argentine Republic to apply its immigration laws generously, in order to encourage at the opportune moment European Catholic immigrants to seek the necessary land and capital in our country.

   Guerra Europea, file 1, vol. 4, cable 1272, archives of the Foreign Ministry of Argentina.

2. Testimony of Walter Schellenberg, Chief of Nazi Foreign Intelligence, Nuremberg, February 6, 1946:

   I believe that under the influence of the Vatican, Latin America, in conjunction with Spain [and] Portugal, should create a new political sphere of influence. It was his idea to unite all the Roman Catholics... Goyeneche [a colleague of Escobar] was a convinced enemy of Bolshevism. He was working for the unification of all Catholics and with that he was trying to see Catholic Europe coming about... [Goyeneche counseled Himmler] to protect the Catholics in Europe because it was his opinion [that] if Europe was to be lost to Bolshevism, then South America, too, would be lost.

   Entry 111, ADC 5691, National Archives and Records Administration (NARA).

B. Transition from Catholic Emigration to Nazi Emigration

1. Note regarding Monsignor Giovanni Battista Montini:

   [Montini participated with] a new group formed in January 1943, in Madrid, whose purpose is to save Europe from Bolshevism, prevent communism in Germany and therefore keep in touch with the German military circles and after the collapse of Germany and the fall of the Nazis, help the military right wing together with a capitalist government seize power.

   RG 226 250/64/26/01, Entry 210, Box 236, NARA.

2. Vatican determines who gets emigration assistance:

    In Italy it is understood that the national [German, under Bishop Hudal and Croat, under Father Draganović, etc.] committee[s] for emigration [are] in charge of emigration with the Pontificia Commissione d'Assistenza [Pontifical Commission of Assistance, i.e. Emigration Bureau] responsible for the resettlement of non-Italians.

    National Catholic Welfare Committee file papers, 10/37/14, archives of the Catholic University of America.

3. U.S. intelligence report from Captain Henry R. Nigrelli, June 5, 1946:

    The Holy See is specifically in agreement with the Argentinian government regarding this emigration project as a cover to allow for counteractive operations against both Communist infiltration and [their] operatives in South America.

    Entry 212, Box 5, RG 256, location 250/64/33/5, NARA.

4. U.S. intelligence report from agent in Madrid, May 29, 1947:

    A valuable source within the group established by Father Boos reports that sometime in April a meeting was held in the foreign office at the request of Boos or his colleague Father Sauer [S.J.] for the purpose of obtaining official approval [for the emigration of Nazis through Spain]. The meeting is said to have [been] attended by Sauer, the Foreign Minister [of Spain], the Cardinal Primate of Toledo and the Papal Nuncio. The report has it that the foreign minister's acceptance was conditioned upon the substitution of the words 'Central Europe' instead of 'Germany'.

    Entry 127, Box 8, File 74, RG 226, location 190/7/21/1, NARA.

5. Report from American diplomat John Moors Cabot, Belgrade, to U.S. State Department, June 11, 1947:

    The Vatican and Argentina [are conniving] to get guilty people [atrocity perpetrators] to [a] haven in the latter country.

    Box 3623, RG 59, location 250/36/19/6, NARA.

6. Report from U.S. intelligence agent Robert Clayton Mudd:

   [Ante] Pavelić tops the list of those that the state department and foreign office have agreed to hand over to [Marshal Josip] Tito for trial. Recommendation: In view of the fact that this man is a criminal, as well as a political criminal, every effort should be made to apprehend him and ship him back to the Yugoslav government for trial.

   Box 173, File IRR XE001 109 Pavelić, RG 319, location 270/84/1/4, NARA.

7. Report from U.S. diplomat John Moors Cabot, Belgrade, to Secretary of State George Marshall, June 25, 1947:

   [War criminals] are slipping through our fingers in spite of our stated support for the prosecution of war criminals. [The guilty,] for whom irrefutable evidence of guilt exists, should be ferreted out and returned to Yugoslavia. I suggest that in addition to taking urgent measures to remedy the above situation, we might ask [the] Vatican, in return for information we are transmitting, for [a] list of Yugoslavs it is sheltering.

   Box 3623, RG 59, location 250/36/19/6, NARA.

8. Report from U.S. intelligence agent Robert C. Mudd regarding the activity of Father Krunoslav Draganovic:

   Draganovic's sponsorship of Croat Quislings definitely links him up with the plan of the Vatican to shield these ex-Ustashi [sic] nationalists until such time as they are able to procure for themselves the proper documents to enable them to go to South America. The Vatican, undoubtedly banking on the strong anti-communist feelings of these men, is endeavoring to infiltrate them into South America in any possible way to counteract the spread of Red doctrine.

   Report with no date or place. Entry A1-86, Box 12, RG 262, NARA.

9. Report from U.S. diplomat John Moors Cabot to U.S. State Department, June 11, 1947:

   [on] the "terrible crimes committed [by Ustashe] in Yugoslavia," affirming that their guilt is "crystal clear."

   Box 3623, RG 59, location 250/36/19/6, NARA.

10. U.S. Diplomat John Moors Cabot warns U.S. State Department of consequences for not extraditing war criminals to Yugoslavia, June 11, 1947:

    How can we defend this record before the UN? If the Yugoslavs take it there I do not know, and there are increasing evidences they will. As I see it we may then be forced either to accept a humiliating decision against us or to manipulate things as to show that we also consider the UN a mere instrument of power politics. I also trust [that] the Catholic Church realized how extremely damaging this affair might be to its position in [Yugoslavia].

    Box 3623, RG 59, location 250/36/19/6, NARA.

11. Memo from Diplomat J. Graham Parsons (presumably to the State Department) regarding the La Vista investigation of the Vatican ratline:

    This appeared to be an inexplicable situation but further investigation indicated that in those Latin American countries where the Church is a controlling or dominating factor, the Vatican has brought pressure to bear, which has resulted in the foreign missions of those countries taking an attitude almost favoring the entry into their country of former Nazis and former fascists or other political groups, so long as they are anti-communist. That, in fact, is the practice in effect in the Latin American consulates and missions in Rome at the present time.

    Entry 1068 or 1069, Box 22, RG 59, location 250/48/29/05, NARA.

12. Diplomat J. Graham Parsons, Vatican City, explaining to Walter "Red" Dowling, U.S. State Department, how the Vatican ratline functions, August 13, 1947:

    Anyone can secure a letter of recommendation...to any welfare group under the protection of the Vatican, stating that his name is so, and his nationality is such, and that he desires an International/ Red Cross identity document... He may be directed to Father Gallov, [the] Hungarian Catholic priest, in temporary control of welfare units operating under the protection of the Vatican. Father

Gallov will either direct [a] subject by letter to his personal contact in the International Red Cross or to Dr. Vida... stating in effect that he has known [the] subject for some time and assistance will be appreciated... to enable him to secure an IRC identity document. This letter will bear the S, an official stamp of the Vatican. UFFICIO ASSISTENZA RELIGIOSA PER UNGAREAL IN URBO.

Box 4080, RG 59, location 250/36/29/02, NARA.

13. Instructions to the British Foreign Office diplomat Francis D'Arcy Osborne, Minister to the Vatican, regarding guilty Ustashe fascists:

[Inform the Vatican secretariat that those] who worked for the Pavelić Ustashe government were giving their support and approval to a regime which flouted humanitarian principles and which condoned atrocities unsurpassed in any period of human history.

The Vatican's appeal to the British may be found in the British Foreign Office 371/67376R6056, PRO. The Foreign Office response above may be found in WO 204/11133, PRO.

List of Contributors

Professor David Bankier (1947-2010) was the Head of the International Institute for Holocaust Research—Yad Vashem from August 2000 to February 2010 and was the incumbent of the John Najmann Chair of Holocaust Studies. He pursued his undergraduate and graduate studies at the Hebrew University of Jerusalem, where he was the Jonah Machower Professor of Holocaust History at the Institute of Contemporary Jewry. Professor Bankier served as visiting professor at universities in London, the United States, South Africa and South America, was involved in developing centers of Jewish studies in Latin America, and promoted academic publications in Spanish. Bankier published 120 scholarly studies, including his notable book, *The Germans and the Final Solution: Public Opinion Under Nazism* (1996). His recently published works include: *Expulsion and Extermination—Holocaust Testimonials from Provincial Lithuania* (2011) and *Lectures—The John Najmann Chair of Holocaust Studies, 2003-2009* (2011).

Thomas Brechenmacher received his title of Dr. phil. habil. in German Language and in Literature of the Middle Ages, History of the Middle Ages, and Modern History. He taught modern and contemporary history at the University of the German Federal Armed Forces. Presently, he teaches modern history and is managing director of the Interdisciplinary Institute for Jewish Studies in the faculty of Philosophy at Potsdam University. He worked in several institutes, including the Forschungsstelle Deutsch-Jüdische Zeitgeschichte e.V. Currently he is working on "Pius XI, Eugenio Pacelli and Germany (1922-1939)". His publications include: *Der Vatikan und die Juden. Geschichte einer unheiligen Beziehung vom 16. Jahrhundert bis zur Gegenwart* (2005); *Das Reichskonkordat 1933. Forschungsstand, Kontroversen, Dokumente* (2007); *Berichte des Apostolischen Nuntius*

Cesare Orsenigo aus Deutschland 1933 (2008); "Pope Pius XI, Eugenio Pacelli and the Persecution of the Jews in Nazi Germany, 1933-1939: New Sources from the Vatican Archives," in *Bulletin of the German Historical Institute in London,* 27, 2005.

Jean-Dominique Durand received his *Agregé* in 1988. He lectures in the Department of Contemporary History at the Jean Moulin University in Lyons, France, where he established the History of Christianity Institute. He was the French Cultural Attaché to the Holy See and Director of the French Cultural Center in Rome from 1998 to 2002. His scholarly research deals mainly with religious history, particularly in Italy.

His publications include: *L'Eglise catholique dans la crise de l'Italie 1943-1948* (1991); *L'Italie de 1815 à nos jours* (1999); *Il fattore religioso nell'integrazione europea* (1999); *Storia della Democrazia cristiana in Europa. Dalla Rivoluzione francese al postcomunismo* (2002); *Quelle laïcité en Europe?* (2003); *Lo Spirito di Assisi* (2004); *Cultures religieuses, Eglises et Europe* (2008). He is the editor of the *Collection Pages d'Histoire* for the Desclée de Brouwer publishing house. He is a member of the Pontificio Consiglio della Cultura, and several scientific committees of historical research centers in Italy, France, and Belgium.

Grazia Loparco is a sister of the Salesian Sisters of Don Bosco (Daughters of Mary Help of Christians). She was born in Locorotondo, Italy, received her Ph.D. in History from the Pontifical Gregorian University in 2001, and currently teaches Church history at the Pontifical Faculty of Education Sciences (*Auxilium*), Rome. She is a member of the Cultural Association for Salesian History and cooperates with various historical institutions. Her publications include: "Gli ebrei negli istituti religiosi a Roma (1943-1944) dall'arrivo alla partenza," *Rivista di Storia della Chiesa in Italia,* anno LVIII, n.1, 2004; "L'assistenza prestata dalle religiose di Roma agli ebrei durante la seconda guerra mondiale," in Luigi Mezzadri and Maurizio Tagliaferri, eds., *Le donne nella Chiesa e in Italia* (2007); "Gli ebrei e molti altri nascosti negli istituti religiosi di Roma," in Giorgio Vecchio, ed., *Le suore e* *la Resistenza* (2010). Loparco was recently appointed counselor to the Vatican department responsible for the canonization of saints.

Dan Michman is Professor of Modern Jewish History and Chair of the Arnold and Leona Finkler Institute of Holocaust Research at Bar-Ilan University and serves as Head of the International Institute of Holocaust Research and Incumbent of the John Najmann Chair of Holocaust Studies at Yad Vashem. He taught at the University of Amsterdam and the Dutch Rabbinical Seminary, and was a visiting professor at the University of Toronto and a Research Fellow at FRIAS (Freiburg Institute of Advanced Studies). His numerous publications, which have been published in 11 languages, mostly focus on the Holocaust (historiography, religious life, refugees and migration, rescue, Jewish Councils, ghettos, Belgium and The Netherlands, the impact of the Holocaust on the Jewish world, Post-Zionism and the Holocaust).

The latest books he authored or edited include: *Holocaust Historiography: A Jewish Perspective. Conceptualizations, Terminology, Approaches and Fundamental Issues* (2003); *Encyclopedia of the Righteous Among the Nations: Belgium* (2004); *Hashoa Bahistoriya Hayehudit: Historiografiya, Toda'a u-Farshanut* [The Holocaust in Jewish History: Historiography, Consciousness, Interpretations] (2005); *Holocaust Historiography in Context: Emergence, Challenges, Polemics and Achievements* (2008); and *The Emergence of Jewish Ghettos during the Holocaust* (2011).

Sergio Itzhak Minerbi received a B.A. in Economics and International Relations from the Hebrew University of Jerusalem and a Ph.D. in History from the Sorbonne in Paris. He was senior lecturer in the Institute of Contemporary Jewry at the Hebrew University of Jerusalem (1972-1978) and visiting professor in the Department of Political Science at Haifa University (1992-1995). In 1961, he entered the Israeli Foreign Office and was Economic Counselor in Brussels (1963-1967), Ambassador to Ivory Coast (1967-1971), Ambassador to the European Communities, Belgium and Luxembourg (1978-1983), and finally Deputy General Director for Economic Affairs until 1989. In that year, he established his own company: Shanti Consultants Ltd.

Minerbi's publications of more than a hundred articles and books include: *L'Italie et la Palestine 1914-1920* (1970); *Raffaele Cantoni, un ebreo anticonformista* (1978); *The Vatican and Zionism: Conflict and the Holy Land, 1895-1925* (1990); *Israele mezzo secolo* (1998); "Pio XII, il Vaticano e il 'Sabato nero': la responsabilità nell'arresto e nella deportazione degli ebrei romani," in *Nuova Storia Contemporanea,* anno VI, 3, 2002.

Matteo Luigi Napolitano received his Ph.D. in 1993. He taught at the University of Urbino (2000-2007) and currently lectures in the Department of History of International Relations at the University of Molise. In 2005, he was appointed delegate of the Pontifical Committee of Historical Science at the International Committee for the History of the Second World War. In 2008, he was appointed member of the Scientific Committee for the Vatican exhibition *Pio XII: L'uomo e il Pontificato*. The various books and articles he has written include: "La Santa Sede e la seconda guerra mondiale: Memoria e ricerca storica nelle pagine della 'Civiltà Cattolica'," in *Studi Urbinati di Scienze giuridiche, politiche ed economiche*, LXVII, nuova serie n. 51.2, 1999-2000; "Pio XII e il Nazismo: Il "silenzio apparente" e l' "azione segreta" del Pontefice," in *Nuova Storia Contemporanea*, V, n.3, May-June 2001; *Pio XII tra guerra e pace: Profezia e diplomazia di un papa (1939-1945)* (2002); *Il Papa che salvò gli ebrei: Dagli archivi segreti del Vaticano tutta la verità su Pio XII* (with Andrea Tornielli) (2004); *Pacelli, Roncalli e i battesimi della Shoah* (with Andrea Tornielli) (2005).

Iael Nidam-Orvieto received her Ph.D. in Holocaust Studies at the Institute of Contemporary Jewry—the Hebrew University of Jerusalem. Her main fields of research are Italian Jews, Jewish responses during the Holocaust, Jewish leadership, and rescue attempts during the Holocaust. She is currently the Editor-in-Chief of the Publications Department at Yad Vashem and teaches at the Hebrew University of Jerusalem. She was a research fellow at the International Institute for Holocaust Research—Yad Vashem and the International Research Institute of the United States Holocaust Memorial Museum in Washington. Her book on the rescue of the children of Villa Emma is forthcoming.

Paul O'Shea has degrees in Theology, Education, and History. His Ph.D. was on Pius XII and his responsibility for Catholic responses during the Holocaust. He is the Dean of Mission at Rosebank College, Australia, a coeducational Catholic secondary school. He is a founding member of the Australian Institute of Holocaust and Genocide Studies, and has contributed to *Genocide Perspectives 2* and *3*. O'Shea has been active in interfaith dialogue for many years and is a member of the Council of Christians and Jews in New South Wales. For over ten years he has taught Holocaust Studies and the role of the Catholic Church during the Shoah in the Mosaic program of the Jewish adult education program at Shalom College, University of New South Wales, as well as team-teaching Politics of Genocide at the University of Technology, Sydney. O'Shea is author of *A Cross Too Heavy: Pius XII and the Jews of Europe* (2011).

Michael Phayer is a historian and professor emeritus at Marquette University in Milwaukee and has written widely on 19th and 20th century European history. He received his Ph.D. from the University of Munich in 1968 and joined Marquette's Department of History in 1970. Currently he is the Distinguished Visiting Professor of Seton Hill University's Holocaust Studies Program. His books include: *The Catholic Church and the Holocaust 1930-1965* (2000), published also in Poland in 2011, and *Pius XII, the Holocaust and the Cold War* (2008). Among his most recent articles is "Helping Jews is Not an Easy Thing to Do," in *Holocaust and Genocide Studies* 21, 3, 2007. Phayer is presently researching Vatican finances during the Holocaust era.

Dina Porat is a Tel Aviv University professor of Jewish history. She has served as head of the Department of Jewish History at Tel Aviv University and the Chaim Rosenberg School of Jewish Studies. She is now head of the Kantor Center for the Study of Contemporary European Jewry, holds the Alfred P. Slaner Chair for the Study of Antisemitism and Racism, and is chief historian at Yad Vashem.

Porat has written and edited a large number of books and articles, including: *The Fall of a Sparrow: The Life and Times of Abba Kovner* (2009), which received the National Jewish Book Award and *The Smoke-smelling Morning Coffee* (Hebrew, 2011). She was a visiting professor at the Hebrew University of Jerusalem, as well as Harvard, Columbia, New York and Venice International universities. Porat was a member of the Israeli Foreign Ministry delegation at four UN world conferences, and served as the academic advisor of the Task Force for International Cooperation on Holocaust Education, Remembrance and Research.

Roberto Spataro was born in Italy in 1965, obtained a Ph.D. in Classics (Naples, Italy) in 1993 and in Theology in 2005 from the Salesian Pontifical University (*Università Pontificia Salesiana*—UPS) in Rome. He taught Church History at the Studium Theologicum Salesianum in Jerusalem (2005-2011), where he was also appointed Dean of Studies. Currently, he lectures in the Faculty of Christian Literature and Classics at UPS. He has published several articles and essays, among which is the noteworthy "Pio XII 'Giusto tra le nazioni'," in *Parola e Storia*, II/2, 2008, pp. 345-359, which has also been translated into Spanish.

Andrea Tornielli received his Ph.D. in Classical Humanities in 1987. He is a columnist for the Italian newpaper *La Stampa* and for the website *Vatican Insider,* and has been following the apostolic pilgrimages of Pope John Paul II and Benedict XVI since 1997. He has edited four books on Pius XII, which include: *Pio XII: Il Papa degli Ebrei* (2001) and *Pio XII: Eugenio Pacelli, un uomo sul trono di Pietro* (2007), a complete biography on Pius XII. He also wrote *Paolo VI: L'audacia di un papa*, (2009) and *Pio IX: L'ultimo papa re* (2011). His research in general deals with the popes of the twentieth century and their contributions to the development of peace and justice in the world.

Susan Zuccotti received her B.A. in history from Wellesley College, and her Ph.D. in modern European history from Columbia University. Zuccotti has taught Holocaust and general Western European History at Columbia and Barnard Colleges in New York City and at Trinity College in Hartford, Connecticut. She has published several books, including: *The Italians and the Holocaust: Persecution, Rescue, and Survival* (1987); *The Holocaust, the French and the Jews* (1993); *Under His Very Windows: The Vatican and the Holocaust in Italy* (2000); and *Holocaust Odysseys: The Jews of Saint-Martin-Vésubie and Their*

Flight through France and Italy, 1939-1945 (2007). Her first book received the National Jewish Book Award for Holocaust Studies in the United States and the Premio Acqui Storia—Primo Lavoro in Italy. *Under His Very Windows* received the National Jewish Book Award for Jewish-Christian Relations and the Sybil Halpern Milton Prize of the German Studies Association. Zuccotti's most recent work, *Pére Marie-Benoît and Jewish Rescue: How a French Priest Together with Jewish Friends Saved Thousands during the Holocaust*, will be published by Indiana University Press in the spring of 2013.

Index

Note: The index does not include the documents in the appendix.